TOP OF THE WORLD

THE INSIDE STORY OF THE
BOSTON CELTICS'
AMAZING ONE-YEAR TURNAROUND
TO BECOME NBA CHAMPIONS

Peter May

Da Capo Press
A Member of the Perseus Books Group

Design and production by Eclipse Publishing Services
Set in 11 point Janson

A CIP catalog record for this book is available from the
Library of Congress.
ISBN: 978-0-306-81810-3
Library of Congress Control Number: 2008935954

Published by Da Capo Press
A Member of the Perseus Books Group
www.dacapopress.com

Da Capo Press books are available at special discounts for bulk purchases
in the U.S. by corporations, institutions, and other organizations. For more
information, please contact the Special Markets Department at the Perseus
Books Group, 2300 Chestnut Street, Suite 200, Philadelphia, PA 19103, or
call (800) 810-4145, ext. 5000, or e-mail special.markets@perseusbooks.com.

10 9 8 7 6 5 4 3 2 1

Contents

Prologue

OR SOME, THE CELEBRATING STARTED AT HALFTIME. The lead in Game 6 of the NBA Finals was 23 points, the Boston Celtics were dominating at both ends of the floor (holding the Los Angeles Lakers without an offensive rebound in the first half), and the atmosphere at the Courtside Club inside the TD Banknorth Garden, was undeniably jubilant.

The Celtics were one half away from winning the 2008 NBA championship, their record seventeenth in the history of the sport's most storied franchise. But it had been 22 years since the last one—prior to that drought, no Celtic team had gone more than five years between championships No. 1 and No. 16—and the relief and elation in the room were palpable. During their playoff run, the Celtics had survived two nerve-wracking seventh games at home. They had played an NBA record 26 playoff games—or two more playoff games than they had had victories in the bleak season before.

Before the game, Wyc Grousbeck, the team's managing general partner, had stuck a cigar into the left breast pocket of his navy blue suit jacket, intending to light it up as a tribute to the immortal Red Auerbach, who had died in the fall of 2006. Grousbeck had had a good feeling going in; the Celtics led the series 3–2. He said, "I told myself that in the Super Bowl, you only get one chance. In the World Cup final, you get only one chance. In the NCAA Tournament, you only get one chance. But we had two chances to win, so I felt lucky. With two chances to win one game, I felt pretty confident."

Inside the club at halftime, movers and shakers from all walks, including Boston Red Sox owners John Henry and Tom Werner, New England Patriots coach Bill Belichick, Pats' owner Robert Kraft, assorted Patriots players, and Wyc's father Irv were equally upbeat—and with good reason. The first half had been a tour de force at both ends of the floor, a display so powerful that the Celtics coach, Doc Rivers, mostly just sat on the bench and watched with transparent pride. Before the game, it was Rivers who had told his team that tonight was going to be the night they put it all together.

"Let's leave no doubt," he said. "We have yet to play a complete game in the playoffs. Not just in this series, but in the whole playoffs. We blew some teams out, but we have been mostly a spurt team and have not put together the product we have been working on all season." Then he said, "What are you waiting for?"

The Lakers scored the first four points of the game, but the Celtics' first basket of the night proved to be a sign of things to come. Point guard Rajon Rondo, who had struggled mightily in Games 3, 4, and 5 in Los Angeles while dealing with an ankle sprain, swiped the ball out of the hands of Pau Gasol. It was the first of his six steals in the game; afterward Lakers coach Phil Jackson said that Rondo "created havoc" on the floor. Rondo then drove the length of the court, went under the basket, and found an open Ray Allen on the left perimeter; Allen made the first of his seven three-point field goals in the game.

The Celtics then blew it open by closing the second period with a 26–6 run to create the 23-point halftime lead. James Posey and Eddie House knocked down big three pointers. Kevin Garnett converted an old-fashioned three play in the final minute after being decked by Lamar Odom.

Still, while many of the Celtics ownership group were early revelers, neither Rivers, nor the man who put this team together, general manager Danny Ainge, were quite as confident. "Because of what had happened earlier in the series, I didn't feel too comfortable," Ainge said.

Indeed, in Game 2, the Lakers had been down by 24 points in the fourth quarter and rallied to cut the deficit to a single point. The Celtics had trailed by 24 points in Game 4 in Los Angeles and then staged the greatest rally in the history of the NBA Finals to win the game. Coaches and general managers are predisposed to *not* feel comfortable until they can look up at the scoreboard at the end of the game. But this was not going to be one of those nights. The Celtics made sure of that.

"I'm thinking the Lakers still have all those great three-point shooters, and Kobe [Bryant] can be a game-changer," Ainge said. "But at the same time, I knew our players were not going to let down. I started to feel really good about halfway through the third quarter."

That was when his cellphone buzzed, signaling a text message. It was from Larry Bird, his former Celtics teammate, who was running the Indiana Pacers. It was brief and to the point: "Great Job Danny. I'm Really Happy For You." When the lead swelled into the 30s and even low 40s in the fourth quarter, a second message popped up, this one from Ainge's close friend, former teammate, and, Lakers fans would say, enabler of the 2008 champions by agreeing to trade Garnett to Boston: Kevin McHale, the man running the Minnesota Timberwolves. It too, was brief and to the point: "Congratulations."

As the game drew to its now foregone conclusion, the scene around the Celtics bench started to resemble a Hieronymus Bosch painting. Families crowded around. Fans crowded around. Hats and tee shirts were distributed. Paul Pierce, who would soon be named the Most Valuable Player of the series, picked up a barrel of red Gatorade and dunked Rivers from behind, a tradition the football-crazy Rivers (a huge Chicago Bears fan) could understand and embrace. The stained shirt later raised an astonishing $55,000 at an auction to benefit the Shamrock Foundation, the Celtics' charitable arm.

It was an incredibly emotional time for the coach, who had played 13 years in the NBA and never won a championship. Until 2008, as a coach spanning seven-plus seasons in two locales (Orlando, Boston), he had never even won a single playoff series. Now, he was on the verge of winning it all, and at the expense of the celebrated Hall of Famer Phil Jackson, who spent the majority of the second half glued to his ergonomically correct chair and watching the carnage unfold with Buddha-like equanimity. Meanwhile, former NBA coach Jeff Van Gundy was telling television viewers, "I'm really tired of this [Lakers] defense right now," as Celtic upon Celtic knocked down baskets from inside and outside.

Rivers started to feel comfortable when there were about seven minutes to play and walked away from the bench to reflect by himself and enjoy the rout. "For me, visually, all the stuff we had worked on all year came together for one night. That was what that game meant to me," he said. "It all came together. Everything worked."

He spotted his family in the crowd. There was one notable omission—his father Grady, who had died the previous November. "He had been to every one of my games when I was a kid growing up, and the one game that I wished he could have been at, he wasn't. And that bothered me," Rivers said. When asked later what he thought his father would have said, Rivers laughed and said, "It's about time."

But as the clock wound down, Rivers said he was surprised by how he felt. Yes, he was happy. But, he noticed, he felt happier for the others. He zeroed in on 38-year-old P.J. Brown, who had joined the team in late February and had played 15 years, never before making it to the NBA Finals. This was going to be his first—and last—shot at a ring; he had come out of retirement to join the Celtics and was likely to go back into retirement now that it was over.

"To me, P.J. was the poster child for happiness that night," Rivers said. "Talk about guys who want to win. He stood out more than any of them. That's what I got out of it and that's was what was so cool. I always thought it was going to be, 'God, I finally made it.' But the other part, seeing P.J. Brown at that moment, is even better."

Miami Heat coach Pat Riley, watching the game from his Coral Gables home, had the exact same feeling, for he too had coached Brown, as well as Posey and House. An admitted and unadulterated Celtic-hater from his many years with the Lakers, Riley nonetheless couldn't help but feel heartened for the Celtics he had coached. That group also included Rivers, who had played for Riley in New York. "My heart was with LA," he said, "but I was really happy for those guys."

It was similar for Ainge as well. He left his courtside seat near the Celtics bench and joined the players and coaching staff in the waning moments. He too saw Brown and had the same thoughts as Rivers. He continued to scan the bench, with each player he saw representing a story of his own.

"I saw Paul and I thought about all the things he has been through and all the discussions we'd had," Ainge said. "And I saw Doc and all that he had been through. And all the others. But probably my greatest emotion was seeing Rondo."

Prior to the game, Ainge had gone up to Rondo and told him that the most important statistic for him in this particular evening was going to be FGA: field goals attempted. That, of course, was a statistic near and dear to Ainge's heart, for he'd had a reputation as a player who loved to shoot the ball. But there also was a pointed message behind Ainge's comments: Rondo had taken 33 shots in the first five games, and the Celtics wanted him to be more aggressive in Game 6 because it would force Kobe Bryant to have to play more defense. Rondo ended up with 21 points, 7 rebounds, and 8 assists along with the 6 steals. More important: he took 20 shots.

"I don't think anyone understands the pressure of being a 22-year-old kid like Rajon who has no real basketball pedigree. I mean, he's not Magic Johnson. He's not Chris Paul," Ainge said. "To have been the whipping boy of the veteran players and the coaches, and to have had all that pressure because opposing teams aren't guarding him, and commentators are talking all about him being the supposed weak link. I was just so happy for him. And when I went over to the bench to congratulate him, I saw tears coming out of his eyes and rolling down his cheeks. I couldn't have been prouder of him at that moment. It was like one of my own children had done some miraculous thing."

When the final horn sounded, the score was a ridiculous 131–92. Grousbeck had been right; it *had* been over at the half. No title-clinching game in NBA history had been decided by such a large margin. When NBA Commissioner David Stern presented the Larry O'Brien Trophy to the Celtics, he noted, "Some place, somewhere, Red [Auerbach] is lighting up a cigar." It was then that Grousbeck pulled the stogie from his suit-coat pocket, only to realize he had no matches. He deftly tucked the cigar in his pants pocket. It was about the only thing that didn't go right for Boston on this particular night.

Garnett ran to center court, knelt down, and kissed the Celtics leprechaun logo and NBA Finals Trophy logo. Pierce clenched his fists and strode out onto the floor, finally in possession of the one thing that, until this moment, had separated him from all the other Celtics greats: a championship. Allen strode around waving a towel in one hand.

The three had appeared in 25 All-Star Games. Garnett had a league MVP award and was the 2008 Defensive Player of the Year. Allen and Garnett won Olympic gold in Sydney in 2000. But none had even participated in an NBA Finals until this season, and now the three 30-somethings were experiencing the ultimate for the first time, together. "Top of the world, man. Top of the world," Garnett screamed into the ESPN sideline microphone of Michele Tafoya.

Garnett soon found Celtic soul mate Bill Russell. The greatest winner in NBA history and, until just now, one of the greatest non-winners in NBA history, were linked together not only by their defensive play, but by their jewelry. "I've got my own," Garnett said while hugging Russell. The reference was to a line earlier from Russell, who saw a lot of himself in the 32-year-old, and who was so impressed by Garnett's game and demeanor, that he said he'd give Garnett one of his rings if the Celtics didn't prevail. He would not have to do that now. "I just want to say, other than my kid being born [earlier in the season], this has got to be the happiest day of my life," Garnett said.

"You know," Pierce said, "I'm not living under the shadows of the other greats now. I'm able to make my own history with my own time here. If I was going to be one of the best Celtics ever to play, I had to put up a banner."

Allen, who had gone through a mysterious and uncharacteristic shooting slump in the playoffs and then had to deal with his son's diagnosis of juvenile diabetes before Game 5, said simply, "Everything we went through was definitely worth it."

And they went through a lot.

The Celtics had completed the single greatest turnaround in NBA history, going from 24 wins in 2006–2007 to 66 wins in

2007–2008. The 42-game swing easily topped the previous best of 36, established by the 1997–1998 San Antonio Spurs, who had a rookie by the name of Tim Duncan. They had done so by playing an 82-game season without a single player scoring as many as 40 points in a game; Pierce's 37 against Seattle two days after Christmas represented the high-water mark. They had done so with a suffocating defense that was anchored by Garnett and which led the NBA in defensive field goal percentage and defensive three-point field goal percentage while being second (to Detroit) in fewest points per game. Three Celtics had been chosen to play in the All-Star Game. They spent the entire season in first place and ended up winning 13 of 14 playoff games in Boston. It had been a wire-to-wire exhibition of teamwork and selflessness.

The partying continued long into the night at the Courtside Club in the Garden with the championship trophy on display for all to see. Champagne and beer flowed freely as the lowest member of the Celtics staff mingled seamlessly with Garnett and Pierce.

Pierce then invited anyone and everyone back to his spacious digs in suburban Lincoln, Massachusetts, a 30-minute drive. Teammates, wives, and friends arrived around 4 a.m., continuing the celebration, but Pierce was not among them. When arriving home, he discovered his daughter Prianna Lee, little more than two months old, had a three-digit temperature. Pierce and his fiancée Julie Landrum got back into his car and, while everyone partied at his house, drove to Winchester Hospital, where their daughter was admitted. (Almost without exception, if a child three months or younger has a high temperature like Prianna's, the child is admitted so doctors can check for meningitis.) Pierce and his fiancée spent the next two days and nights at the hospital, awaiting test results that would confirm nothing more sinister than a fever.

"They didn't find anything seriously wrong," Pierce said. "But the whole thing really scared me. I really didn't have any sleep over those two days, but not for the reasons everyone thinks. I was in the hospital. I didn't have a chance to sleep. You can't sleep when your baby is in the hospital. So I never really got to enjoy the championship until the parade a couple days later. That was when they released her."

Wyc Grousbeck also was not among the revelers at Pierce's home. He left the TD Banknorth Garden around 4 a.m., firmly clutching the championship trophy. He placed it on his breakfast table at home and finally retired. The trophy was still there later that morning when he woke up on his first full day as the man in charge of the 2008 NBA champions.

1

Ping-Pong History

O N THE AFTERNOON OF MAY 22, 2007, Wyc Grousbeck, the Celtics principal owner, put on his favorite green-striped suit, one tailor-made for him by Etro in Florence, Italy, and one he had worn, occasionally to the dismay of his sartorially savvier spouse, to many Celtics games.

It was a month after the last game of the Celtics 2006–2007 season. Although the Celtics had had trouble winning in 2007, they seemed to prevail on the nights that Grousbeck wore the suit, so he thought it was the ideal ensemble to wear to the 2007 NBA draft lottery, where the Celtics were hoping to get either the No. 1 or No. 2 pick.

Grousbeck climbed into the driver's seat of his vintage, silver and gray 1968 Ford Mustang fastback for what normally would be a short drive to Hanscom Field, where a private plane awaited to take him, Celtics broadcaster and Hall of Famer Tommy Heinsohn, and Heinsohn's wife Helen to Secaucus, New Jersey, the site of the lottery. Grousbeck went a quarter of a mile, took a turn, and the clutch blew in his Mustang.

Thinking that this was not the best way to start what was going to be one of the most eventful days in Celtics history, Grousbeck drifted over to the side of the road, knowing that the plane was due to leave in 20 minutes. He decided to abandon the vehicle, walked back home, took another car, and barely made it to Hanscom for the flight.

Grousbeck and everyone associated with the Celtics desperately hoped that the 2007 lottery could do for them what the 1997 lottery did not do for coach Rick Pitino—deliver them a franchise player in either Ohio State center Greg Oden or University of Texas forward Kevin Durant, both considered to be future All-Stars. Ten years earlier, the Celtics had gone into the lottery with by far the best statistical chance to get the No. 1 pick, who that year was Wake Forest's Tim Duncan. Instead, the San Antonio Spurs won the lottery, and Duncan has been an anchor for four championship teams. The Celtics ended up with the third and sixth picks, taking Chauncey Billups and Ron Mercer.

BY ANY YARDSTICK, the Celtics were worthy lottery material in 2007. Their season, a real *annus horribilis*, had resulted in only 24 victories, the second lowest total in an 82-game season in franchise history.

The remarkably durable Paul Pierce, who had missed just 19 games in his first eight seasons, missed a total of 35, cut down by a stress fracture in his left foot. Wally Szczerbiak, another starter, missed 50 games and had season-ending ankle surgery. Al Jefferson, seen as the team's best young player, missed 13 games after an emergency appendectomy. Tony Allen, who had started to blossom after Pierce went down, blew out his left knee in early January in what still ranks as one of the most implausible NBA moments:

coming down awkwardly from a dunk that did not count because the whistle already had blown. Theo Ratliff, acquired for his soon-to-be-expiring hefty contract ($11.6 million), played a total of 44 minutes and eventually had season-ending back surgery.

About the only positive development, if it can be viewed as such, was second-year forward Gerald Green's imaginative routine during All-Star weekend in Las Vegas, which earned him the Slam Dunk Championship. Green was the only Celtic to appear that weekend, unless you counted one of the team cheerleaders.

The Celtics endured a franchise-worst 18-game losing streak from January 7 to February 12 and then immediately after ending it, proceeded to lose four more. Amazingly, the more the team lost, the more people started to focus on the lottery, with Oden and Durant as the obvious attractions. (At that point, neither player had declared for the draft, but the universal feeling was that they would.) National television abandoned the Celtics wholesale; all of their originally scheduled games on ESPN were dropped, and they went the entire season without a network appearance.

The glass-half-full Grousbeck resorted one night to distributing inspirational literature to all of the players before a game against the Miami Heat. The Celtics lost the game by 12 points. Injuries and youth, a deadly combination in the NBA, combined to turn the 2006–2007 season into an unmitigated disaster.

The team's bad luck even extended into the first week of the post-season. Point guard Sebastian Telfair, a New York City high school legend whose game had not successfully translated to the NBA, was arrested. He had been stopped in Connecticut while doing 77 mph in a 45 mph zone. Police also found a loaded handgun in the 2006 Land Rover, and Telfair could produce only a suspended Florida driver's license, even though he listed his address as New York City.

This was not Telfair's first incident with a handgun. While with the Portland Trail Blazers on a road trip to Boston during the 2005–2006 season, Telfair had carried a gun onto the Blazers' charter plane. He said the weapon, registered to his girlfriend, had been packed by accident. The Blazers fined him. Then, during the exhibition season with the Celtics in a game in New York, he was taken to a police station for questioning in the shooting of rapper Fabolous. According to Telfair, the shooting had occurred after a necklace he valued at $50,000 had been ripped off him while outside a Manhattan night club.

The latest Telfair episode infuriated Grousbeck. "I'm very emotional," Grousbeck said. "It's one of my faults. But we had just finished a terrible season, and I had spoken to the team in the locker room along with [fellow owner] Steve Pagliuca, which is rare for me. I hardly ever do that. I said to them, 'I've been on a national championship team in college [rowing at Princeton], and we had an attitude on that team to push for that. And I'd like all of you to have that attitude over the summer and let's come back next fall strong and together.'"

He told the players that with individuals like Pierce and Jefferson, there was promise ahead. He then asked them to remember what team they played for, to stay out of trouble, and keep their noses clean. Less than two days later, Grousbeck was sitting down to breakfast at an owners' meeting in New York when he got the Telfair news. He had to go over and tell NBA Commissioner David Stern, who doesn't like it when his players misbehave. The timing could not have been worse.

On returning to Boston, Grousbeck called the team's equipment manager John Connor at the team's practice facility in suburban Waltham, a state-of-the-art place where a fingerprint ID is required for entry and players have their own gated parking area. He instructed Connor to remove Telfair's name from his locker and then, without the knowledge of Ainge or Rivers, proceeded to email the information to reporters. "Our locker room is invitation only," Grousbeck said, "and he's not invited. It was an emotional decision, but there's emotion at the core of any sports team that wins. I'm not sure if I handled it right."

What was certain was that on that day, April 21, 2007, Telfair had played his last game as a Celtic. Two months later, he would be traded.

———————

A MONTH LATER, Grousbeck was back in the New York City area, but in a much better state of mind. The lottery represented hope for a team that needed it, big time. No one was paying attention to the Celtics in the city of Boston, as both the Red Sox and the Patriots were the 800-pound gorillas who dominated coverage and water-cooler conversation. (Indeed, the Red Sox coverage in Boston was so over-the-top that on the day the Celtics officially acquired Kevin Garnett, the *Boston Globe* equated the signing to the Red Sox's acquisition of relief pitcher Eric Gagne that same day.)

The Celtics' chances of landing either the first or second pick in 2007 were surpassed by only one other team, the Memphis Grizzlies. But neither team had even a 40 percent chance of getting the picks. You could not find anyone in the NBA community who didn't think Oden and Durant were destined to be perennial All-Stars. Oden, a mammoth, athletic presence, was deemed to be a franchise changer/savior, which is exactly what the Celtics needed after going through a dreadful season. Durant was a gifted offensive player, likened to a cross between Tracy McGrady and Kevin Garnett. While the consensus in the NBA is that size rules all, at the time of the lottery Celtics general manager Danny Ainge leaned ever so slightly toward Durant, although he knew that there would be another six weeks to closely evaluate the players if the Celtics received either of the first two picks.

The lottery had been introduced in 1985, supposedly to discourage teams from deliberately losing games. Most drafts reward the worst teams with the best picks, which is what the NBA had been doing since 1966, when the league used a coin flip to determine the No. 1 overall pick. The teams with the worst records in each of the two conferences participated. When there was only one undeniable star available, the coin flip took on added importance. The greatest example of this was in 1969, with the Phoenix Suns and Milwaukee Bucks. The Bucks won the flip and selected Lew Alcindor out of UCLA (he would later change his name to Kareem Abdul-Jabbar). The Suns selected Neal Walk, whose NBA career was over before it ever began.

The lottery has been changed a few times since its introduction, but the basic premise remains the same. All of the teams that do not make the playoffs are involved, and each has a statistical shot at the No. 1 pick. The teams with the worst records simply have more opportunities, but no team can go into the event thinking its percentages are favorable.

The NBA assigns sets of four numbers to all the lottery teams. There are 1,000 such four-number combinations, with the worst team (in 2007, Memphis) receiving 250 combinations. The Celtics received 199 combinations, giving them a 19.9 percent chance at the No. 1 overall pick. Their chances for either No. 1 or No. 2 were roughly double that, but still well below average. For this year, that was deemed to be fine.

The lottery itself is conducted before the televised event in a room in the NBA's entertainment facility in Secaucus. It's a conference room, upstairs from the quasi-stage that television viewers are accustomed to seeing. There are rows of tables to accommodate the 14 lottery teams, and each team is allowed to have one representative in the room.

To keep things quiet, the NBA makes every team representative surrender his cellphone, pager, PDA, or anything else that would allow him or her to communicate the outcome back to the team.

Fourteen Ping-Pong balls, numbered 1 to 14, are placed in a tumbler, and four balls are spun out. Those four numbers are assigned to a specific team and that team is deemed to be the winner. The process is then repeated a second and third time. After that, the Ping-Pong balls are put away, and the draft order reverts to form; namely, the team with the worst record still out there gets the No. 4 pick and so on, down to No. 14. So the team with the worst record can do no worse than the No. 4 pick, the team with the second worst record can do no worse than the fifth pick, and so on.

Grousbeck and the others took their seats and watched a demonstration dry run. The Celtics did not win, not that it would have mattered. Then came the actual lottery, and immediately Grousbeck went from anticipation to devastation. He knew the instant that the balls tumbled that the Celtics were not going to get No. 1. Or No. 2. Or even No. 3. No, they would drop three spots to No. 5, the lowest they could possibly go.

The Celtics needed a No. 1 or a No. 2 to show up on one of the four balls. They didn't get either. The order didn't matter. But there were no No. 1s or No. 2s. Grousbeck shared his misery with Memphis, which fell all the way to No. 4, giving team executive Jerry West, a lottery hater, another chance to stew. Milwaukee, with the third worst record, fell to sixth.

Into the top three spots went Portland, Seattle, and Atlanta. Out in Seattle, Ray Allen, five weeks before he would be traded to Boston, saw the results on television and started thinking the Sonics might be on to something—finally. "There had been so much uncertainty and negativity about the future and direction of the franchise and all of a sudden it was like, 'Wow. Here's a positive story,'" Allen said. "Maybe this will spur the city to try and keep the team there. We had a good young team. Me. Rashard [Lewis]. Now we had a chance to get [Kevin] Durant. It finally looked like we might start winning."

Grousbeck did the diplomatic thing. He congratulated the winners. "Then I sort of sat down, dumbfounded, for I think about five minutes," Grousbeck said. "I said to myself, 'This stinks.' And then I remembered that the news wouldn't be official for another 55 minutes or so and then they are all going to feel as terrible as I am feeling. And that made me feel even worse."

BEFORE THAT FATEFUL NIGHT, the Celtics had had some internal discussions about what they would do should they get the first or second pick. Paul Pierce had already said that the team should trade it; he had had enough of rebuilding and wanted to win right away. Rivers said he proposed trading the pick because, even with Oden or Durant, the Celtics would still be far from a championship. He said he wanted to use the pick to get Kevin Garnett, now widely assumed to be available for the first time, while also being able to keep Al Jefferson. "That was my thinking going in, and that would have made us absolutely remarkable," Rivers said.

But the final call in all such matters falls with Ainge. He had seen Durant and Oden play many times; in fact, the NBA had fined the Celtics $30,000 for "excessive contact" with Durant's family because Ainge sat next to Durant's mother during a Texas game. The reasoning was that Ainge's mere presence might be seen as an inducement to Durant to leave school early. As bizarre as that sounds—many, many other scouts also were watching Durant—it nonetheless warranted a fine from the league.

Ainge had also spent a considerable amount of time watching the others who would likely be in the three-to-seven range in the event of a worst-case scenario in Secaucus. "I figured I would have the next six weeks to focus on those two guys if we had gotten the first or second pick," he said. "So I was focusing on the other guys. You don't allow yourself to get too far ahead of the game," he went on. "I was preparing more for us not getting either pick, because if we had gotten one of them, then it was going to be easy."

Or not. One of the potential downfalls of getting the No. 1 or No. 2 pick, and keeping it, was that it likely would have led to the trading of Pierce. Two years earlier, Pierce almost had been dealt to Portland for a draft pick that would have turned out to be Chris Paul. In the end, the Celtics didn't pull the trigger. But they were close enough to have told advertisers at the *Boston Globe* to have two Celtics ads ready for the morning paper the next day, one with

Pierce and one without Pierce. When the New Orleans Hornets took Paul, the ad with Pierce was put into the newspaper.

"Had we just made the draft pick [in 2007], we might have had to do something with Paul [Pierce]," Ainge admitted. "He was at a point, and rightly so, that he was tired of playing with all these young players. And I was sympathetic to that. I think at some point we would have made that decision."

As THE TELEVISED VERSION OF THE LOTTERY NEARED, Grousbeck was still in the dumps in Secaucus, unable to communicate the bad news back to the home base. Season ticket holders were attending the annual draft party at the practice facility in Waltham, and there was an air of expectation that this time the Celtics would not get screwed, as had happened in 1997. Even the Spurs coach Gregg Popovich had expressed his hope that the Celtics would win the lottery to make up for 1997, allowing them to finally get Oden. When the NBA saw those remarks, the league quickly fined Popovich. While it was common knowledge in March 2007, when Popovich spoke, that Oden was leaving school, until he officially entered his name in the NBA draft in May, he was deemed to be an underclassman and therefore off limits because he might be subject to NBA temptation.

During the hour between the real lottery and the televised version, the NBA's cameras produced an in-house shot of the drawing room where Grousbeck was waiting. He wasn't alone in his exasperation. Jerry West, who had narrowly lost out on LeBron James four years earlier, was bemoaning the inherent unfairness of the lottery to one and all. The Portland and Seattle representatives were predictably exuberant. Atlanta had to get into the top three or it would lose its pick to Phoenix. It did and, as a result, ended up with Al Horford, who had a superb rookie season. Phoenix ended up getting Atlanta's pick in 2008, No. 15 overall.

But the quick camera shot of the room was also beamed to the teams that were participating. Grousbeck's body language, easily seen back in Waltham, was transparent. "I looked like death warmed over," he recalled. Sitting in Danny Ainge's office, which overlooks the practice court, Steve Pagliuca, Grousbeck's ownership partner, said a hush fell over the room. "It was like the air had gotten sucked out," he commented. "You could tell looking at Wyc that we had not gotten the first pick. We knew right then and there."

It soon became apparent the Celtics had not gotten the No. 1 or the No. 2 pick. On stage, Tommy Heinsohn was getting ready to sit down at the Celtics podium on the tiered stage. His wife Helen had brought all kinds of religious paraphernalia to help; Grousbeck had brought a pocket knife given to him by Red Auerbach, the Celtics iconic figure who had died the previous October. Then came the televised event. A camera shot from a bar in Boston captured perfectly the sentiment in Boston, as a Celtics fan clasped both hands to his head in disbelief. Grousbeck did not try to put a positive spin on the evening, for it would have sounded silly. They had gone to New Jersey hoping to come back with Greg Oden or Kevin Durant, and now they were coming back with . . . No. 5? "At no point did we contemplate that," Pagliuca said. "That wasn't even in the cards."

Watching the lottery on television in Los Angeles while hosting a party for his charitable foundation, Paul Pierce had conflicting thoughts. The first was more bad luck for the team that had lost Duncan a decade earlier and, before that, had had to deal with the sudden deaths of two promising young players, Len Bias, who never wore a Celtic uniform, and Reggie Lewis, who was developing into an All-Star guard.

The second feeling, however, was much more positive. Pierce immediately figured that the Celtics in all likelihood would now have to trade the pick. "It was like, here we go again. Bad luck. Len Bias. Reggie Lewis. Tim Duncan. I'm thinking to myself, 'Not again,'" Pierce said. "I'm also thinking at this point that it might be good because now Danny is going to have to trade the pick. There's no way the fifth pick will help us."

———————

PIERCE, AINGE, GROUSBECK, AND PAGLIUCA had had a meeting after the season in which the Celtics owners promised Pierce that they would do everything in their power to get him immediate help and that they wanted him to devote his summer to getting in shape and coming back next season. Indeed, Pierce had kept his end of the bargain by declining an opportunity to try out for the USA Basketball team, which would participate in the 2008 Olympics. But he was skeptical of the promises from management. He had heard them before and seen little to warrant any optimism.

Pierce and his agent Jeff Schwartz had been in constant contact in the weeks leading up to and after the lottery about the 2007–2008 season. Neither was sure Pierce would be back in Boston, management promises notwithstanding. "I thought I'd be a member of the Los Angeles Clippers," Pierce said. "I thought it was over. I thought I was going to be anything but a Celtic.

"My agent and I were talking a lot about which teams I might want to go to. The Celtics knew I had been loyal to them, so he was thinking we might talk to them about a situation where it would work for me and it would work for them, someplace where I'd be happy, but they'd also be happy with what they got for me. We had a lot of those conversations."

Working out in Los Angeles at UCLA in May, he ran into Kobe Bryant, who had publicly demanded a trade in frustration over the lack of activity by the Lakers. They got into a friendly argument as to which player would be traded first. "He had already gone public. I was like, 'Kobe, I m going to get traded before you.'"

As it turned out, both players stayed put. But on that day in May, it would have been hard to convince either of that. Then, when the Ping-Pong balls delivered the No. 5 pick to Boston, the Celtics turned to Plan B: trading the pick. Pierce was right about one thing. There was no way the Celtics were going to get a prime timer or impact player with the No. 5 pick. Indeed, names like Jeff Green of Georgetown, Yi Jianlin of China, and Al Thornton of Florida State were already surfacing as likely candidates to land in Boston. Decent prospects all, but not the kind that Pierce—or Ainge or Rivers—really, truly wanted.

Slowly, reality set in. Grousbeck flew home with the Heinsohns, commiserating all the way, each one telling the other, "You did your best." Ainge predicted that not only would the Celtics get a very good player at No. 5, but that the team's days of being in the lottery were over. Few took him seriously. Rivers, after his initial shock, turned to Ainge and said, "Hell, if we're waiting for No. 1 to happen to become a good team, then we're going to be waiting for a long, long time. We're going to have to go out and make something happen."

And that is exactly what they did.

EVEN BEFORE THE DISAPPOINTING NEWS from lottery night, Ainge had started to zero in on acquiring Kevin Garnett. Several things were in his favor. In his first four years with Boston, while constantly retooling the team, Ainge had drafted well and Rivers had developed what many NBA personnel people thought were very serviceable players.

Jefferson was No. 1 on that list. He had come to the Celtics directly from Prentiss High School in Mississippi and was one of four players on the 2006–2007 Celtics who never went to college. The others were Sebastian Telfair, Kendrick Perkins, and Gerald Green. Ainge had lucked into Jefferson in the 2004

NBA draft; his real hope had been that California high-school player Robert Swift would be available at No. 15, where the Celtics picked. But the Sonics took Swift at No. 13, and Ainge rolled the dice on Jefferson, who had been a prolific scorer in high school but could hardly be expected to make a substantive contribution in his first year in the NBA. But Jefferson got some playing time in his first year, performed well in the playoffs, and after three seasons with the Celtics, by steadily improving each year, had become a beast. He had developed a slew of moves around the basket, drawing comparisons, however premature and unrealistic, to Kevin McHale. He was a rebounding machine. And he was improving on defense, the one acknowledged weakness in his game.

Among young big men in the NBA, few had more promise. He also had a big fan in Minnesota, McHale, who now came to the same conclusion Ainge had come to in Boston a few years earlier: he wasn't going to win with what he had. It was time to rebuild. For Minnesota, that meant deciding what to do with Garnett.

"I thought there was a chance we could get him at the end of the [2006–2007] season," Ainge said. "It was nothing specific that Kevin [McHale] told me, but I thought there was a possibility they might actually move him. I knew Kevin [McHale] liked Al Jefferson a lot and (the Timberwolves) needed to get younger. We had a lot of possibilities to offer them to get KG." (Ainge and McHale remain close friends from their days as Celtics teammates and converse regularly.)

After the lottery, things quieted down in Boston. In Minnesota, however, it was just heating up, as it looked more likely that, for the first time in his life, Garnett was not going to be wearing a Minnesota Timberwolves uniform next season.

For starters, there was an extension coming due for Garnett, who had already earned more than $140 million from the Timberwolves in his first 12 years. The upcoming extension would likely cost another $100 million. While no one complained that Garnett didn't deliver, the team rarely did, and the Timberwolves started to think that the money might be better spent elsewhere.

Garnett was now almost 32 years old and, more worrisome, had played more regular-season minutes in his NBA career than either Larry Bird or Isiah Thomas. He had two more years left on his contract, but the second year was at his option, allowing him to become a free agent at the end of the 2007–2008 season. The Timberwolves decided not to sign Garnett to an extension, a signal to the rest of the league that he was now available.

The Celtics and Timberwolves agreed to a deal before the draft, but the quickness of the negotiations caught Garnett off guard. He had made no trade demands and had been, above all else, fiercely loyal to the Timberwolves. He was not looking to move and felt insulted that he was being shopped around, even though that is commonplace in the NBA.

He also wasn't keen on joining a 24-win Celtics team. He couldn't see how that situation was much better than the one he was already in. So his agent told both teams that Garnett did not want to do the deal and would not sign an extension with the Celtics, a critical component of the trade.

Immediately before the deal was squelched, Rivers finally got Garnett on the telephone, no small feat in the off-season. "He was mad at Minnesota, not at Boston," Rivers said. "He took it very, very personal that they were trying to trade him. He kept saying, 'I'm not mad at you. I'm not mad at Danny.' But he was mad at McHale, which kind of put Danny in a bind because they are such good friends.

"But what impressed me most in talking to him was that he didn't want the state of Minnesota to think he was bailing on them, that was his whole passion. He kept saying, 'I didn't ask to get traded. I didn't want to get traded.' That's what upset him more than anything. I just told him about the opportunity here. He didn't think we had enough and he probably was right."

Andy Miller, Garnett's agent, then went public by saying his client was not coming to Boston. Ainge and Rivers never really believed that, but for now that was the state of things. Boston, however, had company in the pursuit of Garnett.

Phoenix was after Garnett, although the Celtics privately doubted that the money-conscious Suns would give Garnett the contract extension he was going to demand. The Lakers were pursuing Garnett, but their big contract, necessary to do the deal under the NBA's salary cap rules, belonged to Lamar Odom, whom the Timberwolves did not want.

The Mavericks and Warriors were in the chase as well. All those teams had one thing in common: they were in the Western Conference, the same conference as the Timberwolves. Ainge felt all along that if he produced an attractive package—and he felt that he had—then McHale would be more inclined to trade Garnett to the Eastern Conference so the Timberwolves would have to face him only twice a year.

But for the moment, the Celtics had to get better to convince Garnett to agree to a deal and sign an extension. Boston was never going to do the deal without Garnett's imprimatur. The team was giving up too much. So in the weeks before the draft, Ainge set out to improve the Celtics so that Garnett might reconsider.

2

Along Comes Ray

RAY ALLEN HAD BEEN on Danny Ainge's short list for awhile. And why not? Allen, one of the NBA's best shooters, classiest individuals, and most dedicated professionals, was in the same situation as Paul Pierce: a good-to-great player on a team going nowhere.

Three years earlier, the Celtics and Sonics had talked about a trade for Allen, but at that time Seattle wanted Pierce. Talk of a deal quickly ended. Now, in June 2007, things had changed in both locales, making another run at Allen more promising and more realistic.

Ainge kept Pierce abreast of what he was doing, trying to reassure his star player that he was serious about acquiring veteran help for his captain. Pierce liked what he heard, but had to remind himself that it was still only talk. "The names Danny was saying were names that got me really excited," he said. "Shawn Marion.

Ray Allen. Shoot, I'd rather have Ray Allen than the fifth pick. Wouldn't you? That was a no-brainer to me."

———————

WALTER RAY ALLEN HAD BEEN A SEVEN-TIME ALL-STAR in both Milwaukee and Seattle, having entered the NBA in 1996 following his junior year at the University of Connecticut. He had won gold with the U.S. Olympic team in 2000 in Sydney and two other times had helped national teams with NBA players qualify for the Olympics (1999 and 2003).

He was widely viewed as one of the NBA's elite players and was coming off a season in which he (a) averaged a career high 26.4 points a game, but (b) missed 27 games and had double ankle surgery for bone spurs at the end of the season. He was 32 years old, and the Celtics had to weigh his history against their future.

Team doctors, given access to Allen's medical records by the Sonics, looked everything over; in their opinion, the prognosis for recovery from the surgeries was excellent. No one worried about the prolonged period of inactivity resulting in him turning into the slovenly Shawn Kemp; his body is a temple.

The Celtics did not know and could not know, however, if he was going to be available in 2007. He had three years left on his contract, but the Sonics had been sold, had hired a young general manager, Sam Presti, who wanted to improve the team's defense, and then had gotten lucky on lottery night, landing the second overall pick. Presti faced the prospect of losing free agent Rashard Lewis to free agency—which he eventually did—but in June 2007, he still had Lewis, Ray Allen, and the likelihood of Kevin Durant. That didn't appear to be a bad situation.

"Seattle was going to go one of two ways," said Ainge, who re-visited the Allen talks when Presti settled in. "They had the second pick. Either they were going to trade it to add to what they had, or they were going to use it and go young with Durant. I just felt that with a new general manager, it was going to be the latter, that some time, some day, he was going to move Ray."

Allen was aware that his name was out there. "I had heard stuff for about a week, but you always hear stuff when the team isn't doing well," he said. "Every year, it seemed like that was the story."

Talks got serious as the draft approached. Eventually, the Celtics came up with an offer: Wally Szczerbiak, Delonte West, and the fifth pick in the draft, who the Sonics hoped would be Jeff Green. The Sonics countered that they'd rather have Theo Ratliff (and his expiring contract) and Rajon Rondo. Had Seattle insisted on either of those two players remaining in the trade, Ray Allen would never have become a Celtic. Danny Ainge was not going to trade Rondo, and Ratliff's fat contract was being held to entice another team in a possible second deal involving another big-name veteran. The short list included Kevin Garnett, Jason Kidd, Pau Gasol, and Shawn Marion.

Ainge spent significant time briefing ownership on why the acquisition of Allen would be a good thing, even as Wyc Grousbeck expressed initial skepticism. "I must confess, it looked sideways to me," Grousbeck said. "Ray had just had double ankle surgery, so that made me worried. And I wondered how much better we'd really be."

That was fine with Ainge. He told the owners that Allen could really complement Pierce and Al Jefferson with his shooting. He reminded the owners, not that they needed to be reminded, of Allen's elegance, diligence, and high character. He reminded the owners of their promise to Pierce earlier in the spring that they would do whatever they could to bring in some veteran help. But he also told them—and the owners wholeheartedly concurred— that if the Sonics insisted on Rondo or Ratliff being in the deal, there would be no deal.

"That wasn't going to happen," Ainge said. "We needed Theo's contract because if we don't have that, we don't have what

we need to make the next deal. And there was no way we were trading Rajon."

That is why the deal went down to the wire on draft day. The
Celtics held firm, and the Sonics, who really wanted Jeff Green
eventually acquiesced and accepted Szczerbiak and West. The
Celtics also got a second-round pick out of the deal, which they
used to select Glen "Big Baby" Davis. So while it hardly looked like
a coup for Boston on draft night, and Ainge was roundly criticized
for the deal at the time, it was the initial step in what would be one
of the most dramatic makeovers in NBA history.

————————

VERY FEW BASKETBALL PEOPLE IN BOSTON needed an introduction to
Ray Allen. He had spent three of his most formative years honing
his skills less than 90 minutes away in Storrs, at the University of
Connecticut. He had been in the league for 12 years and had made
countless trips through Boston as a member of the Milwaukee
Bucks and Seattle Sonics.

But what the casual fan might not have known was how
fiercely dedicated Allen is both to the game and to his personal
routine. If there's one word that describes Allen's almost maniacal
approach to his profession, it's precision.

"Ray wants everything to be just so," explained former Sonics
coach Nate McMillan, who had Allen for 2½ seasons in Seattle.
"He wants to be able to do his pregame shooting the same
way, every game. He wants the same parking spot, every day. He
wants the same seat on the team plane. He is a total creature of
habit."

That obsession—Allen himself thinks he might have an un-
diagnosed case of obsessive compulsive disorder—has been with
him for as long as he can remember. Even in elementary school,
he would make sure he never left the gym without first making
five layups with each hand. To this day, his game-day routine is

sacrosanct: the same food (chicken and rice); the same number of shots from the same number of places; the shaving of his head; the number of squats, bench presses, and curls (depending on the time of the season); and the same parking space. In the off-season, while in Seattle, he took thrice-weekly bike rides of 30 miles through the mountains to stay in shape. He ran two other days.

Maybe it was his military upbringing. He had moved around as a kid because his father was in the Air Force. One year, home might be California. Another year, it might be London.

"It was probably a combination of my military life and my college life," he said. "I had decided early on that if I was going to be a great player, I had to have a routine. And it had to be something a little different from what everyone else did. That's why a routine is so important. Every game day in the NBA is really Groundhog Day. It's the same whether you're in Portland or Atlanta. It doesn't matter. You walk into the gym and do your thing."

By the time Allen was in high school, however, the family had settled in Dalzell, South Carolina. His father was stationed at Shaw Air Force Base near Sumter, while his mother worked in a convenience store. Allen attended Hillcrest High School, where he was able to stay for the full four years.

He was an almost immediate star there, earning All-State and team MVP honors for three consecutive seasons. UConn coach Jim Calhoun first laid eyes on Allen in 1992, the summer before Allen's senior year in high school, at an all-star camp in Indianapolis sponsored by Nike. Connecticut had a tradition of having big guards who were successful in the pros, and Calhoun thought Allen would fit right in.

Calhoun put Allen's name on his wish list, but it quickly moved to "must get" after he saw Allen a second time, at a tournament in Jacksonville, Florida, where Allen's AAU team was playing one of the country's best teams from New York City. "He scored 63 points," Calhoun said of Allen. "He had this incredible ability not to just catch and shoot, but to catch, then lift, and then shoot.

It was like he caught the ball and then took the elevator to the third floor. It was something to see."

When Allen returned for his senior year at Hillcrest, he finished with a flourish. The team went 27–4 and won the state championship, with Allen collecting 25 points and 15 rebounds in the title game, played before more than 8,000 fans at the University of South Carolina in Columbia. He averaged 28.5 points, 13.5 rebounds, and 5.3 assists a game and won numerous state accolades, including the coveted Mr. Basketball of South Carolina.

But as good as he was, he wasn't what the high school basketball observers would call "a public name" in 1993. There was no invitation to the McDonald's All-America game. There wasn't a slew of attention from many of the nation's more prestigious college programs either. Duke's Mike Krzyzewski didn't even remember Allen being on his radar screen; Allen would have made an ideal Blue Devil just as the classy Grant Hill was getting ready to leave Durham.

"I really didn't know much about what publicity I should be getting or shouldn't be getting," Allen said. "I think it was because I had always lived on a military base and overseas. I just didn't know. I was always on the outside, looking in. I was just happy to be able to go to college and not have my parents have to pay for it."

Connecticut considered itself a national program, however, even though it was a few years away from its first national championship. (It had won the NIT in 1988.) The Huskies played in the tough Big East Conference and were regulars in the NCAA Tournament. Assistant coach Howie Dickerman laid much of the groundwork for UConn, watching Allen play and staying in touch with the family. Then Calhoun stepped in to close the deal.

"I went to make my home visit," Calhoun recalled, "and I was wearing this big red tie. He really liked that red tie. I sat with him and his mom and you could tell, right away, what he was all about. Very, very few kids that I've recruited already had that 'It' thing about them, but Ray did. So did Emeka [Okafor]. You knew you wouldn't have to prod him to work. You knew you wouldn't have to worry about him off the court.

"There was this regalness to him, and I'd say maybe four or five kids that I've recruited had that. David Robinson had it. Emeka had it. Ben Gordon had it. I knew he had visited Clemson and South Carolina, but those programs weren't doing that well. He had visited Alabama and Kentucky. But I just felt connected to the kid right away."

Allen felt it as well. "Coach Calhoun, coach [Dave] Leitao, coach Dickerman, they all had this charisma about them," he said. "And I noticed when I made my visit to the campus that it was out of the city, and that at Storrs, you were going to be with your teammates and your friends all the time. That appealed to me."

Allen chose UConn, where his fastidiousness, good looks, and overall demeanor quickly earned him the nickname "Hollywood." (That would prove to be prophetic when filmmaker Spike Lee chose Allen to play the lead character, Jesus Shuttlesworth, in his movie *He Got Game*, which also starred Denzel Washington.) Allen always wore the right clothes, always looked like he stepped out of an Armani catalogue. Even now, he admits to owning 60 suits.

In what Calhoun calls "the eighth wonder of the world," the neatnik Allen was roomed with Travis Knight, who, Calhoun noted, "could have a three-day-old piece of pizza under his pillow and never know it. I honestly don't know how they coexisted. Ray wants his life neat, his apartment neat, his workouts neat. Travis just wasn't like that."

No, Knight wasn't. Allen would constantly harp on his roommate to clean up his dinner dishes. Knight never did. So Allen told him that the next time he saw Knight's dirty dishes in the sink, he would put them on top of his bed.

"So, right after I said this, I come back to the apartment and there are his dirty dishes in the sink," Allen said. "And he had just had his favorite meal, spaghetti and meat sauce. I took all the dishes and the pots and pans he cooked with and plopped them, right on top of his bed. He walked in with a visitor and was embarrassed by the whole thing. I didn't see any more dirty dishes in the sink after that."

As a freshman, Allen played in the shadow of Donyell Marshall, while diligently working on the arc of his shot with UConn assistant coach Glen Miller, now the head coach at the University of Pennsylvania. Calhoun and Miller felt Allen's shot was too flat, but hours and hours of shooting practice changed that.

Allen quickly became The Man in Storrs as a sophomore, averaging 21.1 points a game. He toyed with declaring for the NBA draft after his sophomore year, buoyed by a call his mother received from an NBA team who told her they would take her son in the first round if he came out. That was after he had scored 36 points in an Elite Eight season-ending loss to eventual NCAA champion UCLA.

"He didn't want to leave college. He was having too much fun," Calhoun recalled. "And I remember Kevin Stacom [a former NBA player and friend] telling me that if Ray waited a year, he'd be a top-five pick the next year and go on to have an All-Star type career. All of those things turned out to be true."

As a junior, Allen led UConn to the Sweet Sixteen, where the Huskies were beaten by eventual Final Four participant Mississippi State. He averaged 23.4 points a game and then he and everyone else knew it was time for him to leave.

Allen was seen as one of the so-called "Super Six" in the 1996 draft, none of whom were named Kobe Bryant, who would end up going thirteenth in a prearranged deal between the Lakers and Charlotte Hornets. The top six picks were universally seen as Allen Iverson, Stephon Marbury, Ray Allen, Marcus Camby, Shareef Abdur-Rahim, and Antoine Walker.

The Celtics had the sixth pick that year, thanks to a trade the year earlier with the Dallas Mavericks. But M.L. Carr, who was then running the Celtics, didn't even bother bringing Allen in for an interview or a workout.

"He was out of our reach," Carr said. "We thought he might go as high as No. 3. Larry [Bird] was working for us then as a consultant, and he was a huge Ray fan. He really wanted him. But we didn't see any way he'd slide all the way to six. We figured he'd be long gone by then. We were zeroed in on [Walker]."

Allen actually ended up going fifth, taken by Minnesota, but quickly traded to Milwaukee in a prearranged deal for Marbury. Thus, when Allen finally did become a Celtic in the summer of 2007, he told Doc Rivers, "This has been a long time coming, because I thought I might be a Celtic on draft day."

In his first five seasons with the Bucks, Allen didn't miss a game. And two years into his NBA career, he was seen as the perfect casting choice for *He Got Game*. Allen spent eight weeks in acting classes before hitting the set and showed every bit as much dedication as he does playing basketball. He received overwhelmingly favorable reviews in the film, in which he plays a high school star who is trying to navigate the sticky world of wealth, privilege, and hangers-on. ("He could pass for 18," Spike Lee said; at the time Allen was still only 22.) He also had a role in the 2001 movie *Harvard Man*, a story about a Harvard basketball player (not played by Allen) who tries to throw games.

Allen had played well enough in his first two seasons in Milwaukee that, after the league-imposed lockout ended in 1999, he was eligible to sign a lucrative contract extension. Because the new agreement between the players and the owners placed a limit on player salaries, Allen decided to go it alone and negotiate his extension directly with Milwaukee owner Herbert Kohl. Both came into the bargaining sessions agreeing that Allen deserved the maximum allowable under the Collective Bargaining Agreement: a cool $70.9 million over six years. The only impediment was Allen's request for an opt-out clause in the final season. Kohl said he didn't do opt-outs, and the six-year deal was agreed to over a luncheon that Allen's mother Flo also attended.

"We had developed a very close relationship at that point. Ray felt comfortable coming to see me directly, and it was something that I much desired," Kohl said. "It was a pretty easy negotiation. There was a feeling of mutual respect and everything flowed from there."

By 2001, Allen's fifth season in Milwaukee, the Bucks were deemed to be a certifiable force. Allen was joined by Glenn Robinson, Sam Cassell, Tim Thomas, and Lindsey Hunter. The team won 52 games, finished first in its division, and took the Iverson-led Philadelphia 76ers to a seventh game in the Eastern Conference Finals. The Sixers won, 108–91, but it had been a tough series that could have gone either way. Cassell remembered going into the Philadelphia locker room after the game to congratulate coach Larry Brown: "And he said to me, 'Sam, thank you, but you all will have a better chance of beating the Lakers than us.' And that was because we could score. They [the Sixers] had one primary scorer. They only had one guy who could get you 20 points. We had three, maybe four, who could do it." In fact, in that season, Cassell, Allen, and Robinson all had had games where they scored 40 or more, and Thomas had one of 39.

"That was such a tough series," Cassell said. "We led 2–1, and then in Game 5 we could have won at the end, but Big Dog [Robinson] missed a ten-foot shot that he makes about 20 out of 20 times."

After the series, Allen and his coach, George Karl, were fined ($10,000 and $25,000, respectively) for saying that they thought the NBA wanted Philadelphia (read: Iverson and a larger TV market) in the NBA Finals rather than small-market Milwaukee. "I thought we had been treated unfairly," Allen said. "In Game 6, our starting [power forward] Scott Williams was called for a foul for elbowing Iverson as he drove to the basket. He stayed in the game. We won. Then we flew to Philly for Game 7 and found out that it had been upgraded to a flagrant foul and that Scott had been suspended for the game. He had been very valuable for us and had had one of his best seasons."

That was as close as Allen would come to the NBA Finals until 2008. "The feeling I had after we lost Game 7 that year was that, well, we'll come back and get 'em next year. But you learn pretty quickly that just because you did it one year, it doesn't guarantee that it will happen the next year."

IN THAT NEXT YEAR, 2001–2002, the Bucks led their division into March, then fell apart down the stretch and missed the playoffs entirely. Midway though the 2002–2003 season, with Allen's relationship with Karl having deteriorated beyond repair, Allen was traded to Seattle for Gary Payton, a longtime Karl favorite.

"I always saw the relationship with George as being a one-sided feud," Allen said. "He always found something negative to say about me when there was a story in the paper. I could never satisfy him, no matter what I did. I felt like I had to defend myself against him, all the time. I tried to handle it the best way I could, but it kept showing up in the papers and my family got fed up with it. It started to hit home.

"It was a bad trade. I liked it in Milwaukee. I had been an All-Star. And Gary Payton was gone the next year. The hardest thing about trades is not the business part of it. You show up and you play," he went on. "The hardest part is having to leave all the friends that you had made over the years. That's where the sadness comes. We had good friends in Milwaukee. We had good friends in Seattle. It's tough."

Of the Allen–Karl relationship, Kohl said, "One of my biggest regrets is that Ray didn't finish his career in Milwaukee. It was a very difficult thing for me to do. I would guess that was the most regrettable transaction we've made in the 23 years that I've owned the Bucks."

The four-plus years in Seattle were equally frustrating, although Allen played well enough to be selected for the All-Star Game each season, the last one as a Commissioner's add-on. He also served as a role model for many of the younger players coming through, his work ethic spreading in the locker room until almost everyone started arriving early to take extra shots.

But in all Allen's time in Seattle, only once, in 2005, did the Sonics even make the playoffs, winning 52 games to take the Northwest Division. They took out the Kings in the first round and nearly upset the eventual champion San Antonio Spurs in the second round; had an Allen three-pointer fallen at the end of Game 6, the series would have moved to San Antonio for a Game 7.

After that season, Allen was a free agent but elected to stay in Seattle, signing a five-year $80 million extension. But coach Nate McMillan, also a free agent, bolted for Portland. The next two Seattle coaches—Bob Weiss and Bob Hill—proved ineffectual, and Allen became disenchanted with what he perceived to be Seattle's inability to get him any help. Sort of how Paul Pierce was feeling in Boston.

"I kept telling them that we needed to get better players," he said. "But they never did. They talked about having this five-year plan and yet they stood still. We would have been right there if they had just added a few players. It was always like there was never enough. They never would put their best foot forward."

Allen thought owner Howard Schultz ran the team not to win games, but to satisfy the bottom line. Then Schultz sold the team to an Oklahoma City-based group, which then cleaned out the front office and hired the highly regarded Presti to run the basketball operations. Presti had been schooled in the San Antonio way, having been a part of the last three San Antonio championships, starting as an intern and moving all the way up to assistant general manager.

He inherited a tricky situation, with many expecting the Oklahoma City–based ownership group to move the team to Oklahoma City in the next year. That came to pass. Rashard Lewis, who Allen described as a "brother," was entering free agency and was deemed to be a decent player, but no one could have envisioned dropping $118 million on him, which is what the Orlando Magic ended up doing. That, however, came well after the Sonics and Allen parted ways.

Presti wasn't initially looking to trade Allen, but the Celtics' persistence eventually paid off. Presti also got future salary flexibility because Szczerbiak's deal wasn't as lengthy or as expensive as Allen's. And Allen was ready for a change of scenery, especially coming back east to a team that was looking to win. Further, he revealed that he actually had been a Celtics fan while at UConn, a real testament given that Boston was pretty bad in those three years. "It just seems like I've been in the doldrums for the last four-and-a-half years,'" he said arriving in Boston. "It's a wonderful, wonderful feeling for me."

———————

WHILE AINGE HAD BEEN BUSY trying to improve his roster in May and June, Doc Rivers had been trying to do the same thing to his coaching staff. Two top assistants would not be returning; Tony Brown had decided to take an assistant's job with the Milwaukee Bucks under Larry Krystkowiak. And longtime Rivers' chum Dave Wohl was being moved into the Celtics front office, where he was given the title of assistant general manager and would help Ainge with deals.

So Rivers had at least one major hire to make, which didn't bother him in the slightest. "Everyone always wants to stick with their staff, and I wondered why," Rivers said. "I think you should be in search of the perfect staff, just like you'd be in search of the perfect team."

At the time, Rivers oversaw a young team that presumably would stay young if the team kept the No. 5 pick, which it was planning to use on the raw but promising Chinese star Yi Jianlin. Al Jefferson was still only 22. Kendrick Perkins was 23. Rajon Rondo and Gerald Green were both 21. Delonte West, 24, and Tony Allen, 25, were the graybeards.

In trying to reshape his staff in the early summer of 2007, he ended up talking with Larry Brown, the Hall of Fame coach who was then working in the Philadelphia 76ers front office following his disastrous one-year tenure with the New York Knicks. "I talk a lot with Larry about two things—basketball and golf," Rivers said.

Larry Brown is a coach, period. That's what he does. That's who he is. Rivers and Larry Brown started tossing around possible replacements for Tony Brown and Wohl, and finally Rivers said, "What about you?" (Rivers had played for Brown in Los Angeles, the two were good friends, and, Rivers thought, who better to work with all the young players than Mr. Fundamental himself?)

A long pause ensued.

"Are you serious?" Brown asked.

"Yeah, dead serious," Rivers said.

"Doc, I'll take the job," Brown said. "Don't mess around with me. Are you really serious?"

"Yeah, dead serious," Rivers said again.

Brown then said the two needed to talk about parameters so he, Brown, wouldn't be viewed as some vulture waiting for Rivers to stumble and fall. Rivers said he thought Brown's penchant for teaching was exactly what the Celtics needed, especially with all of their young talent. "Larry, I'm secure enough to hire you," Rivers said. "I think you'd be great. You'd be allowed to do what you like to do. We have a young team. It's a teaching environment."

It sounded great to Brown, who was desperate to get back on the bench, any bench. "I was ready to come," he said. "I really wanted to come. Doc felt comfortable enough bringing me in, and for me, I don't like the games anyway. I like the practices. It would have been wonderful to go there and to teach, to learn things from a new staff, with so many young players that I'd get a chance to work with. It was a no-brainer in my mind."

Brown then told Rivers he needed time to think about it. There were health issues with his in-laws, who lived in California, and there was Brown's allegiance to Sixers chairman Ed Snyder, who had brought him back to Philadelphia after the two had had a less than amicable parting in 2003.

It was almost a back-to-the-future moment for Brown. Ten years earlier, Brown thought he had the head coaching job of the Celtics. After an early run at Rick Pitino proved fruitless, the Celtics turned to Brown, who had just parted ways with the Indiana Pacers after four seasons, an eternity for the peripatetic coach. Brown basically accepted the job; all he was waiting for was a confirmation call from the Celtics. He never got one.

As Brown tells the story, he ran into Pitino at that time in southern California and mentioned that he was going to take the Boston job. But he also let slip the details of the compensation package, which apparently was much better than the one Pitino had rejected. Pitino then jumped back into the picture and, as he was Boston's first choice, he got the job. Brown ended up going to the 76ers.

This new position in Boston wouldn't be the head coaching job, but it was a coaching job. He would be on the floor. He would be on trips, scouting. More important to him, he'd be able to coach at practice, where Larry Brown is happiest.

Knowing Brown's tendency to change his mind, Rivers had not even brought up the topic either to his immediate boss Danny Ainge or to ownership, who also would have to sign off on it. That changed relatively soon. In July, Brown called and told Rivers, "I'll take it."

Rivers then broached the subject with Ainge, who was receptive. But when Rivers told ownership, there was concern that Brown might be seen as the obvious heir apparent, intent on getting the job.

"We were concerned about Larry," co-owner Steve Pagliuca said. "We felt you have to have a unified chain of command, and it wasn't clear to us initially that there was. But Doc convinced us. There aren't many people who could bring in a Hall of Fame coach to work under him, but Doc could. And we really tried to get him to come after that." All that convincing, however, proved to be unnecessary. Because Brown, living up to his reputation as a man of many moods, called back soon thereafter and told Rivers he could not take the job. Snyder wanted him to stay, and Brown theorized, maybe it wasn't the most prudent of moves to go from one divisional rival to another. It appeared to be over.

Waiting in the wings was tom thibodeau, a longtime lieutenant of Jeff Van Gundy, both in New York and most recently in Houston. He had a solid reputation around the league as a defensive-minded coach; he had been approached by Rivers before the Brown merry-go-round began. But Thibodeau wanted a long-term contract from the Celtics, which, at the time, they were loathe to dispense.

It had not gone as planned for Van Gundy and Thibodeau in Houston in 2006–2007, where the Rockets had had an excellent regular season, but then blew a 2–0 lead over Utah in the first round of the playoffs, dropping an excruciating Game 7 at home. Still, Thibodeau held out hope that he and Van Gundy would be back.

"We had put so much into the situation at Houston," Thibodeau said. "It was very sudden and it was very difficult to walk away from. I felt we were in a very good position, and we were maybe a player away from being really good. And it was a good group to be around. That's what made it so tough to leave."

Thibodeau's reputation guaranteed that he would receive more than a few cursory calls. He talked to the Suns. He talked to the Mavericks. Neither team is known for their defense, so each situation made sense. Then, in the first week of July, he accepted a job as an assistant coach for another defensively challenged team, the Washington Wizards. He was familiar with Washington GM Ernie Grunfeld, who had been in New York when he and Van Gundy were with the Knicks.

Three days later, he changed his mind. "It wasn't right. Not the right fit," Thibodeau said.

He then called Rivers and was told that the Larry Brown situation was still on hold. "Basically, Doc told me he had moved on and, with Larry, how can I fault him for that? I thought it was a missed opportunity, but at the same time, I was still in touch with other teams and I didn't mind the extra time to think things through," Thibodeau said.

But once Brown called and told Rivers he could not accept the job, Rivers hung up the phone and called Thibodeau. It was now late July. Allen was on board. The Garnett deal was percolating, but had not yet been consummated. Thibodeau accepted, and by the time he settled in Boston, Garnett was a Celtic.

Brown called Rivers a few days later. "Did you hire anyone yet?" Brown asked, unaware that Thibodeau had accepted the position. The Celtics did not publicly announce the hiring until August 30.

"Yeah, I did," Rivers said.

"Darn," Brown said, "I would have taken the job."

The team that Rivers and Brown talked about in the spring would not be the same team the following fall, although Brown said it would not have mattered to him who was there. "Who wouldn't want to coach Kevin [Garnett] and Ray [Allen]. I had both of them in 1999 at the [Olympic] qualifying tournament in Puerto Rico and as an assistant to Rudy [Tomjanovich] in the 2000 Olympics," he said. "They were great.

"I just like to coach and teach. The biggest myth about me is that I don't play young guys," Brown said. "I do. And the other myth is that older guys don't want to be taught or coached. That's the furthest thing from the truth. I was willing to do whatever Doc wanted me to do. That's the job of an assistant. It just didn't work out. It's too bad. It would have been neat."

And it might well have worked. Who knows? Had Brown never made that second phone call to Rivers, he might well have been on the Boston bench for the 2007–2008 season, and Tom Thibodeau, the man credited with devising and implementing Boston's league-best defense, would not have been.

Larry Brown ended up staying in Philadelphia for another year and then accepted the head coaching job of the Charlotte Bobcats for the 2008–2009 season. It is his ninth NBA head coaching job.

———————————

In thibodeau, however, the Celtics got exactly what they needed, even though at the time, the team was bereft of defensive-minded players. Ainge made sure that defensive-performance clauses were in the coaching contracts, because "we wanted to emphasize that from the top down." Once the 2007–2008 roster was complete, with defensive stalwarts like Kevin Garnett and James Posey on board, Ainge felt the Celtics had a chance to be one of the top eight defensive teams in the league.

Thibodeau had coached in the NBA for 17 seasons. Defense was his calling card. The year before he came to Boston, the No. 1 team in the league in defensive field goal percentage was the Rockets.

"The key for me with Tibbs [Thibodeau] was to get the veterans to buy into what he was doing because he is so intense, and sometimes with a veteran team, that intensity can result in things going the wrong way," Rivers said. "But early on, I told the players that Tibbs' voice was the one that they were going to hear and listen to when we were going over defenses. I think they hear my voice too much anyway. And when a player came up to me early and said, 'Doc, what if we do this?' I would say, 'What did Tibbs just say?' I made it a very big point early on to get away from doing the defensive part of it. Obviously, Tibbs and I would talk about what we were going to do and how we wanted to do it, but once we made that decision, he was the one who sold it."

Rivers also elevated Armond Hill, who had been on his staff for the previous three seasons, to be his Tim Thibodeau on offense. Unlike Thibodeau, Hill was a certified former player, having starred at Princeton (he was the best player on the team that won the 1975 NIT, a monumental achievement then, especially since it came at the expense of such marquee national programs as Oregon, Providence, and South Carolina). He was a No. 1 draft pick (ninth overall) of the Atlanta Hawks in 1976 and had coached at both the college level (Columbia) and in the NBA as an assistant in Atlanta before coming to Boston.

Although Rivers is more involved vocally with the offense, calling plays on the sideline and drawing them up in the huddles, many of the sets and ideas spring from Hill, who sits to the coach's right during games. Thibodeau sits to the coach's left. It's not a coincidence.

"I've always done that because I didn't want to be way at the end, away from all the players," Rivers said. "I wanted to be in earshot. And I can always turn one way to get answers to any questions I have about the offense and then turn the other way to get answers to any questions I have about the defense."

———————

RIVERS HAD HIS RECONFIGURED COACHING STAFF. He had a new shooting guard. But he figured that with what the Celtics had given away to get Allen, he wasn't going to get a whole lot more in 2007. "When we got Ray, I just didn't see anything more happening," he said. "I thought we had lost the opportunity [to get another big player]. I didn't think we had enough assets anymore."

He was wrong. And he was never happier to be so.

3

The Big Ticket

WITHIN A WEEK OF THE 2007 DRAFT and Boston's acquisition of Ray Allen, Kevin Garnett's agent, Andy Miller,
called his client to gauge whether the new Celtics might
look any more appealing now than before the draft.

Garnett didn't have to be sold on Allen. They had been fellow
All-Stars from the Western Conference for the past four years and
had known each other since high school, when they both played in
South Carolina. One of Garnett's lasting memories of seeing Allen
for the first time was of an almost ultra-composed, to-the-manor-
born teenager who knew what he wanted and how to get it.

But Garnett does nothing on impulse. After receiving the call
from his agent, he said he would think it over. For Garnett, that's a
process than can be measured in weeks, not days or hours.

Meanwhile, back in Boston, Ainge had presented to ownership the current situation about the possibilities. Contrary to what
Rivers believed, Ainge felt he still had the two most important

ingredients to make the trade for Garnett: Al Jefferson and Theo Ratliff's expiring contract. What he did not have anymore was the No. 5 pick, but he could remedy that by sending a first-round pick that the Timberwolves had given in January 2006 back to Minnesota. He could add another as well.

Ainge and Minnesota GM Kevin McHale reconnected in the first week of July in Las Vegas, where the Celtics and Timberwolves each had entries in the Toshiba Summer League. Miller was there as well, and he started the process rolling by informing McHale and then Ainge that the Allen trade had accomplished what Ainge had hoped: ignite some interest in Garnett coming to Boston.

Garnett, back in California at his Malibu home, called friends for their input. He talked to Detroit's Chauncey Billups, who had been a teammate in Minnesota and had remained close after leaving for the Pistons. (The two were featured in the "There Can Only Be One" ads in the playoffs.) Billups told Garnett he should go to Boston, even if it would be bad for Detroit. Things were not getting any better in Minnesota, and the two of them could look forward to meeting in the Eastern Conference Finals.

"I just knew how much of a competitor KG was and he deserved a chance to go deep into the playoffs," Billups said. "And there wasn't going to be that opportunity if he remained in Minnesota. I told him, 'You can't look back on your career one day and say, Damn, I wished I would have done this, or I shouldn't have stayed in Minnesota.' I thought it was a great move for him."

Garnett sought the counsel of another close friend, Tyronn Lue, a frequent summer visitor to Garnett's home who had played briefly for Doc Rivers in Orlando. Lue went to bat for Rivers, which was important to Garnett because the Wolves had already gone through several coaches since Garnett's favorite coach, Flip Saunders, had been fired.

"I just didn't want to rush anything," Garnett said. "I'm a processing kind of a guy. I never speak on anyone's situation. I just worry about my own situation and try to evaluate every side for whatever it's worth. That's just who I am, conservative like that. I try to understand it. I try to view it. I take all the time I need. And then I make a decision."

He knew Boston wasn't the only option, but it looked to be the best one because of their personnel. Both the Suns and Lakers were hot on his trail as well, and he already had received a phone call from Suns' point guard Steve Nash, who made a recruiting pitch to come to Phoenix.

"Steve Nash and I are very close friends. He called me right away," Garnett said. "But the thing was that if I did go there, I wanted to play with [Amare] Stoudemire, and it didn't look like he was going to be a part of the plan. It looked like they were going to trade him. LA was going through some difficulties with Kobe and him not wanting to be there. That put that situation into limbo too, even though I do have a home out there and spend a lot of time there. But the problems he was having with management bothered me a lot. I'm thinking, this is their No. 1 player and he's going through all this? What's it going to be like for me?"

Meanwhile Ainge, trying to keep Pierce abreast of what was going on, sent his captain a text message saying that he thought his chances to land Garnett were much better this time around. Pierce's response: "Yeah, right."

"I didn't want to get my hopes up," Pierce said, noting that he had run into Garnett during one of his sessions at UCLA and didn't even raise the topic of Garnett coming to Boston. "I've been hearing that kind of talk for all these years. We couldn't even get a C-type player to come. How are we going to get an A-type player like KG?"

Doc Rivers hosts his annual charity golf tournament each July in Orlando, and Ainge, an excellent golfer, looked forward to attending. That was until he received word from McHale that Garnett would grant him an audience in Malibu on July 20, the same day as Rivers' tournament. So instead of going to Florida, Ainge boarded a flight in Boston for Los Angeles.

He picked up his rental car at the airport and began the drive north to the posh suburb of Malibu, home to the rich and famous, of which Garnett was both. This was pretty much a temperature-check visit for Ainge. He wanted to know if he was wasting his time and Garnett's by proceeding. He felt that Garnett might be ready for a change of scenery after 12 years in Minnesota.

"I watched that guy play so much over the years that there wasn't any doubt in my mind that he would fit in with Paul and Ray," Ainge said. "Or that he would bring all that energy and emotion. I just think, in Minnesota, he had lost his spirit to play. He has to have that to be the special player he is. So, you wonder, is it because he has made all this money? Or that he's done all this and won those awards? Or is it something else? My thinking was that he still had a lot left and a lot to offer."

The Garnett house, located on a bluff, isn't easy to find. As Ainge drove up the long driveway, he thought to himself, "This is pretty nice." When he went through the front door and saw the whole rear of the house overlooking the Pacific Ocean, he thought to himself, "This is spectacular."

As the two men walked outside for a chat on the patio next to the swimming pool, Ainge had yet another thought: "What a great place to hit range balls! There was nothing between his house and the freeway and the ocean was on the other side of the freeway," he said. "So you could just tee it up and hit it right into the ocean from KG's backyard."

Eventually, the two started to talk the talk. Brandi Garnett, Kevin's wife, brought out fruit and sandwiches—"prepared top notch, like everything they do," Ainge said. Ainge detected a sense of excitement in Garnett.

"In some ways, Kevin is a very mature person," Ainge said. "He's extremely loyal. He has a good heart. He cares about people. He cares about his teammates. There's another side of Kevin in that he's like a 13-year-old with all this energy, hyped up, like a new puppy. He goes nonstop. I saw both sides in our conversation.

I think he knew then that Boston would be a great opportunity for him. I certainly conveyed that to him. At the end, he was trying to control his excitement. But I sensed he had made up his mind."

Garnett had not made up his mind, but he was getting closer and closer to embracing the possibility of being a Celtic.

"They already had Ray, and Danny mentioned the other guys he was looking at, like [James Posey], so he put together this map and left that with me," Garnett said. "I let it brew, so to speak. Let it simmer. Danny was very upfront with me. Very frank. I think I was too in what I was looking for. It was a very, very detailed conversation. I addressed my dislikes about the league and the things I wasn't happy with in Minnesota. He expressed some of his feelings about his team. When he left, I was still in limbo. I wasn't convinced. Then I spoke to Chauncey and Ty Lue again and tried to envision myself making this transition but also trying to weigh all the options at the same time. And at the end of the day, it came down to Boston. It was the best option."

Three-plus weeks after the draft and a month after he first had rejected the notion of leaving Minnesota for Boston, Garnett had now come full circle. But the Celtics and Timberwolves still had to work out a deal.

The basics were already in place: Boston would send Al Jefferson, Theo Ratliff, Ryan Gomes, and Gerald Green to the Wolves. The Celtics would also return the No. 1 they had gotten from the Wolves and add another one to sweeten the deal. But one obstacle remained: the identity of the fifth player (seventh, if you count the draft picks) in the deal. Minnesota wanted Rajon Rondo. The Celtics were offering Sebastian Telfair, who was still on the roster, albeit persona non grata following the handgun incident.

Near the end of July, the players involved in the deal were still being discussed. The Lakers were also in the picture, believed to be offering a package that included Lamar Odom and Andrew Bynum, although they had refused to part with Bynum the previous

February in a deal with the Nets that would have brought Jason Kidd to Los Angeles. (After the Garnett deal went down, LA coach Phil Jackson said, "Red Auerbach came out of the grave and told Kevin [McHale] to give him [Garnett] to the Celtics so the Celtics could get back in the run. That was a blessing. We just didn't have that connection to make that happen for us.")

As D-Day approached, Grousbeck received a phone call from Glen Taylor, the owner of the Timberwolves. The two were friends and had served on some NBA committees together. The call came at Ainge's suggestion. He told Grousbeck that he and McHale had gone as far as they could go, that Taylor wanted to take this to the owner-to-owner level. Grousbeck agreed and took the Taylor call while at his vacation home on Martha's Vineyard.

"Glen called and said, 'Give us Rondo and the deal is done. You'll be the talk of the league. You'll have Pierce, Allen, and Garnett, and you'll be the favorites to win it all. But you have to give us Rondo,'" Grousbeck said.

As in the negotiations for Ray Allen, including Rondo in the deal was an absolute nonstarter. It's hard to fathom that a point guard with one year's experience in the NBA could be deemed so valuable as to threaten trades for both Allen and Garnett, two possible Hall of Famers, but that was precisely the case. Grousbeck said the Celtics considered Rondo their starting point guard, which he would not likely be for Minnesota. The Wolves had Marko Jaric, Randy Foye, and even Troy Hudson (who would eventually be bought out of his contract). Rondo would not be starting ahead of all of them.

"To give up our starting point guard for someone who would be a backup for you doesn't make sense to us," Grousbeck told Taylor, "He's worth more to us as a starter. We have to win now. We need him."

Back and forth it went until Grousbeck sweetened the pot by agreeing to pay a portion of Telfair's salary. Telfair didn't make much by NBA standards—around $1.7 million. Grousbeck then told Taylor that the deadline to get the deal done was 5 p.m. that night, with Rondo staying in Boston. It was the end of July and if the Celtics were going to get Garnett, they needed to start thinking about filling out their roster.

While Grousbeck still didn't know how things were going to turn out, he felt emboldened by a conversation he had had the previous night with the principal owner of the Boston Red Sox, John Henry. He and his wife had been visiting the Grousbecks on the Vineyard. While on their way to dinner, Grousbeck mentioned the deal and asked Henry for his thoughts. "He said, 'I don't know. I'm not a basketball guy. But I've always gone after the best guy in any deal, and I would do everything I could to get Garnett,'" Grousbeck said.

Around 4 p.m., a nervous Grousbeck still had not heard from Taylor, so he took his cellphone and went for a run along the beach on the south end of the island. He was all alone when the phone rang. It was Taylor.

"You've got a deal," he told Grousbeck.

As Grousbeck paused, he reflected on the nearly identical situation May 22, when he had been the only one to know that the Celtics were not going to get Greg Oden or Kevin Durant and how devastating that had been. Now, a little more than two months later, the Celtics had Ray Allen and an agreement in place to get Kevin Garnett. "And, just like in May, I was the only one in Boston who knew," Grousbeck said. "I just let out this roar. But there was no one within a mile of me."

Actually, Pierce had had a pretty good inkling that the deal was going down. The night before, he had been in Los Angeles and had run into old friend and teammate Antoine Walker. "Toine [Walker] had just been with KG and Gary Payton at Gary's wedding [where his vows had been renewed]. He told me we were getting KG," Pierce said. "I was like, are you sure? How do you know? He told me that KG had just told him and I was like, wow! Then, they made it official the next day. I couldn't believe it."

THE CELTICS HAD SURRENDERED SEVEN PLAYERS (the five existing players and the two draft picks) for Garnett. The Celtics also had agreed to a three-year extension for Garnett, who settled for less than he could have received, but still ended up with a whopping $105 million over a five-year period.

When a team trades a superstar, it rarely ever gets anything close to equal value. Such was the case here, with the sole exception being that Jefferson might develop into a first-ballot Hall of Famer, which is what Garnett will be. Of the five players Minnesota received, only Jefferson, Telfair, and Gomes received any meaningful time in 2007–2008. Green didn't even finish the season with the Wolves; he was traded to Houston and then released. He signed a one-year deal with Dallas in the summer of 2008. Theo Ratliff was bought out and ended up playing for the Pistons for the rest of the season. Telfair was allowed to become a free agent, but eventually was re-signed by the Wolves.

McHale was roasted for the deal in Minnesota, but his real crime wasn't that he made the deal, but rather that he never gave Garnett a better supporting cast of players while he played for the Timberwolves. The one year he did, 2003–2004, the Wolves made it to the Western Conference Finals. But too often he accepted mediocre players (often represented by agent Bill Duffy—his college roommate, as many observers have noted). He was fleeced by Ainge on two occasions, to the point where he took on nine Celtics (from lottery teams) in a space of 18 months. One person emailed the *Boston Globe*, commenting, "The Celtics ought to retire his number again."

Now McHale had just traded to Boston the greatest player in Minnesota history and one of the greatest in NBA history. Wrote Tom Powers of the *St. Paul Pioneer Press*, "The sun will come up tomorrow. Unless, of course, Kevin McHale is somehow put in charge of the solar system. In which case the sun will implode and we all will die."

KEVIN GARNETT'S PLACE IN NBA HISTORY is already well established by what he has done on the court. But he is also involuntarily responsible for two other seminal, league-changing events: the 1998–1999 league lockout of the players and the movement of high school players directly to the NBA, which eventually was stopped in 2007 by NBA Commissioner David Stern and National Basketball Players Association chief Billy Hunter.

In the spring of 1995, Garnett was unquestionably one of the best high school basketball players in the country. His games at Farragut Academy in Chicago were must-see events; he ended up averaging 26 points, 18 rebounds, 7 assists, and 6 blocked shots a game. He was hoping to attend the University of Michigan, but did not have the academics to qualify for a scholarship.

He had come to Chicago because, as he put it, "I had to get out of South Carolina and I had to get out quick." While in high school, shortly before the start of his senior year, Garnett and several of his friends had been charged with assaulting a white student who, they said, had been taunting them with racial epithets. The charge was dropped after Garnett entered a diversion program for first-time offenders. But the racial climate at the school was unlikely to change, so Garnett knew he had to leave the area.

He already had been named Mr. Basketball in South Carolina in 1994, the first time a junior had won the award. He led Mauldin High School to the state championship by averaging 27 points and 17 rebounds a game. Garnett needed to leave Mauldin in part because the racial incident might affect his playing status as a senior. But he had nowhere to go.

Then, in the summer before his senior year, he participated in a summer basketball camp sponsored by Nike. Fellow campers included Chauncey Billups, Paul Pierce, and Antawn Jamison. Another was Ronnie Fields, who attended Farragut Academy and was one of the top prep players in the country. He and Garnett became close during the camp.

Garnett's team at the Nike camp was coached by William "Wolf" Nelson, who also happened to be the head coach at Farragut Academy. Garnett loved the way Nelson handled the kids and the system he used. He encouraged Garnett to be aggressive, to have that take-no-prisoners attitude now seen daily in the NBA. "I listened to him. I really liked his freedom of creativity while you played and that gave me a peace of mind," Garnett said. "He allowed me to be myself. I liked that."

He talked to Nelson about his situation in South Carolina and his desire to go elsewhere. Nelson was all ears, but he also knew this was not your ordinary transfer situation. Most transfers came from within the city. Garnett was from out of state.

Garnett had never been to Chicago, had no idea what kind of school Farragut Academy was or where it was located. He had lived in a city environment as a youngster, in a black section of Greenville, South Carolina, before his mother moved the family to Mauldin, a suburb of Greenville. But a move to Chicago was about as big a culture change as one could envision. Mauldin was small, southern, and slow-paced. Chicago was just the opposite.

"When I was younger, I was more of a 'hood guy, living in apartments, that sort of thing," Garnett said. "Later on, my mother moved us to the suburbs and I had better schooling. Chicago was like going backwards. It was *so* 'hood, so urban, so much of a city, it reverted me back to my younger days. But the things I learned in my short time there helped me to this day as a young man. I went up there with damn near nothing, just me and my younger sister. But it was a great experience, a life-changing experience. I saw only one way of life until I went to Chicago and what I saw there and did there helped me be a lot more diverse, a lot more open."

Living in Chicago hardened Garnett. His mother deposited him and his younger sister Ashley on the city's not-so-great West Side and then returned to South Carolina, where she worked as a hair stylist. More often than not, Garnett found accommodations elsewhere with friends or with Nelson. From there or from pay phones, he would seek the counsel of Sonny Vaccaro, then working for adidas and a father figure to many high school basketball players. Vaccaro ran summer camps and staged All-Star games for the best high school kids, with the shoe company paying the freight. Vaccaro knew of Garnett as a player in South Carolina and had rejected Garnett's bid to play in adidas' ABCD camp in the summer of 1994. "He always seemed to have problems," Vaccaro said of Garnett.

But once Garnett surfaced in Chicago, the two struck up a long-term friendship. Time and again, Vaccaro's telephone in his southern California home would ring in the middle of the night. Garnett would be on the other end, often times at Nelson's house. "I wore out Wolf's phone, I'll tell you that," Garnett said.

What Garnett wanted was advice: should he go from Farragut to the NBA? In 1995, this was a huge thing, for no high school player had gone directly to the NBA in almost two decades, and only one, Moses Malone, had ever done it and had any kind of celebrated professional career.

"There was no precedent at that time," Vaccaro said. "He didn't have the scores to qualify [for a college scholarship]. I kept telling him, 'David Stern is guaranteeing you at least three years of very good money if you go into the draft. Even if you're wrong, you'll still collect millions of dollars.'"

Garnett's penchant for taking his time was never more evident than in this instance. Even in June of his senior year, he was still taking standardized tests, hoping to qualify for a scholarship to Michigan. By then, he had won the Most Valuable Player in the McDonald's All-Star Game and had been named National Player of the Year by a number of publications. Vaccaro, who by this time felt he knew the kid, invited him to his Magic Roundball Classic, held in Auburn Hills, Michigan.

He had no idea if Garnett would attend because he felt Garnett had a connection to Nike, having attended their camp the year before. When the competition started at the camp, Garnett, was a no-show. Then, one evening, at the welcome banquet at the Marriott Hotel in nearby Troy, Garnett showed up in a sweatsuit, with a pair of buddies. Vaccaro's jaw dropped. Dick Vitale, the keynote speaker, was briefly speechless—no small feat.

It was the first time Garnett and Vaccaro had met.

"He told me, I owe you this," Vaccaro said. "It shows how much he values loyalty and friendship." Said Garnett, "Sonny was there for me when I needed help. I appreciated it."

Garnett followed Vaccaro's advice, declaring for the 1995 NBA draft. He then absolutely blew the minds of those in attendance with a predraft workout at the University of Illinois-Chicago, a performance so exhausting that he collapsed on the gym floor after everyone had left and gone to sleep. Among those at the workout was Kevin McHale, the general manager of the Timberwolves. His team had the fifth pick in the draft, and after seeing Garnett, he began to seriously consider taking the kid.

It would be a bold move to declare for the draft—and a precedent setter as well. The next year, Kobe Bryant and Jermaine O'Neal came out. Tracy McGrady came out in 1997, Al Harrington in 1998, and Jonathan Bender in 1999. Until the league and union put an end to the practice, starting with the 2006 draft, every year from 1995 to 2005 featured at least one high school player drafted in the first round, where guaranteed money awaited. In 2001, Kwame Brown became the first-ever high school player to be the No. 1 overall pick. Two years later, LeBron James was the No. 1 overall pick, and, in 2004, Dwight Howard was the No. 1 pick. In that year, an astonishing eight high school players went in the first round.

McHale rolled the dice and drafted Garnett at No. 5. Garnett achieved instant-millionaire status with three years of guaranteed salary worth more than $5 million.

GARNETT ALWAYS REFERRED TO HIS PROFESSIONAL HOME as 'Sota. As a rookie, he moved to the Twin Cities with some friends and his mother. He soon became close to a Wolves season ticket holder named James Harris, who would become famous as the recording producer and writer Jimmy Jam. They first met in a parking lot at Byerly's, a 24-hour grocery store in the Minneapolis area. It was late at night, and Harris doesn't remember anyone else being in the lot except the two of them. Harris told Garnett how much he liked watching him play, even if the Wolves were thinking of holding him back as part of the transition process. But all Garnett talked about was the community. How could he be more active? What were the local charities? "You don't usually see that in a rookie," Harris said.

Garnett became a frequent visitor to Harris' house and would eventually meet his wife through Harris; she and Harris' wife were sisters. He also became close to Malik Sealy, who Garnett had watched when Sealy, a high school phenom from New York City, played at St. John's. It was the reason Garnett chose No. 21 in Minnesota, Sealy's number in college. "I wasn't the most confident guy at that time, and I was trying to find someone who was another me. Not the best player, but someone who played like me," Garnett said shortly after Sealy joined the Timberwolves for the 1998–1999 season.

Tragically, the relationship did not last long. Early one morning in May 2000, Sealy was killed by a drunk driver as he returned home from a party celebrating Garnett's twenty-fourth birthday. Garnett was devastated. He paid tribute to his friend by making sure that Sealy's locker at the Target Center remained intact, complete with uniform and sneakers.

As a rookie, Garnett played less than 29 minutes a game, but in his second year, 1996–1997, he played well enough to be named to the Western Conference All-Star team. He has been in every All-Star Game since then. With the addition of Stephon Marbury in 1996 (whom Garnett had come to know through the amateur circuit), the Timberwolves made the playoffs in 1997 for the first time. They lost in three straight games, setting an unfortunate pattern for Garnett that defined his Minnesota post-seasons: one and done. Garnett's Timberwolves teams would make eight playoff appearances. Seven of those resulted in first-round exits.

But a Timberwolves team led by Garnett, Marbury, and Tom Gugliotta appeared to be on the rise in the late 1990s and into the new millennium. Garnett was eligible for his first contract extension starting in his fourth year, and, under the rules at the time, there were no limits on what a team could pay one of its own players. When Minnesota offered Garnett $102 million for six years, he and his agent, Eric Fleischer, rejected it. The final deal was an astonishing $126 million, making Garnett, at age 23, the highest paid player in the league.

The deal sent shockwaves through the NBA. The owners decided they needed cost certainty—a limit on player salaries—and locked out the players when the Collective Bargaining Agreement expired in 1998. The lockout lasted into 1999, forced the cancellation of the All-Star Game, and nearly cost the league a season. But the players eventually settled for a cap on individual salaries (a generous one, nonetheless), and a 50-game season was played.

In his 12 years with Minnesota, Garnett earned almost $200 million; he signed a second extension after the $126 million deal expired in 2004. "He never once made you feel that he wasn't worth the money," Garnett's coach in Minnesota, Flip Saunders, said. "If anything, by the way he played, by the example he showed, by the way he led his life, he was a bargain."

He also had been unswervingly loyal to the Timberwolves, probably to the detriment of his career. No matter how well he played, the team never improved. Minnesota was even stripped of a number of first-round picks after getting caught trying to do an under-the-table deal with Joe Smith.

Toward the end of his days with the Timberwolves, he retreated to the beach near his Malibu home and ran into a neighbor, Hall of Fame coach Pat Riley. What followed was totally unexpected: an all-day, into-the-night discussion between the player and the coach about basketball, life, and everything in between. The two drank bottled water, sent the wives out for Chinese food, and later ended up at Riley's house, continuing their dialogue.

"I didn't think any player would want to talk to a coach for 12 hours," Riley said. "That just doesn't happen in the NBA, in or out of season. But in listening to him, I sensed his passion, his enthusiasm, his knowledge, but also his desperation because things were not going well in Minnesota."

But Garnett never publicly vocalized the desire to play elsewhere, although he did wonder if McHale was ever going to get some good, complementary players. He would have signed another extension with the team had one been put forth.

"I never wanted to leave Minnesota. I never thought I'd leave Minnesota. I'm all about loyalty. But I wasn't into young. I wasn't into rebuilding. That was the direction they were going to go. And I knew that it was time for me to leave," he said.

Said Saunders, "He gave everything he had to that organization. Everything. What were the Timberwolves before he got there? When people think of the Minnesota Timberwolves, who do they think of? They think of KG."

The one great run Garnett had in Minnesota came after McHale acquired Latrell Sprewell from the Knicks and Sam Cassell from the Bucks prior to the start of the 2003–2004 season. It was the answer to Garnett's hopes for more talent, much the same way Danny Ainge answered Paul Pierce's hopes four years later. Minnesota instantly became a favorite to challenge the defending champion Spurs and the rebuilt Lakers, who had added Karl Malone and Gary Payton to a team that still had Shaquille O'Neal and Kobe Bryant. Minnesota responded with the best season in franchise history, winning 58 games, tops in the Western Conference. Garnett was a near-unanimous choice for the league's

Most Valuable Player. It seemed as if the Timberwolves finally had taken their place among the league's elite.

The Timberwolves made it to the conference finals by beating Denver in the first round and then eliminating Sacramento in the conference semifinals in seven games, with Garnett delivering a monster performance in the series decider: 32 points, 20 rebounds, and 5 blocks on his twenty-eighth birthday. After the game, Garnett was given a standing ovation when he strode into his favorite Minnesota dining establishment for a post-game repast.

But the Wolves couldn't get past the star-packed Lakers in the conference finals, falling in six games. Cassell was dealing with a sore back and was severely limited in the series, making many believe that, had he been healthy, the result might have been different. Cassell certainly believes that. "I thought we were the better team," he said. "We had the best record. But I couldn't play the way I wanted to play the whole series."

Unfortunately for Garnett and the Timberwolves, that proved to be the high-water mark for the franchise. The team dropped to 44 wins in 2004–2005 and didn't make the playoffs. It failed again in 2005–2006 and 2006–2007. In those down years, there was always interest in Garnett. Other teams felt he might need a change of scene and would try to entice Minnesota into trading him. But Garnett didn't want to leave.

"I wanted to make it happen there," he said. "When things aren't going the way you want them to go, the easiest thing is to say, 'Get me out of here.' The hardest thing is to stick around and try to make it work. That was my mind-set. I wanted to make it work."

But seeing where the Timberwolves were headed and seeing his chances in Minnesota getting slimmer by the day, Garnett finally decided he'd have to make it work somewhere else.

LIKE ALLEN AND PIERCE, both All-Stars yet both playing on lottery teams the year before, Garnett was coming to Boston at the right time in his career. He had his MVP Trophy. He'd been an All-Star Game regular, an All-NBA regular, and an All-Defensive Team regular. Now he was joining a team with two players on board who were better than any pair he'd ever had in Minnesota. He was going to the weaker conference. Almost automatically, the Celtics went from being long shots to win the NBA championship to Las Vegas favorites.

When the trade was announced, the Celtics set up a bank of operators to field requests for season tickets. There was a 60 percent increase. Team president Rich Gotham said, "The number one reason for selling tickets is success. Number two is the hope of success." The team would end up selling out all 41 of its home games, something it had last done in the old Boston Garden in the heyday of Larry Bird, Kevin McHale, and Robert Parish.

The impact was felt everywhere. In the Boston suburb of Dedham, restaurant owner Frank Santo had to add the Celtics cable channel to his television at the bar because people were coming in to see the games. "I didn't get one request for that last year. Not one," Santo said.

In addition, Celtics ownership had done what a lot of other ownership groups would not have done—agreed to trades that would make them luxury tax payers for the first time. In the NBA, if a team's payroll exceeds a certain amount, then every dollar over that has to be paid back to the league at the end of the season. The Garnett deal and extension put the Celtics over that threshold, and they still needed to add players.

Celtics owners allowed Ainge to pursue free agents, knowing anyone they signed would essentially cost them double.

The Celtics ended up sending a check to the NBA in July 2008 for more than $8.2 million for their luxury tax payment. To the owners, it was money well spent.

4

Setting a Course

CAMERAMEN WERE DISMANTLING THEIR TRIPODS, reporters were heading back to write their stories, and many members of the Boston Celtics ownership group were still accepting congratulations shortly after the press conference that had introduced Kevin Garnett. He, Paul Pierce, and Ray Allen had all been on the podium at the Legends Club at TD Banknorth Garden, and the sense of anticipation and expectation could not have been greater.

As people started to file out, Garnett and his wife Brandi went out onto the arena floor, then just a big slab of cement, and looked up to see thousands of empty yellow and green seats. It would never look that way again when Garnett came to play wearing a Celtics uniform. He had chosen No. 5 because No. 21 had already been retired (for Bill Sharman). No. 5 represented the fifth pick in the 1995 NBA draft. Almost overnight, the Celtics replica jersey with the No. 5 became one of the top sellers at the NBA Store.

Celtics coach Doc Rivers had dinner plans in the North End of Boston that night, but he also had something else in mind for the trio of players that were now being dubbed the "Big Three." That had been the moniker attached to Larry Bird, Kevin McHale, and Robert Parish, who teamed to win three titles in the 1980s. These three hadn't won anything yet, and they reminded anyone who asked and more or less tried to bury all the Big Three talk before it even began.

Rivers summoned the trio to his office at the arena, sat them all down, looked them in the eye, and told them how happy he was to have them here. Then, he went on. "I'm going to be frank," he remembered telling them. "This is not going to work if you do not commit to playing defense, because we can't be just a good defensive team. We have to be a great defensive team."

Rivers brought up the names of a few NBA players who say they want to win, "But most of you guys, when you say that, you're really full of shit. You all want to win. Everyone wants to win. But most of you want to win as long as you're comfortable with the way things are done for you, as long as you can still do the things you've always done."

He told them the Celtics would not win if they didn't trust his offense, his defense, and most important, one another. "I don't care how good you are or how good you think you are," Rivers told them. "You guys might think I'm tripping a little here, but you only have one shot. I don't want to hear about next year, because that's a total fallacy. You'll be hurt. You'll be tired. You'll be too old. You don't know about next year. You've got this year to get it done and there is no other year. That's the sense of urgency that you have to have. But again, it all comes down to defense. We have to commit to that right here, right now."

This was preaching to the chorus for the defensive-minded Garnett. "I'm in," he told Rivers. Then he turned to the other two, neither of them known for their defensive prowess, and said, "Paul, Ray, y'all got to start playing some defense this year."

Allen chalked it up to being on a new team with a new coach and new system. "I'd heard it before from just about every coach I ever had," he said. "They all say, 'We're going to play defense.' But what I took away from that meeting was that it wasn't just going to be the coach. It was going to fall on the players as well. We were going to be held accountable."

All three were on board at that very moment. They understood. What they didn't know, nor did Rivers at that time, was who else was going to be on board with them.

———

Just getting garnett and allen had cost the Celtics seven players from their 2006–2007 roster. First-year player Allen Ray was headed to Europe, and Michael Olowokandi, who had appeared in only 24 games, was not coming back. At the time of that news conference, the Celtics had a roster of only eight players. One through three looked pretty good. Beyond that, there were plenty of questions.

The Celtics faced a couple of problems in filling out their roster. One was money; they already had crossed the luxury tax threshold in acquiring Garnett.

There also was the available pool of talent. Ainge knew the kind of players he wanted—veterans—but he also knew it might be hard to entice a veteran without a lot of money to offer. All he had available was the so-called "mid-level exception," worth around $5 million, which he could offer to anyone in full or which could be split up any number of ways. There also was the so-called "million dollar exception," which now was worth $1.8 million and could be used to sign a player. There also was the veteran's minimum, which could be offered any number of times, with the NBA paying a percentage of the contract. The amount depended on how many years of service the player had in the league.

But Ainge has never been one to think inside the box and he had one player in mind as he began the month of August: Reggie Miller. The great Indiana Pacers star would turn 42 in three weeks, had finished a distinguished 18-year career in 2005, and was living the comfortable life in Malibu, doing television work as an NBA analyst for TNT.

"I felt we needed more shooting, more leaders, more guys who have made big shots in big games, and I thought Reggie would be perfect for us in the locker room, in fourth quarter play, and in the playoffs," Ainge said. "I thought he'd be a huge asset."

Shooting was, of course, Miller's calling card. He retired as the NBA's career leader in three-point shooting both in attempts and conversions. He loved to take big shots at the end of games, and he made his share. He was close to Garnett; both had houses in Malibu. Garnett even helped in the recruiting process, trying to coax Miller back to the court for a shot at the one thing that had eluded him: a championship ring.

Miller had won gold as a 1996 Olympian in Atlanta and as a member of the 1994 World Championship team in Canada. But in his 18 seasons with the Pacers, only once, in 2000, did they make it as far as the NBA Finals, where the Lakers, led by Shaquille O'Neal and Kobe Bryant, beat them in six games.

This wasn't the first time Ainge had reached out to retired veterans. Two years earlier, he had contacted former Utah point guard John Stockton about possibly coming out of retirement. But Stockton, who retired in 2003, wasn't interested.

Doc Rivers was all for the Miller chase as well. He called up Rick Carlisle, Miller's last coach in Indiana; Carlisle said he thought Miller was far from done. Carlisle urged the Celtics, for whom he once played, to make an all-out run at Miller, believing like Ainge that Miller would be a great addition on and off the court.

Miller reached the point where he said he'd consider it. He and Ainge then came up with a plan: a ten-day stretch of two-a-day workouts to see if Miller could handle the grind and if his body was still NBA-ready. The workouts took place in Malibu. Garnett participated in one and reported back to Ainge that he was impressed with Miller's energy and conditioning. Ainge checked in by phone at the end of each day.

At the end of the ten days, Miller figured he was healthy and still good enough to be able to do what the Celtics wanted him to do: come off the bench for maybe 15 to 20 minutes a night, while mentoring the younger players. But his heart, he told Ainge, just wasn't in it anymore. The thought of playing in the playoffs and winning a championship was alluring, but it couldn't trump the idea of having to play four games in five nights or making midwinter trips to Milwaukee or taking red-eye flights back from the West Coast.

He told the *Indianapolis Star*, which had faithfully covered him throughout his career, "Physically, I know I could have done it. But mentally, when you do something like this, you've either got to be all in or all out. And I've decided I'm all out."

Ainge understood, although he was disappointed. "He's always been an intense worker. That was his last try," Ainge said. "He got it out of his system. He has such high expectations. He was such a great player for so long, and he knows what you have to do, day in and day out, to be your best and to make the commitment. I think he had already moved on mentally in his life, but he wanted to make sure that was the case. He did. After that, he was sure."

But when Miller made his first visit as part of the TNT broadcast crew, Ainge went out of his way to ask Miller if he was still sure. "Yeah, I'm sure," Miller said. To which Ainge shrugged and said, "All right."

AINGE HAD NOT BEEN solely on Miller Watch during those first couple weeks in August. He needed veterans and he needed shooting and he thought he got both when the team signed journeyman Eddie House on August 9. Also signed was longtime backup big man and free spirit Scot Pollard, a teammate of Pierce's in college at Kansas.

Pollard never made much of a contribution; injuries shelved his season before it ever had a chance, and he eventually underwent two ankle surgeries. House, however, was a different story. Ainge likened House to a "special weapon" because of his ability to shoot the ball. House has a tattoo on his left arm that says "Lethal Weapon." When Ainge approached Rivers to see what the coach thought, he didn't get any objection.

"I love him as a shooter," Rivers said. "When I was coaching against him, it always scared the hell out of me when he came into a game because he makes shots. The only downside as I saw it was Eddie's size. We already had a small point guard [Rajon Rondo], and I was worried about Eddie's ability to handle the ball. I figured we'd be able to get away with it in the regular season. I wasn't as certain about the playoffs."

Ainge wasn't worried about that now. He had made a conscious decision that he was not going to bring in a veteran point guard to help Rondo because he wanted to see if Rondo was up to the task of running the team. He didn't want Rondo always looking over his shoulder or Rivers going with a veteran for short-term success. House, he felt, was not that kind of player.

"I was a fan of Eddie's when I was in Phoenix and he was at Arizona State. I used to watch him play all the time," Ainge said. "He's a little like a third-down receiver in football, a specialist like Troy Brown or Kevin Faulk [of the New England Patriots]. It's a luxury to have someone like that. You put up with what he doesn't do because the one thing he does do is special."

House agreed to a one-year deal worth $1.5 million, continuing a trend in his career at that point that had seen him bounce around from team to team, year to year, never staying in one place more than one season. It wasn't always for lack of interest either. The Suns, who had him in 2004–2005, wanted to make a run for him in 2007, but were hampered by finances. The Nets, for whom he had played the year before, would have liked to have had him back too.

"He doesn't fit the mold," said House's agent, Mark Bartelstein. "He's not the perfect size. He's not the perfect shape. He's kind of like the ugly duckling. But everywhere he goes, the team gets better. He's a great locker room guy, a great energy guy, and he waves a towel whether he's playing two minutes a game or 30 minutes a game. He does what he does as good or better than anyone else. He can win games."

Eddie House is the NBA equivalent of the great line from Joni Mitchell's "Big Yellow Taxi": "Don't it always seem to go that you don't know what you've got till it's gone." He's also the quintessential survivor; the Celtics were House's eighth team in eight years.

"What's hard about all that is picking up the family every year and having to move," House said. "If it was just me, it wouldn't bother me. I'm good enough to get a job in the league somewhere, and I'm doing something I love to do. But for the kids [he has three sons], it's hard. They go to school, meet some new friends, are all cool with that, and then they have to do the same thing the next year all over again. That's what's tough."

House attended Arizona State, where he was seen as equal parts wild child and go-to guy. There was an altercation in a restaurant in Oregon with A.J. Bramlett of Arizona; both teams were dining there. There was an arrest in the summer after his freshman season for taking part in the theft of a CD player; the charges were dropped. His first coach at Arizona State, Bill Frieder, was gone after one year. His replacement, Don Newman, was gone after one year.

"It was a bit of a culture shock for me, going to college," House said. "I made mistakes and I have no one to blame but myself. It was different, being on my own. I was outspoken. I spoke my mind." He remembers speaking his mind when it appeared that Newman was going to be replaced by Rick Majerus, who had had a successful college coaching career at Marquette and Utah. House and most of his teammates wanted Newman to stick around. The team, in its second season, had made it to the National Invitation Tournament in New York.

"I was outspoken saying we didn't need Rick Majerus," House said. "We did pretty well with coach Newman, and all of us had a good relationship with him and felt good about him. We had come in and committed to Arizona State, and my thought was that Rick Majerus was going to come in and weed us out. He didn't like this. He didn't like that. He didn't like guys with tattoos. Everyone on the team had a tattoo. It didn't seem like it was a good fit."

Majerus didn't get the job. But Newman didn't either. Arizona State hired Rob Evans, who had been the head coach at the University of Mississippi for the past four years. One of Evans' players at Ole Miss had been a guard named Michael White, whose father Kevin White happened to be the athletic director at Arizona State. Evans was a disciplinarian, and he immediately laid down the rules and the law. House acquiesced, sort of. "One of the rules was that we had to go class," House said. "So, yeah, I missed a couple of those." Evans had heard the stories about House. "He was a live wire when I got there and had had a few issues. I called him in and told him how things were going to be," Evans said. "I told him I wanted him to live on campus. He said, 'I can't do that.' I told him, 'That isn't a multiple-choice question.' And he did it."

But there were still dustups along the way. House missed a class in summer school, and the penalty was what Evans liked to call "5 at 5": a five-mile run at 5 a.m. House showed up 30 minutes before he was supposed to and completed the run. When House didn't keep up with his schoolwork the summer before his senior year, Evans wouldn't let him try out for the USA Team competing at the World University Games. Evans was on USA Basketball's board, and he was desperate to get some exposure for House and the Arizona State program. But a rule is a rule, and when he confronted House, he said House was contrite and understanding.

"For the first six months I had him, Eddie was a headache. For the last 18 months, he was an absolute joy to coach," Evans said.

Said House, "Coach Evans gave me structure in my life, and I needed that. And he challenged me to become the best player I could be. I needed that too."

Evans pushed and prodded House in practice, sensing there was more than what he was seeing or getting. One day he said to House, "Eddie, if you want to make it in the NBA, you cannot continue to wallow in mediocrity." Toughness was never the issue. As a freshman, House had to undergo three root-canal procedures after chipping his teeth in an afternoon game at the Great Alaska Shootout. He was back to play the next game, at noon the following day, and had seven three-pointers. As a junior, he broke his jaw taking charges during a practice drill. He had it wired shut and for six weeks lived on a diet of soup and milkshakes.

In four years at Arizona State, playing for three different coaches, House never missed a game or a practice. He left Tempe as the school's all-time leading scorer and gained PAC 10 Player of the Year honors as a senior, when he led the team in scoring, assists, and steals.

As a senior, he scored 61 points against California, a game witnessed by Pat Riley. He had 46 against San Diego State. Evans remembered getting a call from the coach of Penn State, who vowed House wouldn't get 40. He didn't. He got 42.

"Then they run a triangle and one (a special defense designed to stop a scorer) on Eddie when we played Washington State, and we ended up winning. So I asked their coach why he did that and he said, 'We didn't want to be on [ESPN's] SportsCenter the next night,'" Evans said. "You couldn't guard Eddie." House also had 40 points against UCLA, becoming the first player in PAC 10 history to have four games of 40 or more points in a season.

In the 2000 NBA draft, House was chosen in the second round by the Miami Heat, whose coach, Riley, regards rookies as little more than pond scum. But House's enthusiasm and visible love for the game gained one big fan in Miami—Riley's then 11-year-old daughter Elisabeth. She would come to Heat games with a sign—"Free Eddie House"—that got a reaction from the rookie guard. "I played in 50 games as a rookie," House said with pride. "Pat doesn't play rookies. I was the only rookie on that team, and it was unheard of for Pat to play rookies or even acknowledge that you were around. I got to play during the season [an average of 11 minutes a game] and in the playoffs [18 minutes per game in three games].

"His daughter wanted me to play. And I was so hungry to get out on that court and play basketball that when my number did get called, there was this burst of energy, like a bird coming out of a cage. I guess that's where she got the 'Free Eddie House.'"

House spent his first three years in Miami and still has a fan in Riley.

"He's one of the greatest competitors I have ever been around," Riley said of House. "He's a great practice player. When he went too far out, you had to bring him back in, but he wasn't afraid of anything or anyone, didn't back down, dependable. He's like that gunslinger that comes into town, fires 'em up, and then sleeps on the street."

Starting in 2003, House's professional odyssey began in earnest. He spent one year with the Clippers, who traded him the next year to the Bobcats. Early in December 2004, Charlotte coach Bernie Bickerstaff called House into his office and told him that he was going to be replaced.

"It wasn't that they didn't want me exactly," House said. "Bernie told me they were thinking of getting a bigger guard. At this point of the season, I'm averaging 11 points a game. I'm third in the league in steals. I'm in the top ten in three-point field goal percentage. I'm starting, and I'm having a career year for me. But they wanted Kareem Rush. Bernie said to me, 'If we get him, your minutes will go down, and you will barely play, if at all.' He said they could waive me, and I'd still get paid because I had a guaranteed contract. So I told them to waive me."

They did. The Bobcats signed Rush, who played two largely forgettable and underwhelming seasons in Charlotte. Milwaukee picked up House two weeks later, waived him three weeks after that, after he appeared in five games. House finished the season with Sacramento, where one of his teammates was his brother-in-law and Arizona neighbor Mike Bibby. "It was a tour that ended up pretty well," said House, who played in 50 games for the Kings and appeared in three playoff games.

He then had his best statistical year for the Suns in 2005–2006, as Phoenix got to the Western Conference Finals and House played in 81 games. He was an ideal fit for the way the Suns played, and it seemed as if he had finally found his niche. "I thought so, too," House said. "But they were having money concerns and couldn't bring me back. It wasn't that they didn't want me."

His agent, Bartelstein, said, "Everywhere Eddie has gone, the team that let him go wants him back. Mike D'Antoni [then the Suns coach] told me one of the biggest mistakes he made in Phoenix was letting him go."

House ended up in New Jersey, where he played shooting games at practice with Jason Kidd (and won his share) and appeared in 56 games, losing time to injuries. New Jersey, like so many teams before, didn't do enough to entice House back, so when Danny Ainge and Doc Rivers called him in the summer of 2007, House eagerly accepted yet another one-year offer.

"It seemed like a logical spot for me," House said. "They had the three guys and they're going to command double teams, so it's like, who are they going to leave open? Me. I can shoot it from the outside and knock it down."

Gradually, the roster was being replenished. The Celtics liked what they saw from their two draftees, Gabe Pruitt and Glen Davis, in Summer League play in Las Vegas. House was on board, as was Pollard. But there was still another player Ainge had targeted who remained unsigned; Ainge figured he would be the perfect addition: James Posey.

———————

In the summer of 2007, James Posey was one exasperated and confused individual. He was a free agent with eight years of NBA experience, one championship ring (Miami, 2006), and a reputation and résumé that were solid and well-known. When Celtics assistant general manager Dave Wohl started to investigate Posey for the Celtics, he called the trainer for the Miami Heat, Ron Culp. The word from Culp was that Posey was one of the best and most positive forces he had ever seen in all his years in an NBA locker room. And Culp went back to the early days of the Portland Trail Blazers in the 1970s.

"It was a long summer for me, not knowing what was going to happen," said Posey. "I was starting to have some bad thoughts. My mind just wasn't in the right place."

He had earned $6.4 million the year before in Miami, but in his exit interview after the season with coach Pat Riley, he was told he'd likely not be re-signed because of Miami's luxury tax concerns. Riley admitted as much, but also said, "I would have loved to have had him back, but I didn't want him to have to take a big pay cut and resent the hell out of it. I know he would have, even though he said he wouldn't. I had to let him go. He might have been able to accept that pay cut somewhere else, but it wasn't going to be in Miami."

Posey wasn't sure what was happening. He saw Miami teammate Jason Kapono sign with Toronto. Eddie Jones, Gary Payton, and Posey were still waiting to be signed.

"I thought it would be a good chance to stay," he said of the Miami situation. "I know it hadn't ended well, but we still had Shaq at the time. We still had D-Wade [Dwyane Wade]. I thought we could come back, be more committed and give it one more shot. But as things dragged on, I could see that wasn't going to happen. I was getting frustrated. I finally told my agent, I'm not going back to Miami."

There was something else that might have been at least partially responsible for Posey's limbo status. In April 2007, he had been charged with DUI in Miami, even though he had not been driving at the time of the arrest. Police said Posey, observed from outside his vehicle, appeared to show all the signs of being intoxicated: bloodshot eyes, slurred speech, and alcohol on his breath. Posey posted a $1,000 bond and was released. The case hung over him for the rest of the season and into the summer, until he finally decided to plead no contest in August simply to resolve the matter.

"It wasn't the legal stuff," Posey said. "It wasn't a factor for me, although I can't say that it wasn't a factor for someone else. Sometimes, you know your reputation, but there are murmurs out there, and the wrong thing gets said and people start to believe it. So that might hurt you. I've never been a problem for any team I've played for. It's tough. Some of the things I heard and people were talking about, it was hard. Miami knew what happened. Riles knew what happened. He didn't suspend me. He let everything play out."

Finally, in August 2007, Posey reached an agreement to play for the Nets. "It was basically a done deal," he said. "I was just frustrated, a lot was going on in my mind, and I wanted it to be over, so I just said, screw it. I remember it was on a Saturday and I called my agent and told him to call New Jersey and tell them I was coming. He said, 'Are you sure? I'll give you some more time.' He mentioned Boston."

Then Posey heard from Eddie House, who said flatly, "Pose, what are you doing?" Coach Doc Rivers was in Florida at a coaching retreat with his staff at an Orlando hotel. He received a call from Danny Ainge, who urged him to call Posey pronto or else the Celtics were going to lose him to the Nets.

"'Listen,'" Rivers told Posey. "'You're not getting off this phone until you tell me you're playing for us.' So I talked for a long time. Then I handed the phone to each coach, who had kind of rehearsed what he was going to say. And when I got back on at the end, you knew he had changed his mind. It was, 'I'm coming, but how am I going to tell New Jersey?' I said, 'You haven't signed a thing yet. Take care of James Posey.'"

Posey's signing was announced on August 27. It was a two-year deal that started at $3.2 million. Or the same figure that Pat Riley figured he could not offer, having had Posey for two seasons. Riley knew him as well as anyone, and at the end of their disastrous (15–67) 2007–2008 season, he figured Posey ended up in a much better spot. "When it's going good, James is right there. But it's a whole different story when it goes the other way," Riley said.

Said Ainge, "I like his demeanor. I like his toughness. He lives for big games, sort of like a Robert Horry type who will make the big shot or the big play. But he's a guy I wouldn't want to be around all that much if we weren't winning."

James posey had built a solid nba career out of being the consummate role player, be it in Denver, Memphis, or Miami. That is how he saw himself early, before he even played a game in the league.

He had carved out a solid, if not spectacular career at Xavier, playing three years for Skip Prosser, who was the only coach who stood by Posey when his grades slipped so badly as a high school senior that he didn't qualify and couldn't play as a freshman.

"I was recruited pretty heavily out of high school [in suburban Cleveland] until my grades got involved. You know how that goes.

It goes the other way," Posey said. "But [Prosser] stuck with me, and me and my family appreciated it. It was hard. The only thing I could do with the team that first year was go to study hall. I couldn't practice. I couldn't travel. I did play intramurals, and there was sort of a recruiting war to get me. That was my season—16 intramural games."

Xavier welcomed Posey back for the next three years, and as a senior, he had turned himself into a legitimate first-round pick, averaging almost 17 points a game. On the night of the 1999 draft, he crossed his fingers that his hometown Cleveland Cavaliers, who had two first-round picks, would use one of them on him. The first pick Cleveland had that night was courtesy of one of then Celtics coach Rick Pitino's impulsive and ridiculous trades. Obsessed with having a "true" center, Pitino, in March 1999, traded Andrew DeClercq and the unprotected No. 1 in 1999 to the Cavs for Vitaly Potapenko. The Boston pick ended up being No. 8 overall. The Cavs' own pick in the first round was No. 11.

"Being from there, I knew the Cavs needed a small forward," Posey said. "They took a point guard, Andre Miller, with their first pick, and then I thought I might go for a second pick."

But the Cavs, looking for outside shooting, opted for Duke's Trajan Langdon.

"That killed me right there," Posey said. "I'm like, wow! They took him? He wasn't even in the league very long."

The Denver Nuggets, choosing eighteenth, selected Posey, and he decided then and there how he was going to make his pro basketball career work. "I figured things happen for a reason," he said. "If Cleveland had taken me, maybe I would not have gone to Boston. Maybe I would not have gotten a ring in Miami. I told myself that night that I was going to keep working hard and try to put myself in a good situation where I can keep a job and stay in this league as long as possible. I accept my role. I play hard. It's about winning, and I know and I believe I'm a winner. I know what I bring to the table when I'm out there competing."

Posey played well enough as a rookie in Denver to make All-Rookie second team. He spent three-and-a-half seasons with the Nuggets and then was traded to Houston in a three-way deal. In an interesting footnote to that season, Posey appeared in 83 games because of the deal. He then became a restricted free agent in the summer of 2003 and gained immeasurable cachet when the Memphis Grizzlies signed him to an offer sheet. At the time, longtime NBA executive Jerry West was calling the shots for the Grizzlies, and the Rockets declined to match Memphis' offer sheet.

West called Posey "a great athlete who can play multiple positions. We have another veteran who coaches can expect to provide leadership and experience, and we value his ability to play defensively."

Posey lasted only two seasons in Memphis, however, before being dealt to Miami in August 2005, part of the largest trade in NBA history. Five teams were involved: Miami, Memphis, Boston, Utah, and New Orleans. Thirteen players changed teams, with Posey, Jason Williams, and Antoine Walker going to Miami. The big deal came one year after Miami had acquired Shaquille O'Neal and was done with the intention of adding veterans to the Heat roster to make a championship run. The year before, Miami had had the best record in the East, but had lost to the Pistons in seven games in the conference finals.

Posey was Pat Riley's kind of player. "He's a gamer," Riley said. "I never had any problems with James. He was great to have with all the other veterans we have, the same way he was in Boston with Kevin, Paul, and Ray."

Posey also had no trouble adapting to Riley. He was a starter for most of his first season in Miami and a reserve in most of his second year there. "I learned a lot from him not just about basketball but about life, just listening to him talk," Posey said. "He's a great coach. He's a great motivator. The mental aspect of how you approach every game. He has a system that's proven. It's all about buying into it. But why wouldn't you listen to him when you know he's done it?"

He was a huge factor in Miami's run to the 2006 title. He led the team in three-point shooting in the playoffs and played almost 30 minutes a game. Unfazed by a chorus of boos in Chicago, he scored a playoff-high 18 points in the Heat's series-clinching victory over the Bulls in the United Center in the first round. The following year, however, the Chicago fans got their revenge as the Bulls swept the Heat in the first round, Posey's last season with the Heat.

If he thought his stressful summer had come to a close with the signing by the Celtics, Posey was to find out otherwise within just four days. The NBA decided to suspend him for one game because he had pleaded no contest to the DUI charge in Miami from the previous April. It was one of the very few things that went wrong for James Posey during the 2007–2008 season.

THE ROSTER WAS NOW PRETTY MUCH INTACT. The Celtics had signed a couple of undrafted rookies—University of South Carolina's Brandon Wallace, who had impressed them during Summer League, and former North Carolina guard Jackie Manuel, who had spent the previous year in the NBA's Development League in Los Angeles. They would add a couple more "camp bodies" before they opened training camp in October.

All that remained now was for Doc Rivers and his staff to make it all come together. And the Celtics coach had an idea of how to do just that, an idea that had been brought to his attention at a most unlikely occasion.

5

Ubuntu

THERE ARE 33 MEMBERS of the Board of Trustees at Marquette University, a Jesuit institution in Milwaukee. Included in that group is one Glenn "Doc" Rivers, Class of 1985, who earned a degree in political science.

Board of Trustee meetings can be lengthy and boring and can cover a number of topics. In the fall of 2007, the meeting was in its second day when the members took a break after a long discussion about public safety at the school. Rivers remained seated and pulled out some of his coaching notes for training camp, which would be starting in a few weeks.

Stephanie Russell, the school's executive director for mission and identity, who was attending the meeting, wandered over to him, tapping him on the shoulder. Previously she had heard Rivers talk about Marquette's student work-study program in Africa and his desire to go there with his family. She had a question for him: had he ever heard the word *ubuntu*? Rivers shook his head. Russell explained that Bishop Desmond Tutu had used the word in a speech at the Marquette campus a few years earlier and it had made a big impression on her. She went on to explain to Rivers that *ubuntu* roughly translated means "I am because we are" or "I am because of you." Or, an African variation of "all for one and one for all." It is a philosophy of life that Tutu described as, "I want you to be all you can be because that's the only way I can be all that I can be." "But," she added, "it can be a lot deeper than that. It can be a way of life." "I'm like, oh my God," Rivers said. "That's my team. I've got to get my team to see that."

That very night, he flew home and immediately went on the Internet, staying up all night, excited about finding a way to bond a team that would have eight new players, many of them veterans. He had his assistant Annemarie Loflin research the topic even further. When he had gotten as much information as he could, Rivers knew he had struck gold.

"It was perfect," he said. "The more you read about it, the more you understood how perfect it was, about overcoming adversity, about sacrificing, about everyone needing and depending on everyone else. It was perfect. The only question I had then was how was I going to sell it?"

Rivers decided to wait until the official opening of training camp to unveil his latest message. He kept it to himself, not even telling his assistant coaches. He wanted it to be new to everyone.

The Celtics were scheduled to fly to Rome for their training camp, a decision that had been announced the previous February by the NBA. Some years, the league sends teams to Europe for exhibition games with other NBA teams and also with the better European teams. The Celtics would spend about ten days in Rome and London and would play two exhibitions, one against the Toronto Raptors and the other against the Minnesota Timberwolves, a team that contained a slew of ex-Celtics.

Although Rivers viewed the trip as an excellent bonding opportunity, he wanted them to board the plane with the word *ubuntu* in their collective minds. The team was scheduled to have a Media Day and its first practice at its Waltham, Massachusetts, training facility before flying to Italy. That was when Rivers decided to let the players in on *ubuntu.*

"There's a word *ubuntu*," he told them, "that will symbolize our season, our success. The word will take on its own life in meaning as the season goes forward. And tomorrow before we leave, our rookies will give us an amazing presentation of what the word means."

That was all he said.

This was news to the four rookies: draft picks Glen Davis and Gabe Pruitt and free-agent signees Jackie Manuel and Brandon Wallace. Like their teammates, they had no clue as to the meaning of *ubuntu.* After practice, Rivers gathered the four players and briefly explained what the word meant. He then said that each one of them was to give a short presentation on the word the following morning.

"This is not freshman hazing," Rivers said. "This is deadly serious and is not to be taken lightly. This is your exam. I am not screwing around, and I don't care if you have to stay up all night. But when you come to practice tomorrow, each one of you will give a presentation on *ubuntu.*" Rivers told the players they could make it short, using phrases. Two or three sentences would suffice. But they had to be earnest and they had to be on topic.

Davis left practice that day thinking, "Is this school here?" He said, "It was kinda weird, but being a rookie, you've got to do your duty. And one of those duties was going to be to tell the other guys the true meaning of the word."

The next day before practice, Rivers got the players to form a circle near the center of the court and announced that the rookies had a presentation to make. All four spoke. All were "phenomenal," Rivers said. He singled out the fun-loving Davis.

"He was as serious as he's ever been in his life," Rivers said of Davis. "I think he really thought he might get cut if he didn't do it right. They must have stayed up all night because each one of them spoke from memory, each one spoke about a different part of the word, and when one finished, the other one stepped right in."

The players started applauding, and the word did take on its own life. The Celtics had tee shirts made with just the word on it. When they broke a huddle, they chanted, "one, two, three, *ubuntu.*" Rivers even brought a man from Africa to personally address the players about the word, adding to what the rookies had said.

Davis had been almost Shakespearean in making his presentation. "I just told them it was a word that represented the start of a journey, that we were all in this together, and we were going to stand by this word and live by this word, verbally and nonverbally, if we had any hope of winning a championship," he said.

But he had not stayed up all night, as his coach had thought. "I just Googled it," he said.

———————

Rivers had one more psychological card up his sleeve, which he was saving for Kevin Garnett, Paul Pierce, and Ray Allen. The day before the team left for Rome, the coach told them to meet him at his apartment in downtown Boston at 8 a.m. Understandably, all three players wanted to know why they were being summoned from their comfortable suburban domiciles at such an ungodly hour. "I told them it was important, that there was someone I wanted them to meet, and that it would be cool," Rivers said.

Garnett, new to the area, left his home with a 90-minute cushion so he would not be late. "It's the summer, so I don't think any of us were really anticipating getting up and being at his place, you know," Garnett said. "I don't even know where the place is, to begin with, so that means I had to get up at 6:30, you know what I mean? I don't think the three of us were real happy about that."

The three were in the lobby on time, when a Duck Boat pulled up in front. These are World War II–style amphibious landing vessels that take passengers on tours of the historic sites in downtown Boston. The 80-minute trip culminates with the boat splashing into the Charles River. Until recently, the boats had been used for tourists. But with the successes of the New England Patriots and the Boston Red Sox in their respective sports, the boats have taken on a new identity—as the official vehicle of Boston championship parades. So-called "rolling rallies" have featured a number of Duck Boats carrying players, wives, and team officials through the streets of Boston.

Pierce recognized the boats, having seen previous championship parades, but admitted he'd never ridden in one. Garnett and Allen had no clue. "All of a sudden this boat on wheels pulls up, and Doc was like, 'This is what we're going to do this morning,'" Garnett said. "I was looking at him like, 'Are you serious?' This could have waited till the sun came out, you know. We got on, and he told us, 'This is the goal. This is the goal right here whenever you're successful in this city and you've won. This is what you take. This is the Duck Tour right here.'"

So, for the next 80 minutes, the four of them went on a special tour, the one that the Boston championship teams take. Few busy Bostonians noticed the four celebrities on this autumn morning. Which was fine by Rivers. He wanted to reiterate what this season was going to be all about.

"I told them that I felt it was important that they give up the phrase, 'What I used to do.' And I used that a lot on them," Rivers said. "'How I used to do it.' Those are phrases you are going to have to give up because it's not going to matter. I told them what you used to do is whatever you wanted to do because you were the only guy. With this team, that is not going to work. All of you are going to sacrifice.

"The second thing was trust," Rivers went on. "The only way to win is to trust my system, and it's not going to be tailored exactly to you. It's going to be tailored to the team. They all said, 'Cool,' and I told them, "It's easy to say 'cool' in this boat now, but when the season starts, and I'm telling you to move the ball and you want to shoot it, that'll be different. They agreed. A player will agree to anything in September. But it's different in November and far different in April and May."

The message hit home, again. This was another version of *ubuntu*, but aimed at the three public faces of the team, the ones on whom the fortunes of the team would hang.

"At first I didn't grasp it," Garnett said. "It was kind of weird. But as he talked in depth and got real and then later on in the year [in October], you saw the pictures of some of the parades and you really begin to understand what it is. It's really tradition and Boston's way of celebrating when you've won or you've achieved something as a whole."

Said Pierce, "It kind of set the foundation, like 'Hey, this has got to be our motivation.' You see pictures in our hallway and our practice facility of the guys celebrating, and it was just like, man, to be able to do this the second time will be great, because the first time was obviously with Doc. And I said, 'Next time I get on this Duck Tour, it's going to be when we win the championship.' And I promised that."

Before the team left for Rome, Rivers added one more motivational touch. Around the practice basketball court hung the 16 championship banners that the team had won from 1957 through 1986. There was room for one more on the wall, and he had a spotlight focus on that bare portion of the wall for the whole season.

————————

That rivers' apartment was in boston said a lot about who he is and how he decided to live his life. He is married, the father of four, yet when he took the Celtics job in 2004, he and his wife Kris made a decision: They would not move their family again. He would go to Boston. She would remain in their home outside Orlando. They had settled in the area when Rivers accepted the Magic head coaching job six years earlier and had no desire to relocate.

At the time, it made sense because Rivers' oldest son Jeremiah was finishing up high school and would be a good enough basketball player to receive a scholarship to Georgetown, which made it to the Final Four in his freshman year. He later transferred to Indiana University. His daughter Callie was a terrific volleyball player and earned a scholarship to the University of Florida. His third child Austin is one of the highest-rated recruits in his class and plans to play basketball at Florida as well.

During his first two years in Boston, Rivers would charter a flight home to Florida, usually at his own expense, to see his son or daughter play. His daughter's games were easier to make; they were mostly in September and October. He thought long and hard about moving the family to Boston after his daughter graduated, but decided against it.

Rivers understood that there was a perception when he was traveling to Florida during the season to see his children play that he was somehow giving his job the short end. He didn't feel that way. Danny Ainge didn't feel that way. And while the owners would have preferred him to move the family to Boston, they too came around. This was hard enough on Rivers as an individual, and he didn't need anyone else passing judgment on his career choice or the way he chose to live his life.

"It is hard to be separated from the family, and it'll be the reason I don't do it [coach] someday," Rivers said. "But when I got the Boston job, our kids had been in Orlando for six years. It was the longest they had been in one place in all their lives, and they didn't want to leave. I thought it was healthier for them to stay, but not as healthy for me to be away from them. It's very difficult for me. But when I look at them and see how happy they are, it was clearly the right decision for them. For me? I don't know. It's not the greatest, family-wise. And," he continued, "if I'm going to live alone, it's going to be somewhere I can eat, because I don't cook. I'm a city kid. I like that life and it's easier for me."

———————

He is indeed a city kid, born and raised in the Chicago neighborhood of Maywood, the son of a police lieutenant. Early on, Glenn Rivers wanted to be a professional basketball player. When he was in the third grade, his teacher asked all the students what they wanted to be when they grew up. Each child was to write his or her future profession on the blackboard.

"I wrote that I wanted to be a professional basketball player," Rivers said. "The teacher said, 'No, put something attainable, a real goal on the board.' So I wrote 'professional basketball player' again. She said she knew all the boys wanted to play professional football or professional basketball, but that I had to be more realistic. I would not back down. I was not going to change anything. And I was kicked out of class."

When he told his father what had happened, his father walked him back to school, telling his son, "'I don't know if you're going to be a pro basketball player. That's up to you. But whatever you do, just finish the friggin' race.' I had no idea what he was talking about at the time, but what he meant was finish what you start. Everyone always starts stuff, but not everyone finishes."

Playing professional basketball was not such a far-fetched notion in the Rivers' family, in which there was a discernable athletic strain. Rivers was the nephew of Jim Brewer, who played at the University of Minnesota and went on to play for four NBA teams in the 1970s and 1980s. One of his cousins was Byron Irvin, who also played in the NBA for two teams. Another cousin was Ken Singleton, a major league baseball player in the 1970s and 1980s.

By the time Rivers reached high school, he was almost universally known as "Doc," a nickname bestowed on him by coach Rick Majerus, who had Rivers in his basketball camp. Rivers came to camp wearing a shirt that said "Doc," a reference to the great Julius Erving whose nickname was Dr. J.

He also was on track to achieve his goal. He became the first freshman since his uncle, Jim Brewer, to start for Proviso East High School. He played for a no-nonsense, ex-Marine drill sergeant named Glenn Whittenberg, a Caucasian in charge of a team from the inner city. "It was like the White Shadow," Rivers said, referring to the television show that portrayed a Caucasian head coach, played by Ken Howard, with a team of mostly African-Americans.

Rivers loved the discipline of Whittenberg's system. "Before you could even go out on the floor, you had to do 500 jumps with a jump rope and do 50 bench pumps with weights. And when you did the bench pumps, he had this sign on the wall above a bucket of water that said, 'If you think you are so important to the team, stick your foot into the water and pull it out. The hole that you leave is how important you are to the team.' I loved that stuff."

And you wonder why *ubuntu* resonated with this guy?

By the time Rivers left Proviso East, he was a big name in Chicago basketball circles and had generated interest from a host of Midwestern colleges. But he had always had his eyes on Marquette, dating back to Rick Majerus' camp. Majerus was then an assistant at Marquette. Rivers also loved the uniforms (always critical). Back then, Marquette was a true national power, having won the NCAA championship in 1977. Rivers was in high school at the time. He enrolled at Marquette in the fall of 1980, choosing the school over DePaul, Indiana, Notre Dame, and Michigan.

He played three years there for Hank Raymonds and at the end of his junior year faced a decision. Raymonds was leaving, and Majerus was slated to replace him. Despite his affection for and history with Majerus, Rivers was uncertain if it would all work out.

"I love Rick, but I also was thinking, 'He is going to be the coach for my senior year, and it is going to be my most important year, playing with a new coach,'" Rivers said. "I think I was scared things were going to change so much. So I left. And, honestly, I had a guarantee from a team that was in the top 20 that they would draft me. And then they reneged on it."

There also was a more personal reason. Rivers had been dating Kris Campion, who is Caucasian, and the idea of a mixed couple at the school didn't sit well with some at the time. Kris' family home in Milwaukee was spray-painted. There were other ugly incidents. To this day, Rivers' wife thinks the relationship played as much, if not more, of a role in Rivers' decision to leave Marquette early.

Rivers ended up being drafted by the Atlanta Hawks in the second round, the thirty-first pick overall in the 1983 NBA draft. His celebrated toughness and grit would be put to an immediate test, as the Hawks had a new coach, a defensive-minded disciple of Hubie Brown named Mike Fratello. The Hawks also had an abundance of guards on the roster (and a forward named Armond Hill, who would play 15 games for the team).

"I remember it was about the fourth day of training camp, and Wes Matthews was just trash talking me and trying to get into my head. He was trying to keep his job," Rivers said. "I was in his way and he elbowed me in the back of the head. The first time, I let it go. But he did it again and I just turned, picked him up on my back and body-slammed him to the floor. He was hurt. He couldn't get up. But he stopped elbowing me in the head.

"Then after that practice, Mike [Fratello] came over, and I'm thinking he's about to cut me and he said to me, 'You are on this team. You can relax. I haven't made up my mind about everyone else, but you are on this team.' I think he saw that I had some fight in me, that I wasn't intimidated, that I wasn't going to back down," Rivers said.

So began a terrific, 13-year NBA career for Rivers, who played the first eight with the Hawks. Atlanta had some good years in the 1980s, but they could never get past the Celtics or the Pistons. The Hawks won 50 games in 1985–1986, but lost in five games to the eventual champion Celtics in the second round, getting humiliated in the final when the Celtics outscored them 36–6 in the third quarter.

The Hawks won 57 games the following year, but lost to the Pistons in five games in the second round. They won 50 again in 1988, but lost to the Celtics in a spectacular seven-game series, climaxed by the famous Game 7 shootout between Larry Bird and Dominique Wilkins. A 52-win season in 1989 resulted in a first-round loss to Milwaukee.

"There was always some team in the way, usually Boston," Rivers said. He was right, although the Hawks had the Celtics down 3–2 in 1988, but lost Game 6 at home. In 1987, the Hawks had the home court advantage over the Pistons in the second round, but lost twice at home.

Even with a roster featuring future Hall of Famer Dominique Wilkins and players like Rivers, Kevin Willis, Randy Wittman, Antoine Carr, Cliff Levingston, and Tree Rollins, the Hawks always came up short. Playing under Fratello was no walk in the park for Rivers. The coach could be merciless on his point guard, and Rivers was not always receptive to the coach's "suggestions." "He was tough, brutal on me, brutal on all the point guards," Rivers said. "For those first couple of years, I didn't know if my name was Doc Rivers or 'MF asshole.' I was the whipping boy. He would always come up to me, Mike being a Jersey guy, and say, 'You Chicago guys all think you're so tough.' I heard that every day. Finally, one day I just exploded, swore back at him, and everyone was looking on thinking, 'What the hell is going on?' But the next day, Mike took me out to dinner. We worked things out, and it was good from that point on. He had such a passion for defense, but we were pretty good at the other end, too."

Fratello also saw something else in Rivers besides the kid's toughness and determination. He saw a future head coach in the NBA. "No question about it," Fratello said. "I always thought Doc was going to coach when he finished playing."

But before that happened, Rivers would be traded to the Clippers, unhappily for him. He was 30. He had spent his entire career in Atlanta and was established there. The Hawks received one first-round pick and two second-rounders for Rivers, who threatened not to show up for what was then one of the more hapless outfits in the NBA.

Concerned about his situation, the Clippers requested that Rivers come out for a meeting with owner Donald Sterling and his executive henchmen, but then made things hard by also requesting he fly coach instead of first class, where the NBA players were accustomed to sitting. By the time Rivers showed up, along with his agent, the two had already decided that if Sterling or the others started to jive him, or talk double-talk, which the Clippers were famous for doing, he was going to leave. And that is what happened. During the meeting, Rivers heard enough, bolted out of his seat, hailed a cab, and flew back to Atlanta.

Eventually tempers cooled, and Rivers did report. Then halfway through the season, the Clippers fired coach Mike Schuler and replaced him with Larry Brown. Rivers and Brown were together for only that half-season, but Rivers came away with some appreciation for the way Brown coached.

"I loved Larry, but he was crazy," Rivers said. "We had started the year with Mike Schuler and we were OK, then Larry came in and we took off. His practices go on forever, but not because you're playing. It's because he's always stopping things and then explaining things. It got to the point where Ron Harper and I would go to a sports club after practice just so we could get our conditioning in. I mean, Larry came in and he changed his whole offense. He'd say, 'Forget everything I put in three days ago. We're changing.' It was the middle of the season," Rivers said.

The 1991–1992 LA Clippers won 23 of their last 35 games and became the first Clippers team in 15 years to qualify for the playoffs. They took the Jazz to the five-game maximum in the first round before bowing out.

That would be it for Rivers in Los Angeles. He was traded to the Knicks the following year, and it was during his two-year stint there that he came the closest to winning a championship ring.

The 1993–1994 Knicks reached the NBA Finals, but coach Pat Riley had a decision to make when he submitted his playoff roster to the league. Back then, you submitted 12 names before the start of the playoffs, and that list was sacrosanct. If someone got hurt, he could not be replaced. Someone who had been hurt and had recovered could not be activated.

Rivers had missed 63 games that season with a knee injury, but was recovering and would be able to play at some point in the post-season. That wasn't good enough for Riley, who figured he needed 12 healthy bodies out of the chute. "I've always told Doc that I made a huge mistake in 1994," Riley said. "He wasn't ready, but it was still stupid on my part because I knew he would be if we advanced. We might have won it that year if I had put him on. And every time I see Doc, I tell him that. And he gives me that look."

Rivers soaked up everything from Riley, from the mind games to the preparation to the coaching style that stressed team over individual agendas. Riley was also a conditioning fanatic. In Miami, he suspended Antoine Walker and James Posey for being one percent over their allowable body fat quotient. While with the Knicks, Riley had the team take a bus into Manhattan, where they would be tossed into a water tank and told to hold their breath for a minute. That would determine what their body fat percentage was.

But it was Riley, like Fratello, who also saw a future coach in his point guard. When it came time to part ways—the Knicks waived Rivers early in the 1994–1995 season—Rivers recalled Riley's last words and remembers them to this day. "He said, 'You may be grooming for a job in the media, but you are going to end up coaching,'" he said. "He was so important to me because he had this ability to reach players through commitment."

Rivers' playing career ended in San Antonio. He played for Bob Hill, but the man who brought him to San Antonio was then the Spurs general manager, Gregg Popovich. He signed Rivers as a free agent 11 days after being waived by New York. "I wanted to change the culture and environment there, and I wanted to surround David [Robinson] with a different group of players," Popovich said. "Guys who were veterans. Guys who had class. Guys who showed leadership. People who fit in well with David. Doc was one of those guys. He had the kind of personality we wanted at that time. We also brought in Avery [Johnson], and we got Sean [Elliott] back from Detroit. Really, that's where it all started."

The 1995 Spurs won a league-best 62 games, but lost in the Western Conference Finals to the eventual champion Rockets. To this day, Rivers feels the Spurs were the better team. But they had no answer for Hakeem Olajuwon, who was unstoppable and basically willed the Rockets to victory.

When it was time to retire, Rivers had a standing offer from Popovich to coach. By then, Popovich had replaced Hill as the head coach. But Rivers instead went into broadcasting for the Spurs, a job that allowed him to stay current while getting a good look at the league. He knew instinctively then that he was going to coach. He just didn't know when or where.

But while doing television work for the Spurs, another racial incident occurred that was far more horrific than the reaction to his dating a white woman in Wisconsin. While Rivers was away at a charity golf tournament in June 1997, and his wife was with their children at her parents' home, someone torched their home in San Antonio. All was lost, including the pets. No one has ever been charged with what fire officials determined was arson. But, in yet another indication of Rivers' inner determination, the family built a new home near the one that was burned down.

The coaching call came three years later. The Orlando Magic had gone 33–17 in the lockout season, but coach Chuck Daly was retiring. GM John Gabriel was in the process of turning over his roster to make a run at Tim Duncan in 2000 and had a history of somewhat unconventional hires in Daly (67 at the time) and before him, Brian Hill, who had had no head coaching experience. He had seen Rivers on television and had had a long history dealing with Rivers' agent, Lonnie Cooper, who represented both Daly and Hill. There were rumors at the time that Rivers might end up on the San Antonio bench, so Gabriel figured, "We were looking for that young, up and coming coach who had hopes and dreams. Why let someone else have him?"

A couple of interviews into the process, Rivers and Gabriel were already on the topic of assistant coaches. It also didn't hurt that Rivers had a relationship with Duncan from his broadcasting days with the Spurs. Rivers took the job knowing he'd have a roster mostly of players in the final years of their contracts, freeing up money the following summer for the assault on Duncan.

Orlando went through 19 players in Rivers' first season, most of them in the final year of their contracts. Included in that group were Corey Maggette, Chauncey Billups (who was injured and didn't play), Ben Wallace, Chris Gatling, Pat Garrity, Ron Mercer, Chucky Atkins, and John Amaechi.

"Looking back," Gabriel said, "that might have been the best team Doc ever had in Orlando."

Despite all the comings and goings, and with Milwaukee coach George Karl criticizing the 1999–2000 Magic from afar for taking players they didn't want or need and planned to discard, the team still managed to win 41 games. Rivers earned Coach of the Year honors without even making the playoffs, the only time in NBA history. It was an astonishing achievement and the kind of acclaim and recognition that he and the Magic thought would go a long way toward landing Duncan. Gabriel also was named Executive of the Year.

Orlando had cleared out enough salary cap space to make a full-tilt run not only for Duncan, but also for another marquee player. The Magic were in the Eastern Conference, deemed less demanding than the Western Conference, and

Duncan would be closer to his native St. Croix. After a recruiting visit to Orlando, Rivers said he felt the Magic had won the battle for Duncan. "He got on that plane and he told us he was coming," Rivers said. "I wish he had. Who knows what would have happened?"

"Orlando was a very attractive option for Tim, and one of the reasons was Doc," Popovich said. "We took it very, very seriously. People outside the loop might have thought it was a no-brainer that Tim was staying in San Antonio, but we didn't. We worked very hard to keep him."

That included sending David Robinson to talk to Duncan. Eventually, Duncan was convinced to stay. Orlando ended up with Tracy McGrady and Grant Hill, who seemed at the time to be a dynamic duo. But Hill never was fully healthy. For awhile, Rivers would have two game plans ready for each game, one with Hill and one without him. The Magic were just good enough to make the playoffs, but never good enough to do any damage when they got there.

After blowing a 3–1 lead against the Pistons in 2003, Rivers returned for a fifth season in the fall. The Magic won their opener, in overtime at New York, then lost ten straight games. The losing streak cost Rivers his job. After he left, there were stories of discontent among some of the Orlando veterans, namely Darrell Armstrong and Horace Grant, and there also were stories that Rivers wanted more control in the decision-making part of the operation. He quickly found employment in what many people feel is his natural calling—television—where he was elevated to ABC's No. 1 broadcast crew with Al Michaels.

Then the Celtics came calling in the summer of 2004. The man who pursued him with the most ardor was Danny Ainge, Rivers' nemesis from their playing days. Now, however, they were "on the same page."

THREE YEARS INTO RIVERS' SECOND COACHING INCARNATION, the fans of Boston wanted his head on a platter. After a particularly embarrassing home loss to the Knicks early in the 2006–2007 season, there were chants of "Fire Rivers" at the TD Banknorth Garden. No coach of a nonexpansion team that lost as many games in a row as Rivers' 2006–2007 Celtics did—the franchise record 18—ever survived to return with the same team. Publicly, he continued to show the resolve he had needed back in high school, in college, and in his early years in Orlando. He knew he was no Phil Jackson. He also knew Phil Jackson couldn't win either with the lineup he had. He just asked for patience—and players.

Now, 12 months later, he had the players and forgot about the patience. The Celtics were preseason favorites to win it all, in the minds of many. They were the unquestioned "It" team with their celebrated trio of stars. Garnett made sure the trio did things as a trio, refusing individual interviews unless the other two were present. He pretty much maintained that posture throughout the season, always accompanied by someone to the post-game interview room.

The three shot humorous commercials for ESPN and were seen together in a number of photo shoots. And when they left for Rome, all three sported shaved heads. That was a change for Pierce. The other two always had shaved heads.

The trip to Rome was seen as an excellent chance for the team to bond as a unit. There were trips to the Vatican, the Forum, the Spanish steps. There were motorcycle escorts to exhibition games with wide-eyed Italians gawking at the team bus as it traversed the streets of Rome.

The Celtics had a total of 17 players on the roster; all but Scot Pollard made the entire trip. That included a couple late signees: Uruguayan center Esteban Batista, who had played well at the FIBA Olympic Qualifying Tournament that summer in Las Vegas (although his team did not), and former Duke star Dahntay Jones, who had actually been a Celtics No. 1 pick in 2003, although Boston had made the pick in a prearranged deal with Memphis.

The four rookies who had made the impressive *ubuntu* presentation also were present. One day after practice, Garnett told them to assemble in the room of Glen Davis at the team's headquarters, the Exedra Hotel. Then, as the four sat there with jaws dropped, an Italian tailor wheeled in racks of suits and shoes for the rookies. Three per rookie. All paid for by Garnett.

"I'm thinking, so *this* is how it's going to be as a rookie? Oh my God, these were such nice suits and so much money and at first, you feel a little iffy about it," Davis said. "But the guy kept saying, 'Don't worry about it. You better do this. You better do that.'"

Said Gabe Pruitt, "I had never worn suits like that, so it was pretty nice. The guy told us that if what he had didn't fit, he'd fix that and have the suits for us the next day. To have someone of KG's caliber do something like that, it tells you what kind of guy he is. It meant a lot."

Rivers would also be the beneficiary of Garnett's largesse later on in the season. He had heard the suits story and, after being around Garnett for awhile, became less and less surprised about it. "The best part of Kevin is his character, not his talent," Rivers said of Garnett.

For years Rivers had carried around the same tattered briefcase. Then, just before Christmas, he walked into his office and saw a brand new, obviously very expensive leather briefcase sitting on the floor next to his desk. But he too has his habits and superstitions. The team was winning, so he stuck with the old one. He brought the new one home to his apartment, where it stayed unused, until his wife Kris, up for a holiday visit, asked where it had come from and how long he had had it. He told her that Garnett had bought it for him as a Christmas present.

"Wow, that's really nice," she said. "You haven't used it?"

Rivers said it had been a gift.

"When people buy you something nice like that, you have to use it. It brings them joy," Kris Rivers told her husband. "You are going to empty that old briefcase right now, and you're going to put all of your stuff into the new briefcase."

Rivers did as he was told. That night, the Celtics won the game, and Rivers' executive assistant, Annemarie Loflin, called to tell him how excited Garnett had been about the game. "Yeah, we won. He played great," Rivers told Loflin.

"No," she laughed. "He saw you walk out of there with his briefcase."

The next day, Brandi Garnett, Kevin's wife, sent a text message to Loflin, saying, "Tell Doc he looks great with the new briefcase."

THE TEAM BONDED WELL IN ROME. The bonding process had actually started in September, when most of the veterans showed up for player workouts at the training facility. "We were there early, hanging out together, playing cards, going out to eat, getting a feel for each other," Posey said. "And to see the way the Big Three approach the game, approach the practice sessions. They didn't take any short cuts. They competed hard, they pushed their teammates, they did what they were supposed to do."

Celtics principal owner Wyc Grousbeck recalled watching—with a CEO and his wife, who were in town for a visit—a players' workout in September. All three zeroed in on Garnett. "He's taking shots and he's missing them," Grousbeck said. "Then, all of a sudden he lets out this huge roar. And he starts running wind sprints, all by himself, almost as a form of punishment. I had never seen anything like it. I turned to the couple and said, 'Wow. What have we got here?'"

He—and the rest of the basketball world—would soon find out.

6

Shot from Guns

THE TRIP TO EUROPE gave the Celtics their first two exhibition games—both victories—and also a glimpse of the team's newfound energy and intensity, largely the work of the ultra-hyper Garnett.

In their exhibition opener in Rome against the Toronto Raptors (and local hero Andrea Bargnani), Garnett, Pierce, and Ray Allen all were seen diving on the floor after a loose ball. They did it again in the Celtics next exhibition game, a victory in London over the Timberwolves. That game served as a reunion of sorts for the number of ex-Celtics on Minnesota.

It was pretty clear to Rivers early on that Garnett was something special. He had talked to Flip Saunders about Garnett after the deal had been made. Saunders had told him that Garnett was an absolute pleasure to coach, a great teammate, and most of all, a guy who sets the agenda with his selflessness and his intensity.

The difference in the team was palpable. Gone were the clueless kids from a year ago. As Rivers noted, "This year, when I tell them to pick and roll, they know what they have to do. Last year, I had to tell them what a pick and roll was." There also was a focus, a resolve, and a commitment that had not been there the year before.

"You knew [Garnett] had great intensity," Rivers said. "You didn't know he had it full-time, on and off the floor. His intensity in shootarounds and practices spread to our entire team. Our shootarounds were phenomenal. They listened to every word. There was no talking. They were focused. That's all from Kevin Garnett and that changed our team. And the biggest thing I didn't know is that he is such a great teammate. The best player on the team also being the best teammate is very important. And very rare."

Garnett on game days is like a man possessed. He does not speak to reporters, which is not all that uncommon among the elite players. (Allen, however, always has time for questions before a game, on topics ranging from Bruce Springsteen to current events. Pierce and Garnett nicknamed him Ray Obama and figure Allen is a lock to run for elective office once his playing career is over.)

Like many, Garnett has a pregame ritual that drives home his focus and intensity. All season, when the Celtics ran out onto the floor, Garnett was the last player through the runway tunnel. After warm-ups and the National Anthem, but before player introductions, Garnett sat on the bench by himself, eyes closed, head down, as if in deep meditation or prayer. He remained in that position until his name was called for the starting lineup by public address announcer Eddie Paladino. Ignoring the music, pyrotechnics, and even his own face on the video screen, he raised his arm to acknowledge the other starters and went out to the floor.

Once the introductions were finished, he returned to the bench and sat some more, rising to listen to any final pregame thoughts the coach might be inclined to dispense. He then went back to the bench, took off his sweatsuit, and walked over to the basket stanchion nearest the Boston bench, where he tightened the laces on his shorts and then stared into the stanchion for several seconds. It was then over to the bench to get some hand powder, which he spread by clapping his hands in front of the radio broadcasting team of Cedric Maxwell and Sean Grande. Then it was onto the floor (after a hug from James Posey and a quick fist-bump from Eddie House). Garnett would then exhort the crowd before the ball was thrown up for the opening tip.

Where does this all come from?

"I have no idea," Garnett said. "My mom is pretty intense. My grandmother, God rest her soul, was pretty intense. My sister is pretty intense. I guess the best way to explain it is that it's a level of energy that I have, and luckily I have basketball to channel it and use it for something positive and good."

By Opening Night 2007, it was clear to Danny Ainge that Garnett had regained whatever spirit he had lost in the previous down years in Minnesota. But that's not to say there weren't big questions in Ainge's mind as the season was about to start. "I wondered if Rajon [Rondo] was ready," Ainge said. "I wondered if Perk [Kendrick Perkins] was ready. I wondered if Leon [Powe] was ready, and if Big Baby [Glen Davis] would be able to give us anything. There were a lot of unknowns. But one thing I was never concerned about was Paul, Ray, and KG getting along and being able to play together. There was so much passion and so much excitement that I was just hoping they wouldn't all burn out using up all that energy. I felt at that time that we were as good as any of the other top seven or eight teams, that we could win or lose a seven-game series against any of those teams."

"But I'll tell you what I never expected. I never expected 29–3 out of the gate." No one did.

No one was thinking such grandiose thoughts when the Washington Wizards arrived for Opening Night. Gilbert Arenas had already stirred the pot by predicting in his personal blog on the NBA's official Website that the Wizards would ruin the debut of the new Big Three.

There was undeniable electricity in the TD Banknorth Garden, prompting the Wizards Caron Butler to say, "It was like a college game." The Celtics had imported a few members from the World Champion Boston Red Sox to gin up the joint, as if anything more was needed.

Pierce addressed the crowd before the game and promised the fans they would finally be rewarded with a championship-caliber team after so many down years and false hopes. "I couldn't ask for anything better," he said.

The Celtics were without Posey, serving his one-game suspension, but that in no way dampened the enthusiasm of the evening. Then Garnett got the ball in the paint, turned for a fall-away jumper, and launched one of the most brutal shots ever seen in any gym. It missed the rim. By a lot. "I think I hit the logo," said Garnett, a reference to the NBA logo of Jerry West, which is in the lower corner of the backboard.

It was about the only thing Garnett did wrong in his first game wearing the Celtics green and white. He finished with 22 points, 20 rebounds, and 5 assists in 38 minutes. The Celtics outscored the Wizards 38–17 in the second quarter and led by as many as 27 points in cruising to an easy 103–83 victory.

"The only thing I wish," Pierce said after the game, "is that Red [Auerbach] could have been here. You know how much he would have loved to have seen this atmosphere and to see us try to turn this thing around."

Only one Celtic could have made that statement, because only one, Paul Pierce, had any kind of meaningful relationship with the late, great Celtics patriarch. Among the celebrated new Big Three, Pierce had the fewest All-Star appearances and tied with Ray Allen for the fewest playoff games in his career. But there was no question among the trio who was going to be the public face of the 2007–2008 Celtics. Pierce retained his role as team captain. Pierce would be the last player introduced at home games. Pierce would be the one to address the crowd before the home opener.

He had earned that right because he had been through so much just to get to this point. When he talked about 2007–2008 being "the end to one hell of a journey," people who had been with him through thick and thin could identify. A Californian by birth, a Midwesterner in his college years, and a Celtic for all of his professional life, Pierce had been through more than most. A lot more.

ROY WILLIAMS, THE HALL OF FAME COACH at the University of North Carolina, was at Kansas in the summer of 1994 when he first set eyes on a promising swingman from Inglewood, California. Williams had targeted California as one of his recruiting bases. He had ceded the east to Duke, North Carolina, and other powers and had been successful in getting the likes of Jacque Vaughn (Pasadena) and Scot Pollard (San Diego) to choose Lawrence, Kansas, as their college destination.

"I fell in love with Paul the first time I saw him," Williams said of Pierce. "He had grown from this little fat kid who didn't play, into one of the best players in the country. I recruited him as hard as I have anyone. I saw him again later that year and I think he had 26 points in the fourth quarter alone. I'm thinking to myself, 'This guy is going to be a big-time player on game days.' We were lucky to get him."

Pierce had honed his games on the mean streets of Inglewood, playing pickup games in Rogers Park or the playgrounds of St. Anthony's elementary school and the local Y. His mother worked two jobs and steered her son into sports in hopes it would keep him off the streets and out of trouble. Pierce's two male mentors were Patrick Roy, his high school coach, and Scott Collins, an

Inglewood police officer who doubled as Roy's assistant and the father figure that Pierce never had.

On many mornings, well before the start of school, Pierce would climb into his Datsun 210 and drive to the gym, where Collins was often waiting. There Pierce would shoot free throws and work on his game, well before his first class. "It was kind of nasty because you went to class all sweaty," Pierce recalled.

"But it helped me. It helped me develop a work ethic. It helped me learn how to sacrifice," he went on "I mean, who wants to wake up at 5:30 to get to the gym? But back then, I was a kid who had dreams. That was what you needed to do, get to the gym early because you didn't have a chance once school began. It started just being disciplined. And it helped me stay away from the ghetto."

Pierce became a McDonald's All-Star in his senior year, and there was interest from many schools in the west, including Los Angeles' two biggies, UCLA and USC. There was interest from Nevada–Las Vegas, which only a few years earlier had won a national championship. Fresno State was in the mix.

"He was always a good player, but he never seemed to get the proper amount of credit. I think that's why he has always had this kind of chip on his shoulder," said adidas' Sonny Vaccaro, who came to know Pierce quite well when he was in high school. Pierce participated in Vaccaro's All-Star games and was tempted to remain in Los Angeles for college. But he instinctively knew that might not be the best thing for him.

"I needed to get away from Los Angeles. It was tough going to Kansas, but I had to get out," Pierce said. "I remember making my official visit there over Thanksgiving. All the students were away, but there still was a game, and I had never seen anything like that before, the fans, the enthusiasm. All I had known was USC and UCLA. You know LA fans are not real fans. Everyone knows that. I'm thinking to myself, 'I can play on national television, be on a national championship contender, and be in a place where I can focus on nothing but basketball and school work?' That was the best thing.

"Until then, I had just looked at Pac 10 and Big West teams. But my senior year, my grades started to slip because I just started ignoring stuff and went out, hanging around. I had already signed, and I'm thinking, I still have to go to class? I think if I had stayed home and gone to UCLA or USC, things would have gotten even worse. The hard part about leaving was my mom. She was going to be all by herself and she was never going to see me play. But I just felt it was the important thing for me to get away."

Pierce and Kansas were a good fit. In addition to Vaughn and Pollard, Williams also had recruited a lanky Iowan, Raef LaFrentz, and a guard from California, Jerod Haase. It was the situation Pierce had envisioned when he saw Lawrence for the first time—exposure galore and a chance to win a national championship.

Kansas never won a title in Pierce's time in Lawrence, despite winning 98 games in three years and being a No. 2 seed in the NCAA Tournament when Pierce was a freshman and a No. 1 seed in his sophomore and junior years. The Jayhawks never even made it to the Final Four while Pierce was there, which an emotional Williams noted in his induction speech at the Basketball Hall of Fame in 2007. With Pierce and some other former players watching, a tearful Williams apologized to them. "It's something I'll never get over," Williams said. "It was tough. You had to admit your failure in front of all these people you cared about."

Pierce remembered not losing all that often at Kansas (11 times in three years), and "Coach Williams cried after just about every one. He is a very emotional coach. But I learned so much from him, and he really gave me everything, made me who I am."

The last loss was, however, so unexpected and devastating that it still lingers. The Jayhawks were upset in the second round of the 1998 NCAA Tournament by the University of Rhode Island (led by Cuttino Mobley), a loss Williams said ranks as one of the three worst in his career. The other two were the Sweet Sixteen loss to eventual champion Arizona the year before and the 2008 shellacking administered by Kansas to North Carolina in the national semifinals in 2008. (Williams had moved from Kansas to North Carolina in 2003.)

By then, however, Pierce had made up his mind to turn pro. He had toyed with the idea after his sophomore year, but decided he wasn't ready to leave such a talented team. But the loss to Rhode Island—"a tough one, brutal," Pierce said—forced his hand. "I knew it was time to move on and try to take my game to the next level," he said.

The 1998 draft will go down as one of the more intriguing ones in history. The overall No. 1 would turn out to be Michael Olowokandi, as once again height triumphed over all (Olowokandi was a raw seven-foot center). Vince Carter, Antawn Jamison, Pierce, and Dirk Nowitzki were all on the board that night—and none went in the top three.

The Celtics had the tenth pick and had zeroed in on Nowitzki, trying to keep their interest a secret. Coach Rick Pitino had had Nowitzki work out in Germany and had come away determined to take the kid. The only possible spoiler to Pitino's plans was the Dallas Mavericks, whose coach, Don Nelson, was also smitten with Nowitzki. The Mavericks had the sixth overall pick.

Pierce didn't know what to expect. He was rumored to be among the top five for sure, so he didn't even work out for a number of top ten teams, including the Celtics. Boston GM Chris Wallace had spoken to Roy Williams about both Pierce and Raef LaFrentz, but that was the extent of their research. They never gave Pierce a serious thought; their minds were focused on Nowitzki. Thus, when Pierce began to slide, they initially did not notice, because Nowitzki was still on the board as well.

In Philadelphia, the 76ers were poised to take Pierce. He was No. 2 on their draft board (after Vince Carter), and it seemed to one and all a no-brainer, especially with coach Larry Brown's Kansas ties. (He had won a national title coaching the Jayhawks in 1988.)

"I had watched Paul a lot," Brown said. "But we also had Timmy Thomas [from the year before], and we didn't think we were deep enough to get another small forward. And we also were concerned that Pierce might be good enough to beat out Thomas, so that played into our thinking as well."

The Sixers wanted a bigger guard to possibly play alongside Allen Iverson and settled on Larry Hughes, who had played one season at the University of St. Louis. Then, the following March, they turned around and traded Thomas to the Milwaukee Bucks. A year later, they traded Hughes to the Golden State Warriors after Hughes had expressed some disappointment at not being able to start ahead of Aaron McKie or Eric Snow.

After the Sixers took Hughes, Wallace turned to Pitino and said, "We're either going to get Dirk or Paul Pierce." Milwaukee, picking ninth, took Nowitzki in a prearranged deal with Dallas, who had taken Robert Traylor at No. 6. The Celtics were heart-broken about losing Nowitzki. But, as Wallace noted, "We did get a pretty good consolation prize. He had been a big-time player in college," Wallace said of Pierce. "It was sort of like a draft perfect storm for us to get him. Kansas had not had a good NCAA tourna-ment, and I firmly believe that if they had gone to the Final Four, or even won it, then Paul would not have slid to No. 10. There were reports that some of his workouts weren't great. And a lot of people jumped into the top ten who, a couple weeks earlier, we didn't think would be top ten guys."

It would prove to be yet another perceived snub for Pierce. He rode the bench as a sophomore in high school. He would be re-membered as one of the great players at Kansas who couldn't get to the Final Four. And now he was going behind the likes of Michael Olowokandi, Raef LaFrentz, Robert Traylor, and Larry Hughes in the 1998 draft.

"You just use it as extra motivation," he said. "People always have doubted me, and it just makes me try that much harder. It just makes me that much hungrier."

Pierce had to wait, along with everyone else, for the 1998–1999 season to start, because of the lockout. When it ended and he did report, he was not prepared, nor were many of his teammates, for the conditioning drills that Pitino put the team through. The year before, many players had needed intravenous fluids and couldn't practice. It was no different the second year.

"That first training camp was brutal," Pierce said. "There were like five guys who were getting IVs because they were so dehydrated. One time, we were at Brandeis [practice facility], and there were only nine of us who could practice. So [assistant coach] Lester Conner had to practice so we would have ten guys. He ended up guarding me. And I scored just about every time I got the ball. And there's Pitino, yelling at Lester, cursing him out. It was wild."

When Pierce wasn't being run roughshod by Pitino, he was partaking in a shooting drill of his own design. Before taking the shot, he would announce the name of every player taken before him in the draft. Then he'd make the shot. It was one more way to remind himself not only that he had been overlooked, but that he would make those who overlooked or bypassed him in the draft live to regret it.

"I will never forget that night," he said of the draft. "I was sitting in the green room with my mom, my high school coach, my brothers, and I'm hearing all those names called ahead of me. I couldn't believe it."

In his very first month as a Celtic, Pierce played well enough to be named the NBA's Rookie of the Month. The award had originated in 1981–1982, and only one other Celtic, Dino Radja, had ever won it (November 1993). After getting the news, Pierce was called into Pitino's office where, he presumed, congratulations awaited. "With all the coaches there, he sat me down and said, 'We shouldn't be starting you anymore, because we don't want you to get a big head,'" Pierce said. "That guy. He could really mess with your head."

Thus began a relationship that was on-again, off-again. Pitino was at his fatherly best when Pierce found himself in the wrong place at the wrong time on the night of September 25, 2000, and ended up getting stabbed multiple times in a Boston nightclub. He almost died. He still sports scars above his right eye and across his upper back from the attack (covered now by a huge tattoo). Pitino was a daily visitor to the New England Medical Center where Pierce was treated. He was shocked like everyone else when Pierce was back at practice in three weeks and on the floor for the Celtics first exhibition game a week later. He started all 82 games that season.

"I still can't believe it happened to me, but it did," Pierce said of the stabbing incident. "It was definitely a shocker for me. It taught me that I had to be really careful where I went and who I hung around with. As an athlete with a lot of money, you are a target to some people."

That season, 2000–2001, would be the last full one for Pitino in Boston. Pierce saw first-hand the utter mental deterioration of a man whose hallmarks had always been confidence (some might say arrogance) and success everywhere he'd been. He took Providence to the Final Four and won a national championship at Kentucky. He'd resurrected the Knicks in his previous NBA head coaching job. Surely, he would do the same thing with the Celtics, or so the thinking went.

Midway through Pierce's third season, with the Celtics continuing to lose and Pitino starting to point the finger at the impatient fans, it became so bad for the coach that his family stopped attending games. His son, attending a Boston-area private school, was getting abuse simply because of his father. The players stopped playing for the coach, and it was only a matter of time before Pitino resigned. "I've never seen anything like that. But it was time for him to go," Pierce said.

Before a game in Miami in early January 2001, Pitino told Pierce that he was going to resign after the game. It showed how far they had come; Pierce doesn't believe any other player was similarly informed. When Pierce came out of the game in the fourth quarter, the coach gave him a hug. He hugged him back. It was a sad ending to what once had been a very promising story—Rick Pitino returning to Boston to bring the Celtics back to glory.

The Celtics rallied around Pitino's successor, Jim O'Brien, advancing to the Eastern Conference Finals in O'Brien's first full season, 2001–2002. The following year however brought an ownership change and the hiring of Ainge to do what Pitino had failed to do. In 2004, O'Brien resigned. Later that year, Rivers was hired.

It did not go well between the new coach and the returning veteran. Pierce always has believed he is one of the game's elite players, although some others around the league do not share that view. Pierce also had an image problem, having been seen as one of the scapegoats of the 2002 World Championship team, which finished in sixth place and became the first U.S. national team with NBA players to lose in international competition.

U.S. coach George Karl blamed Pierce and Baron Davis for being bad influences on the team. Neither has played a minute for any USA Basketball team since then, although Pierce was invited to try out for the 2006 World Championship Team but was prevented from doing so by injuries.

The Celtics were not close to being a championship-caliber team in 2004. Pierce knew it. Rivers knew it. But Rivers knew if the Celtics were going to do anything, he and Pierce had to be simpatico. They were anything but in that first year.

"I knew we were not going to get along at first, because I was going to ask him to play differently," Rivers said. "In our very first meeting, I said to Paul, 'I love your talent. But I think you should be more efficient.' Then I asked him if he thought he was a great shooter, and he said, 'Yeah, I am.' I asked him, 'How does a great shooter shoot 40 percent?' He explained that he didn't have a lot of help, which was true, but I said, 'No, wait. You just told me you're a great shooter. Either you are or you aren't. Great shooters don't shoot 40 percent. And with your shot selection, you're never going to be a great shooter. We're going to change that. You're going to take less shots.'"

You can imagine how that went over.

"We definitely bumped heads at the beginning,'" Pierce said. "There was a lot of yelling, screaming. No fights. But a lot of rebellion on my part. I didn't think it was going to work between me and him."

When Pierce snapped, Rivers snapped right back. "I'm thinking, who the hell are you to talk like that to me? I'm the coach," Rivers said. "He tests you early and I think he found out that my whole thing with him was that every decision I made was for the good of the team and that might not have always been what's best for Paul. But you could see a little in that first year that his numbers [percentage] did start going up. He still bucked it at times."

For instance, Game 7 of the Celtics–Pacers playoff series. Pierce had already embarrassed himself by getting ejected from Game 6 and then showing up at the post-game news conference with his jaw taped, faking an injury. It was embarrassing. Rivers didn't see any of it until later, and he was mortified. Then, with the Celtics holding the home court advantage in Game 7, Pierce "went the other way," Rivers said. Pierce made only 6 of 13 shots, and the Celtics were humiliated, losing 97–70.

When the Celtics did not deal Pierce to Portland on the night of the 2005 NBA draft, it was a milestone of sorts for the team. Whatever lay ahead, and in June 2005, the view was not pretty, Pierce was in all likelihood going to be a part of it.

Meanwhile Pierce and Rivers met a week after the 2005 draft in Las Vegas, where Pierce has a home and where the Celtics were participating in the NBA's Summer League. Two months after the bizarre jaw episode, Rivers saw a changed man, both in attitude and in body. Rivers had told Pierce at the end of the season that he needed to be in better shape, that there was no savior around the corner, and that, yes, he knew more talent needed to be added. But he also told Pierce that the young players looked up to him and everything he did, from staying in shape, to body language, to how he handled things great and small. Gradually, Pierce came to understand what Rivers meant.

"It was just about me maturing," Pierce said. "After that first year (with Rivers), I had to go home and grow up. It's a difficult situation. I had to stop pouting and work hard, help out the young guys, and hope that things will work out. That was my mind-set. You're the captain and they still pay you to play, so go out and play to the best of your ability, and whatever happens, happens. I think that helped our relationship and them [the Celtics] wanting to keep me around because they saw that change in my attitude. I had a whole summer to think about it. You start getting advice from family and friends, but at the end of the day, it's a decision you have to make. It's growing up. That's all it is. When I look back on all the dumb stuff I did, I was still a young player, wet behind the ears, learning the NBA. That's what helps you grow, learning from your mistakes."

Two years later, he was no longer "a great player on a bad team," as he had famously referred to himself in a *Boston Globe* story in 2006. Now he was on a team that many picked to win it all. He pretty much had seen everything in Boston, from the low years of the Pitino regime to the brief resurgence under O'Brien to fans clamoring for the team to lose in 2006–2007 to enhance its draft odds, a clamor Pierce saw as he sat on the bench in street clothes while missing 35 games with a stress fracture in his left foot. That all seemed so remote, so far removed, when the 2007–2008 season began. For once, Pierce thought, "I have a chance."

"It's a hell of a journey," he said. "You don't really understand it until you get close to where you want. There are times you want to give up and times you want to move on. But there's so much satisfaction in staying with it and sticking things out and seeing things turn around after all the things you go through. That's gratification for me. That's what I think about now."

THE SEASON-OPENING VICTORY over the Wizards unveiled an old/new phenomenon as well—Gino. During the past few years, the Celtics JumboTron had shown clips from a 1977 episode of American Bandstand with kids dancing to the disco beat. Fans for some reason started cheering when a bearded dancer wearing a tee shirt with the name "Gino" appeared, and eventually the whole thing became almost cultish. Fans wore Gino tee shirts to games. Gino became must-see video during timeouts, and in 2007–2008 the video became the equivalent of the lighting of one of Red Auerbach's old cigars—shown only in the fourth quarter when a Celtics victory was assured. Eventually, the players started to notice, as many of the starters were on the bench when the video was shown. (Doc Rivers, still in coaching mode, claims to have never even seen the video.) They too became enamored of Gino.

The name "Gino" on the tee shirt referred to Gino Vannelli, a pop singer from the 1970s. He was astounded at all the attention. But who was the bearded man wearing the shirt that inspired such loyalty and interest? Celtics president Rich Gotham said the team thought about trying to find the man, only to be dissuaded by Kevin Garnett.

"It's perfect right now the way he is," Gotham remembers Garnett telling him. "If we find him, he'll be old and fat and bald, and it will ruin the whole image."

The *Wall Street Journal* then asked Dick Clark Productions, the producers of American Bandstand, to try and find the man. Eventually, the woman with whom Gino was dancing in the video was located, and she delivered the tragic news: the man everyone knew as Gino was actually one Joe Massoni, who had died in 1990 of pneumonia. But the clip lives on.

FOLLOWING THE CELTICS SEASON-OPENING VICTORY, the team journeyed to Toronto to play the defending Atlantic division champs.

When the team gathered for its pregame meeting at the Four Seasons Hotel, Doc Rivers delivered some bad news. He would be leaving for Chicago because he had just learned that his father Grady had died. Rivers had heard that his father was not doing well and had been hospitalized while the team had been in Rome. He thought about returning home then, but his father told him not to bother, that it was no big deal.

"He told me, you stay your butt where you are. I'll be fine," Rivers said. "And then when we got to London, he was already out of the hospital and was back home, doing fine, so I didn't go home."

When he returned to the United States, Rivers repeatedly checked in by phone and then learned that his father had once again taken a turn for the worse. There had been a drop in blood pressure, but Rivers still didn't expect the worst-case scenario. Then at 5 a.m., the phone rang in his hotel room. It was his brother. "We lost daddy," he said. And Rivers broke down. "I was so upset because I didn't think he was that sick. No one did, because my dad kept everything inside," Rivers said.

At the Sunday morning team meeting, Rivers told the team about his father. He mentioned the "finish the race" story and said that it could apply to this team and this season. He brought up *ubuntu* to drive home the fact that they needed to unite to withstand adversity. He told them how his father hated the use of the phrase "you know" and would count how many times his son said the words during an interview. That elicited a few laughs. Rivers then said he was leaving the team, and he did not know when he would be back. Tom Thibodeau, the team's associate head coach, would be coaching the game against the Raptors.

"Those things are always difficult to deal with," Thibodeau said. "You could feel Doc's pain. It had been so sudden. We were all shocked. That was a tough day. But Doc had already set the tone. He had to take care of his life, and we had to carry on the way he would have wanted us to. All the work for the game had already been done. It was just a matter of going out and executing the game plan."

The Celtics won, 98–95, in overtime. The winning shot was a three-pointer by Ray Allen off an out-of-bounds play. Paul Pierce made the pass. Kevin Garnett set the screen that sprung Allen free.

Back in Chicago, Rivers prepared to bury his father. Grady Rivers had rarely missed any of his son's games and coached his youth baseball team for three years. Grady Rivers had a rule—everyone played, even the lowest of the low. The team won three straight league titles. Grady Rivers would be a regular at his son's high school basketball games, an intimidating presence, rivals would charge, because he would always sit under the basket in the first row of bleachers, in his police uniform.

Now his son was trying to juggle work and life as his father had always done seamlessly, or so Rivers had always thought. Once plans were made, Rivers' mother Bettye took her son aside and said, "Glenn, you are going back to your game in New Jersey when this is over." In fact, a close friend of Rivers from New Jersey had chartered an airplane for the funeral service and was flying back after its conclusion. Bettye Rivers wanted her son on that plane.

Her son wasn't all that sure. He had managed to coach two games that week, easy home wins over Denver (in which the Celtics had led by the rather amazing score of 77–38 at halftime) and Atlanta. After the Atlanta game, he had flown to Chicago for the Saturday morning burial service.

Immediately after Grady Rivers' casket was lowered into the ground, Bettye Rivers came over to her son and told him, "Now get in that car, go out to the airport, and go coach your team. This is not a debate. This is what you have to do. You can come back after the game. But you have a job to do. Go do your job."

And he did. In what early on appeared to be a test for the Celtics, Boston won, 112–101. They did so without James Posey, who missed his second straight game with back spasms. The Celtics were 5–0.

Posey had missed three of the first five games—he would miss eight games all season—and his absence removed one very key part of the Celtics pregame ritual: the hug. Before every game, Posey would walk to half court and wait for all the starters to emerge from the huddle, ready to take the court for the jump ball. But before any of them could get onto the court, they first got a warm embrace from Posey, along with some words of encouragement. It wasn't just a regular hug. It was one of those hugs you witness when a parent sees his child for the first time in a long time. Every starter got one. Every starter got a different message.

Posey started the routine when he was in Miami. "At first, I would just say something," he said. "Something positive. Let them start the game with something positive in their minds." Garnett said Posey's embrace and message "reminds us what we need to do to be successful. It's motivating. It's all positive. It really means something."

Think about it. Five starters. In Posey's case, 74 games. That's more than 350 individual, specialized, motivational speeches that Posey delivered in 2007–2008 during the regular season. They're the last words the players hear before they take the floor, and Posey made sure the message was one of encouragement. Rivers had no problem with it, especially since Posey already had established himself as one of the team's regulars. "If he couldn't play, no one would listen," Rivers said. "But the reason they do listen is because he walks the walk."

————————

The celtics didn't lose their first game until November 18, in Orlando, after starting the season with eight straight wins. The Lakers came in for a visit on November 23, the day after Thanksgiving, and it was a Boston runaway. Kobe Bryant missed 12 of 21 shots. Andrew Bynum was neutered by Kendrick Perkins, who had 21 points and 9 rebounds. The Lakers never even got a lead, and Boston led by as many as 22 before settling for a 13-point victory.

"Since I've been in the league, they've sucked," Bryant said of the Celtics. "Now, they're kicking our butts. They are a very well-built team. Hopefully, we'll get to the point where there's some parity between us. That would mean we'd be competing at a championship level." He had no idea how prophetic those remarks would be.

A few things were coming into focus by then. The defense that Rivers had demanded be the focal point of the team was indeed terrific. The Celtics were leading the league in a number of defensive categories, from points allowed to defensive field goal percentage. This had never been the Celtic Way. But with Garnett anchoring things and Tom Thibodeau's schemes, the Celtics were becoming one tough team to score against.

The defense wasn't all that complicated. The plans called for the team to keep the ball out of the paint, the interior area around the basket. The players then would overload one side of the floor and force teams to beat them with outside shooting. They were to go after everything, every shot, every rebound, every loose ball.

In Garnett, Thibodeau had the ideal player to make it work. You can have all the schemes you want, but if the players don't buy into it, the whole thing falls apart. Garnett bought it and, in so doing, demanded the others buy into it as well. Neither Pierce nor Allen was considered a particularly strong defensive player before 2007. After the season was over, both were on the receiving end of unsolicited comments of praise from opposing coaches.

"When we played them, Ray picked up Brandon Roy full court and pressured him the whole way," said Allen's former coach in Seattle, Nate McMillan. "He never did that, not one time in his career did he ever do that."

Both Milwaukee's Larry Krystkowiak and Detroit's Flip Saunders singled out Pierce for his new attention to defense. Pierce had always been one of the better players in the league in coming up with steals, but he was never known for his defense. Like Allen, he had to save a lot because the offense was so dependent on him.

Now, Pierce, Allen, and all the perimeter defenders could dog their man because Garnett had their backs. Perkins, a solid defender and underrated shot-blocker, had their backs too. It was a system that worked as long as the players stuck to the system. That was Thibodeau's responsibility.

"It's a combination of things," Thibodeau said. "You have to have the players committed. It can't just be hype. All coaches talk about wanting to play defense. But how many teams actually do play good defense? I knew about Kevin. I knew Ray was capable of it. Paul had shown the capability as well. And when your three best players are committed, that's huge. They never once looked to get out of anything, not a drill, nothing. That set the tone for everyone else.

"When we started, there were three things I thought about," Thibodeau said. "Would the Big Three be willing to sacrifice? Would it come together quickly with all the new players? And would there be a continuous commitment to defense? We knew we'd score. But we'd have to have that commitment at the other end."

And almost immediately Thibodeau and everyone else had answers for all three of those questions: yes, yes, and yes.

The first day together as members of the Celtics. They hadn't done anything—yet.

A group photo in front of the Colosseum in Rome, where the team spent part of training camp and went through the bonding process.

Kevin Garnett shows Kenyon Martin why he's among the best defenders in the NBA.

James Posey delivering his trademark bear hug and positive message, a sight before all Celtics games.

Center Kendrick Perkins came into his own in his fifth year, helped enormously by the presence of Kevin Garnett.

No one came up bigger (20 points) than rookie Glen 'Big Baby' Davis in this early January victory over the Pistons at the Palace of Auburn Hills.

Former Celtic Joe Johnson showed his versatility in a first-round matchup and nearly led the Atlanta Hawks to a stunning upset.

Paul Pierce helped the Celtics rally from a 22-point deficit in San Antonio. The Celtics did something no team had done in seven years in sweeping the three Texas teams on the road in successive games.

Whether gambling for a steal or driving into the heart of a defense, Rajon Rondo was absolutely fearless.

P.J. Brown's biggest basket in his short stay in Boston, a short jumper in Game 7 against the Cavaliers with 1:20 remaining.

Paul Pierce said he was ready for a massage after going mano a mano with LeBron James for seven games in the conference semifinals.

A hamstring injury to Pistons' All-Star Chauncey Billups, here getting his shot blocked by Kendrick Perkins, helped the Celtics in their much-anticipated Eastern Conference Finals series with Detroit.

Eddie House was a key role player doing what Eddie House does best—shooting from the outside.

The Celtics beat the Lakers in Los Angeles in December, a physical game as evidenced by a cut above Kevin Garnett's right eye that required two stitches to close.

One year earlier, both Paul Pierce and Kobe Bryant had thought they'd be elsewhere when the 2007-2008 season started.

Ray Allen went 48 minutes in Game 4 and scored 19 points, the final two on this layup with 16.4 seconds left. The Celtics overcame a 24-point deficit to take a 3-1 series lead.

With the title assured, Paul Pierce went into football mode and doused his coach with Gatorade. The stained shirt then sold for $55,000 at a charity auction.

Danny Ainge won two titles as a player for the Celtics, but this one was every bit as meaningful, given the work he had done to assemble the team.

Bill Russell and Kevin Garnett shared an intensity for the game and an appreciation of the importance of defense.

It was a tough year for Doc Rivers, but he could savor a victory cigar when it was all over, much like Red Auerbach used to do.

7

Growth Spurts

IN ANY SEASON of high expectations—and 2007–2008 certainly qualified as one for the Boston Celtics—there are always going to be "temperature-check" dates along the way. These usually come in the form of significant games, which, in an 82-game schedule followed by almost two months of playoffs, tend to be few and far between.

Some of these games are obvious once the schedule is released. Some are not, which would be the case for Boston's first visit to Charlotte on November 24, the night after they had dismantled the Lakers. Charlotte was on a mild winning streak, but no one felt the Bobcats were any match for the 10–1 Celtics, who had not trailed in either of their previous two games, while leading by as many as 22 in each one.

The word *dominance* would accurately describe their play in the first few weeks of the season. They could even be faulted for possibly looking ahead to their next game, November 27 at

Cleveland, their first matchup against the defending conference champions.

Charlotte, which would turn out to be one of the tougher matchups for the Celtics all season, gave Boston everything it could handle, even without its leading scorer, Gerald Wallace. The game was close throughout, with the Celtics never leading by more than four points. The Bobcats took control at the end and, leading by two points, appeared to have the game won when Paul Pierce missed a short jumper and Raymond Felton got the rebound.

The Celtics quickly fouled Felton with 4.7 seconds left, but Boston was not in the penalty so the Bobcats got the ball out in front of their own bench, near the basket they were defending. For reasons never fully explained, Charlotte coach Sam Vincent, a rookie coach (and a member of Boston's previous championship team in 1986) did not call a timeout. That would have allowed his team to move the ball up the court for the inbound play, while also perhaps recognizing that Emeka Okafor, a brutal free-throw shooter, should not be in the game at this time.

But Vincent neither called time nor pulled Okafor. The Celtics ignored Okafor when Jason Richardson was making the inbound pass because they figured correctly that Richardson would not pass to him. Richardson tried instead to feather a pass to Jeff McInnis, but Eddie House got his hand on the ball and tipped it. Pierce came up with the ball. In the past, that would have likely meant a wild turnaround heave at the buzzer. Instead, Pierce found a wide-open Ray Allen on the other side of the floor and unhesitatingly sent it Allen's way, even though Allen had missed 11 of his 14 shots in the game, including all five of his three-pointers.

Allen calmly knocked down the game-winner as time expired and then was carried off the floor by Glen "Big Baby" Davis, as the stunned Bobcats tried to figure out what had just happened. It wasn't that the Celtics had stolen one. It was *how* they had stolen one. Watching back home in his suburban Boston house, co-owner Steve Pagliuca thought to himself, "Wow. We have one superstar who gives up the ball for the other superstar who is wide open. We got a chance." To Pagliuca, that one play epitomized what Rivers and everyone else had been preaching since September. "It was the ultimate display of team chemistry," Pagliuca said.

Pierce downplayed it, asking how could he *not* pass to Allen, one of the greatest three-point shooters of all time? But it was proof, yet again for Pierce, how much different things were this time around. He was always the one who was perceived as selfish, who took too many bad shots, and missed more than he should. His response always had been, "Who else do you want taking them?" Now, there were actually legitimate options.

"When we [he, Allen, and Garnett] first got together, we talked about all these things. But at the end of the day, what's the goal? The goal is to win," Pierce said. "Who cares who gets the last shot? Who cares who gets the most points? Who cares who gets the credit? Because if we win, we're winners.

"We've all got individual accolades, but we hadn't won any-thing," Pierce continued. "So were we willing to sacrifice those things to win? I always thought it would work. Kevin, Ray. These guys are unselfish. You saw how they played. And I knew the way I could play. A lot of people didn't think I could adjust to them. I was like, 'It's going to be easy because I got somebody I can pass the ball to.' Before, it was hard for me to trust an 18-year-old kid out of high school. I was surrounded by players like that, and it's hard for me to trust them. But you surround me with Kevin, Ray, Posey, and Eddie House, and I'm going to give it up without a second thought. Once we got those players, I knew this whole thing could work because we all were unselfish."

The Celtics luck lasted until they played Cleveland three nights later. Allen, one of the most accurate free-throw shooters in NBA history, missed two at the end of a tie game, and the Celtics lost in overtime, as LeBron James accounted for 35 points and 13 assists. Two nights later, they were back at home, for a much anticipated game against the Knicks, not so much because it was New York, but because it was being played on Thursday night. In the NBA, that usually means one thing: national television on TNT.

It had been awhile since the Celtics had been on TNT. Their season opener had been on ESPN, but the boys from Boston had not been subject to the interesting insights of Kenny Smith and Charles Barkley for some time. "Since Danny Ainge was doing the games," Rivers joked, referring to Ainge's stint with TNT some five years earlier.

The Knicks were coming off a pair of wins following eight straight losses, but were widely seen as inept and poorly managed. General Manager Isiah Thomas had put together a roster of highly paid individuals (by far the largest payroll in the league) who didn't mesh. Thomas also coached the group, and not very well either, judging by the record.

What ensued that night won't soon be forgotten by either team, although it probably forced a mass exodus from TNT by channel surfers. The Celtics won, 104–59. The Knicks needed a last-second half-court heave from Nate Robinson to avoid their lowest scoring game since the NBA introduced the shot-clock in the 1954–1955 season. And he got a chance to shoot only because the Celtics deliberately turned over the ball on their final possession with two seconds left.

The lead reached 52 points in the game. Garnett played only 22 minutes, his shortest stint in years. "I can't remember getting that kind of rest," Garnett said. But the Knicks, while embarrassed about being thoroughly outplayed, were not about to ordain their longtime rival as the team to beat. In fact, one of them, Quentin Richardson, had made a statement before the game that strangely enough still resonated throughout the league and had more than a few believers. "They're not that deep of a team," Richardson said. "After those three, there's a significant drop-off."

A few days later, Rajon Rondo, most definitely not one of "those three," appeared for a photo shoot for *DIME Magazine*, wearing a borrowed suit. One of the photographers referenced the Knicks blowout. "They didn't even show up," Rondo said of the Knicks that night. "It was crazy."

RAJON RONDO HAS ALWAYS had an air of confidence that has served him well. Occasionally, one might confuse the confidence for cockiness. Or, occasionally, insubordination. But if the Celtics did indeed have a "significant drop-off" in talent after the Big Three, Rondo was determined to squash that line of thinking in 2007–2008. And by the time the season ended, no one was talking about a drop-off, significant or otherwise.

The Celtics clearly thought they had something in Rondo, which is why Danny Ainge refused to even consider putting Rondo in either the Garnett or Allen trades. There was much to like about Rondo just by appearances: he isn't tall, but he has ridiculously long arms and huge hands (which is why he almost stuck to football in high school because he was a good quarterback). He is quick. He has great instincts.

He was discovered by the Celtics almost by accident, although there are very few scouting "accidents" in this day and age. Ainge dispatched Jon Niednagel, a brain-typing expert who predicts success by reading facial expressions and physical traits, whose opinion about players Ainge values, to see a high school game in 2004 featuring powerhouse Oak Hill Academy in Mouth of Wilson, Virginia.

Niednagel was sent to scout Josh Smith, an athletic high-flyer who was rumored to be considering declaring for the NBA draft. Niednagel sent back a message that while Smith was fine, he also liked this little point guard they had, Rajon Rondo. From then on, Danny Ainge started tracking Rondo.

Oak Hill Academy is literally in the middle of nowhere, but it possesses a second-to-none list of graduates who have gone on to play in the NBA. Since 1980, the school has had 11 of its graduates become first-round picks in the NBA, ranging from Rondo to Carmelo Anthony, Jerry Stackhouse, and Rod Strickland. Josh Smith and DeSagana Diop both went directly from Oak Hill to the NBA; the other nine did at least a year of college or something akin to college.

"It's almost like a college," Josh Smith said. "We traveled a lot. We played a lot of games. We played only the best high schools in the nation. We went to Spain. We went to LA. We traveled and still had to do our schoolwork. There are no distractions out there—none," Smith went on. "It's strictly basketball and books. You can't do anything else. It's co-ed. But you can't cross that line or it's big trouble. We had to go to church every Sunday. It was so strict. It may be known for basketball, but it's also a boarding school where kids get the discipline they need."

In Rondo's case, his arrival at Oak Hill was one of mutual need. The program needed a point guard for the 2003–2004 season. And Rondo needed a place to play in 2003–2004 because his former coach and mentor, Doug Bibby (cousin of Mike Bibby) had switched high schools in Louisville, and Rondo couldn't transfer.

"I knew about Oak Hill, of course," Rondo said. "Their coach was coaching this All-Star team at a shootout, and I went to the game to watch. I didn't know him. But he knew about me. He said to me, 'We're looking for a point guard. Would you be interested in coming?' I said, 'Probably not.' At that point, I didn't want to move. I was real close to my mother, and it was too far from home. But then Josh Smith called me and convinced me, so I decided to go. I knew I'd get more exposure if I went there and that my game would probably improve. I never realized how much. Before I went to Oak Hill, I was ranked one hundred and eighty-ninth in the country. When I came out, I was in the top ten."

Rondo believed that basketball was not necessarily his best sport, but was the one that gave him the best chance to make a livelihood. He said he was thinking those things well before high school, just as his Celtics coach was thinking those same things years earlier in a third-grade classroom in Chicago. Rondo was a Louisville city kid, but at first preferred football to basketball.

"I didn't start playing basketball really until I was about 10 or 11," he said. "I had a cousin who was two months older and played a lot of basketball, so one day I just started playing with him, and I fell in love with it. But I also played football and ran track in my first year of high school and found out that was too much. I wanted to focus on football, but I wasn't a big guy. And it seemed like all the quarterbacks were six-four or six-five, and that wasn't me. So I decided basketball was my best way to try and get to the pro level."

In his one year at Oak Hill, 2003–2004, Rondo was part of a national championship team that went 38–0. He still holds the school records for assists in one game (31) and in a season (494).

"When he first got there, he was a scoring point guard," Josh Smith said. "When you come to Oak Hill, you've usually been The Man on your team, so sometimes you have to change your game. He turned into a great playmaker and passer. I knew if the Celtics let him do what he can do and play his game, he'd be doing exactly what he's doing now."

While at Oak Hill, Rondo ended up rooming with Smith a month into the school year. Neither had lived away from home until then (Smith had attended high school in Powder Springs, Georgia, before heading to Oak Hill). They were starry-eyed kids, dreaming of the NBA, with high-profile college programs (Indiana, Kentucky) courting them as recruits.

There were the usual food fights and hanging out at the local gas station, which qualifies as entertainment in Mouth of Wilson. It was Smith who tried to steal his roomie's Raman noodles, but backed off when he realized that was pretty much the only sustenance Rondo had. He wouldn't eat the food at the school. Rondo liked the room neat, maybe not Ray Allen-neat, but something above Cockroach Central. Smith remembers "fighting like brothers" on occasion, but the two of them emerged from their year together as fast friends. They still communicate regularly.

Smith spurned Indiana and went directly to the NBA, where the Hawks took him with the seventeenth pick in the 2004 draft. Rondo knew he wasn't ready to make that jump quite yet and had both Louisville and Kentucky very interested in his services. Louisville was also recruiting a New York City phenom named Sebastian Telfair, who also would jump to the NBA.

"Louisville offered me a scholarship the year before I went to Oak Hill," Rondo said. "[Rick] Pitino invited me, my mother, and coach Bibby over when he offered it, but I didn't want to take it. It was too early. I felt it was a great school, but it was in my hometown. I knew I wanted to get away, but not too far. When I was at Oak Hill, my mother couldn't get to a lot of the games because it was too far, and I wanted her to see me because she's been my biggest supporter all along. We even played a couple of home games in Louisville when I was at Oak Hill, just as a payback sort of thing I guess. But I wanted to stay off the streets, and Kentucky fit the bill. It was 50 miles down the road. It wasn't home. But it wasn't too far from home. I had a good time there. I'm glad where I am, but I wouldn't mind still being a kid, having fun with my teammates and classmates."

The Celtics continued watching Rondo from afar and occasionally in person. In 2005 Ainge sent scout Ryan McDonough to see the Global Games in Frisco, Texas, a competition that featured a select U.S. team and teams from other nations. The U.S. team, which won all four of its games, would then head off to Argentina to participate in the FIBA U–21 World Championships. There were a lot of familiar names on that team as well—Rudy Gay, Allen Ray, J.J. Redick, and Glen "Big Baby" Davis. But McDonough called Ainge to rave about one player in particular— Rajon Rondo.

That team would finish fifth in Argentina, even though, at 7–1, it matched gold medalist Lithuania for the best record in the tournament. The difference was that the sole U.S. loss came at the wrong time, in the first segment of the medal round. (Spain suffered a similar fate at the 2004 Olympics in Athens.)

USA Team coach Phil Martelli of Saint Joseph's University still remembers Rondo as "very introspective, a deep thinker. You had to be sure how you spoke to him. But what you saw him do in Game 6 against the Lakers, he did in Argentina. He stole the ball, not from the guy he was guarding, but from other people. I had never been around anyone who did it like he did."

FIBA no longer conducts a U–21 championship tournament, so Rondo is in the record books for what he did in Argentina. He had 27 steals in the tournament, a record, and he had eight against China, a single-game record. He also tied the record for most field goals in a game (nine) against Nigeria. The tournament was held after Rondo's freshman year at Kentucky, where he set a school record for steals (87) that year, including eight in one game. He was second in the conference in steals as a freshman.

"Going into his sophomore year, we were really high on him," Ainge said. "Then we saw he wasn't playing well. He was benched. He was moved to shooting guard. You could tell something was wrong. There was bad body language. The feedback from the crowd wasn't good. I could sense something was wrong. We had concerns."

Rondo was showing his headstrong side, a side that also caused him to clash with Doc Rivers when Rondo was a rookie. University of Kentucky coach Tubby Smith chalked it up to "publicity from being in a high-profile program." But it was more than that. It was your classic coach-player friction.

"He gets emotional at times, and we work on that a lot with his teammates and his coaches," Rivers said. "He had that problem at Kentucky. Someone would tell him something, and he always saw it as criticism instead of coaching or even teammates trying to help him. And he would close down. That mental toughness part might hurt him at times because he's always fighting everything."

The Celtics interviewed everyone, from Smith to Rondo's Kentucky neighbors to the longtime equipment manager at Kentucky, Bill Keightley, who gave Rondo a ringing endorsement. But even after all the interviews, the Celtics still had concerns. They concluded that Rondo was emotional, stubborn, and not easy to coach; he needed to mature and had not fit in well at Kentucky, all of which raised red flags. But they also concluded he would be an ideal addition to their team. He had undeniable talent. Ainge trotted out a statistic showing Rondo stole the ball from the man he was guarding 16 percent of the time. No one else they were considering for the 2006 draft did it more than 2 or 3 percent.

Rondo declared for the 2006 draft after two seasons at Kentucky. Despite his problems with Smith and the system, he had still managed to lead the SEC in assists, was second in steals, and incredibly, led his team in rebounding. The kid had a knack for the ball, of that there was no doubt. The only question facing Ainge & Co. as Draft Night 2006 approached was how to get him.

THE CELTICS HELD THE SEVENTH PICK in the 2006 draft. There were six, widely perceived, really good prospects at the top: Andrea Bargnani of Italy, Tyrus Thomas of LSU, Brandon Roy of Washington, LaMarcus Aldridge of Texas, Adam Morrison of Gonzaga, and Randy Foye of Villanova. You might have even added Rudy Gay of Connecticut to that mix. (Only the Atlanta Hawks saw Duke's Shelden Williams in that mix. The team that had passed on Chris Paul and Deron Williams the year before picked Shelden Williams No. 5—ahead of Roy—then traded him after less than two seasons.)

Ainge loved Rondo, but not at No. 7. He was working with Portland on a deal that would (a) get the Celtics a point guard in Sebastian Telfair, and (b) allow them to rid themselves of Raef LaFrentz's onerous contract, while inheriting a similarly cumbersome deal but, critically, one that had one year less remaining—Theo Ratliff's contract. Telfair had been underwhelming in two seasons in Portland, but the Celtics thinking was that maybe a change was what he needed. Portland would get the No. 7 pick in the deal, which it used to get Brandon Roy, who would end up being the Rookie of the Year. (Roy was actually the sixth pick by Minnesota, but was quickly traded to Portland for the seventh pick, Randy Foye, and some of Portland owner Paul Allen's cash, of which he has plenty.)

Then, as the first round continued, Rondo was still on the board. Celtics principal owner Wyc Grousbeck, who knew how much Ainge liked Rondo, told Ainge to see if there was a team that would do a deal and surrender a pick that would get Rondo. The LaFrentz deal already had saved the team millions. He would spend a little to make a deal.

"Danny had just spent the last month telling me how much he liked Rondo," Grousbeck said. "I turned to Danny and said, 'You just saved us all this money. If you need to go buy a pick to get Rondo, do it. And he looked at me and said, Are you sure? I said, You love the kid. You've engineered a great business deal here. You've never been wrong on this stuff.' All of us in ownership agreed."

The draft went deeper into the teens, and still no one had drafted Rondo. Ainge finally connected with his old team, Phoenix, where he had coached and which had the twenty-first pick. Ainge had a No. 1 pick, belonging to Cleveland, in the 2007 draft, widely assumed to be one of the deepest in years. He proposed giving that to the Suns and agreed to take on the final year of Brian Grant's salary in exchange for the twenty-first pick. The Suns accepted, provided of course that Rondo was still on the board.

Picks 17, 18, and 19 came and went; then, at No. 20, stood the Knicks. Isiah Thomas, a former point guard, was making the decisions for New York. The Celtics immediately thought, "He is going to screw this whole thing up." Thomas would grow to love Rondo as a pro, but on this night, his eyes were elsewhere. He drafted Renaldo Balkman, who had gone through four high schools and then declared early for the draft after his junior year at South Carolina.

The Suns then picked Rondo. Phoenix has taken some ill-advised heat over the years for drafting Rondo and then trading him to Boston. The truth is that the Suns made the pick for the Celtics, having already agreed to a deal. That stuff happens all the time on draft night. But Rajon Rondo will go down in NBA history as a No. 1 pick of the Suns, even though it was the Celtics who made it all happen.

Rondo, Sebastian Telfair, and Delonte West vied for the point guard minutes in 2006–2007, even as the Celtics' season was in freefall. Rondo appeared in 78 games, and by the second half of the season, it was clear to just about everyone that he was the best of the three and the future point guard of the team. It just took time.

"What we went through that year, and it being my first year, losing so many games, you can lose your focus and your confidence and what it's all about," Rondo said. "If I had had more veterans around me, I would have been further on with my development. But everything happens for a reason. I went through a lot of adversity that year and that made the next year ten times better."

Rondo worked tirelessly on his shooting, taking as many as 500 shots a day in the off-season. That was always seen as one of his weaknesses and he sees that as a challenge. When the Celtics first worked him out before the 2006 draft, they noticed he held the ball in a peculiar way when he shot it. While he always shot a high percentage in college, most of the baskets were from in close, after he had beaten his man off the dribble.

Ainge and Doc Rivers both wondered if Rondo might have any more success with his outside shot if he changed the way he gripped the ball. He kept shooting the same way. "People may say I have changed, but it's just more confidence," he said. That's the kind of stubborn streak the Celtics both feared—and loved—about the kid.

"He put in so much time," Rivers said. "It's nice to see a guy who works at it and see it come to fruition. When he first got here, I didn't know what to think other than he had a great IQ, so you had something to work with. And he had the self-motivation to be good—he really wants to be great—and he had that stubborn streak that got in the way. But he allowed that [streak] to be moved out of the way, and he allowed himself to be coached. He has great natural abilities, and he's one of the few I've ever had in all my years of coaching where I've had to learn to trust those natural abilities. He has such great instincts, and he needs to let them take over."

By the time the Celtics were into the second month of the 2007–2008 season, there was no more concern about Rondo. Yes, teams would sag off him defensively, allowing him open shots. That would be the case all year. "Even when he makes them, they're not going to stop either, because they won't believe it," Doc Rivers said.

The Celtics finished the month of November with a 13–2 record and a second victory over the reeling-and-soon-to-keel-over Miami Heat. Rivers was named Eastern Conference Coach of the Month, the first time in 15 years that a Celtics coach had been so recognized. In those 13 wins, the Celtics had enjoyed leads of 20 or more points on nine occasions. Four of the wins came without the Celtics ever trailing at any point.

They then ripped off seven straight wins to open the month of December and stood at 20–2 when the vaunted Detroit Pistons made their first visit to Boston. This was unquestionably a big game. The Pistons were 18–6 and had a veteran-laced roster filled with guys who had been where the Celtics wanted to go. As good as Boston had played, as strong and as overpowering as the Celtics had looked, the mantra of the day was, "We ain't done nothing yet."

The Pistons had won a title in 2004, almost repeated in 2005, and got to the past five Eastern Conference Finals. They seemed to have an edge about them at the start of the 2007–2008 season, perhaps owing to their collapse in the conference finals the previous spring, where they had led the Cavaliers 2–0 and then proceeded to drop four straight.

The two teams appeared destined to play in the spring; they were both a notch better than anyone else in the conference, or so it seemed. Preseason favorites Chicago, New Jersey, and Miami were all underperforming. While Orlando was playing well at the time, few took the Magic seriously. The Cavs had personnel problems. The Pistons and Celtics stood above it all, guaranteeing a certifiable "big game" on the night of December 19.

The Celtics had not yet lost a home game. They had really only been tested once—a squeaker over Miami—in TD Banknorth Garden. In their first 12 home games leading into the Detroit contest, the Celtics' average margin of victory was an astounding 24 points. That included the epic rout of the Knicks, but also featured a 28-point pounding of Toronto, a 26-point dispatching of the Denver Nuggets and a 23-point victory over the Golden State Warriors.

Into that atmosphere came the Pistons, undeterred and undaunted. They were content to be, as Chauncey Billups liked to say, "Flying under the radar." Everyone was fawning over the Celtics. That was fine with Detroit. Everyone else was talking about the supposedly all-powerful Western Conference. That also was fine with Detroit. They liked the underdog image. It fit their personality.

The game didn't disappoint. The atmosphere was once again electric. Red Sox slugger David Ortiz sat courtside wearing a Ray Allen replica jersey. Allen had missed the previous two games nursing an ankle sprain, but was back and ready for the Pistons. The game featured only a pair of lead changes, as the Celtics led throughout. The Pistons then overtook Boston in the fourth quarter and seemed safe with a six-point lead, only to see the Celtics square things with two long three-pointers, one by Allen and the other by Eddie House.

Billups, normally Mr. Reliable in tense end-of-game situations, then lost the ball in the final ten seconds, giving the Celtics a chance to regain the lead. But Pierce missed a short jumper and the Pistons rebounded and called time with 1.7 seconds left. Billups again got the ball, and this time he caught Tony Allen on an upfake, earning two free throws with one-tenth of a second left. He made them both, and the Celtics had their first home loss of the season.

"We looked forward to this game," Billups said afterward. "It was definitely a playoff-type atmosphere. I think you're looking at the two best teams in the league."

Rivers used the game as one of those "teachable moments" that come along every so often. At the shootaround that morning, he had reminded his team that Billups likes to pump fake and not to fall for it. He had reminded them more than once. Tony Allen, known for his defense, presumably had been listening. But he still fell for it.

After the game, Ray Allen said, "Losing games levels you out. As much as you don't like it, it always humbles you. And it makes sure that you put the work in and cross your T's and dot your I's. We've all lost games. It's how you move forward that counts, how you learn from it."

Two easy home victories followed the Pistons loss, and the Celtics were set to do what just about every Eastern Conference team had done to that point—go west. There was a certain "yeah, but" attached to Boston's torrid start—the Celtics were 23–3 overall when they left for Sacramento on Christmas Day—because of a lack of road wins in the tougher Western Conference. They'd only played ten road games, and all had been against Eastern Conference opponents. At the same time, Orlando had played 10 of its 15 road games against the West.

EARLY IN THE SEASON, Rivers had come to realize the type of team he had and how it was so different from the ones he had the previous two years. One of the concessions he made to the players was that they could do pretty much whatever they wanted on the team charters. If they wanted music, fine. Card games? No problem. As long as there was a certain degree of civility and decorum, that was fine with the coach.

It soon became apparent that Kevin Garnett and Eddie House were 24/7 yakkers. House says, "Most of the time, I'm chill. I relax. I'm only like that when I'm around the guys. No one believes that, but it's true."

Card games became the norm on just about every flight, long or short, win or lose. There were usually two games going on at the same time. There was what the players jokingly called the "Billionaires Table" at which sat Garnett, Pierce, Ray Allen, James Posey, and Kendrick Perkins. They were the five highest-paid players on the team. Then there was the "Poor Man's Table," where the others would play.

"They play every flight, from the beginning of the flight to the end of the flight," Rivers said. "Didn't matter what happened if we'd had a game. A couple of times after a bad loss, no one really wanted to play, but they played anyway, probably because they thought they had to, because it was what they had done all year. That comes from Kevin. Kevin is so respectful. At the beginning of the year, one of the players brought on some iPod speakers, and the music was loud. And I mean loud. And some of the TV guys are saying, 'Jesus, do we have to listen to this all year?' And I said, 'Yeah,' and I let it go because Kevin had asked me if it was OK, if I had a problem with any of this.

"I know the music is loud, but I'm up at the front of the plane, and they're in the back. I decided that would become the players' sanctuary. That's kind of been taken away from them for whatever reason—more media—so the only time they are truly together is when they're at the practice facility or on the plane. Armond [Hill] said to me, 'Boy, that's something new. You never allowed that before.' He was right. I hadn't. But I made the decision that the plane is going to be their locker room, and whoever else comes aboard—

media people, sponsors—is going to have to deal with it. I'm sure for a lot of people it wasn't all that much fun listening to that music. But I think for the players, it was a great bonding thing."

For Christmas, Rivers gave each player a framed photograph of the team taken in front of the Colosseum in Rome the previous October. The picture brought back memories of a great trip and a time when the team had come together out of necessity. They had chatted with each other on the bus rides to and from practice and games because no one used his cellphone overseas. Normally, on most bus rides, there are 12 to 15 cellphones on, with family, friends, or agents telling the players how well they played or complaining to them that they weren't getting enough time or touches. Those are what Rivers calls "peripheral opponents."

And he had plenty of actual opponents to worry about in the days and weeks ahead, including a western swing and a rematch against the Pistons at the Palace of Auburn Hills.

8

Highs and Lows

THE FIRST VENTURE the Celtics made outside the cozy confines of the Eastern Conference proved to be an unqualified success. The team played four games in five nights for the first time and won all four.

The trip featured the team's only visit to Seattle, where Ray Allen had played the previous four-and-one-half seasons and was still immensely popular. He did exactly what he had done all those years when he lived in the area—he showed up early to get his shots in and then headed for the Sonics locker room. Oops!

The fans at sold-out Key Arena—a rarity for the struggling Sonics—gave Allen two standing ovations, the first when he was recognized for his community work and the second when he was introduced in the Boston starting lineup.

Allen then proceeded to score 10 points and miss 9 of the 13 shots he attempted, including the first two—badly—but the Celtics found a way to win. This time Pierce came to the rescue, scoring 26 points in the second half and 37 in the game. It would represent the most points scored by any Celtic in the 82-game regular season. The victory was No. 24 for the Celtics, which matched their win total from the year before. "All that means is that we were bad last year," Doc Rivers said.

Two Sonics could attest to that. Wally Szczerbiak and Delonte West, who had come to Seattle in the trade for Allen, came off the Sonics bench that night and combined for 33 points. West in particular seemed determined to make the Celtics pay for dealing him, with 19 points and 8 assists in just 25 minutes. The two would see the Celtics again in May when the games and the stakes were exponentially higher, but in late December, neither of them had any inkling that might happen.

The Celtics then went to Utah and won a closely contested game, although the Jazz were celebrating the arrival of Kyle Korver, who had just been obtained in a trade with the 76ers. Korver did not play that night, nor did Jazz defensive whiz Andrei Kirilenko, who had a tendon injury in his arm. The Celtics then boarded a flight after the game for a rematch with the Lakers, who were in Los Angeles ready and waiting.

The Celtics learned before the game that Rajon Rondo could not go due to a sore right hamstring. Tony Allen started in Rondo's place and acquitted himself well. The Boston defense once again clamped down on Kobe Bryant, who was a horrid 6-of-25 from the field. The Celtics built a huge lead (25 points) and cruised to an easy victory, 110–91, in a game that featured the Lakers wearing throwback "short shorts" in the first half. Bryant compared wearing the shorts to what it must feel like wearing a thong.

The game also featured some chippiness; seven technical fouls were called, and Lamar Odom was called for a flagrant foul when he tackled Ray Allen.

For the second time in as many meetings, the Celtics had had no problems with the Lakers. Bryant couldn't get comfortable.

Odom couldn't get comfortable. And for all the promise that young center Andrew Bynum showed to that point, and he was showing a lot, he was once again badly outplayed by the Celtics young center, Kendrick Perkins.

Like Rondo, Perkins was determined to make people understand that there was no "significant drop-off" after the first three players. One newspaper poll before the season had Perkins ranked as the fifteenth best starting center in the Eastern Conference. There was no No. 16. But he would become a very valuable player on the 2007–2008 team, willingly accepting his role while also, like Rondo, undeniably benefiting from the more talented players around him.

OF ALL THE CELTICS, probably no one had better basketball genes than Kendrick Perkins. His father Kenneth Perkins ranks as one of the best players in the history of Lamar University. He played at the Beaumont, Texas, school from 1980 to 1984 and still ranks among the top ten in several categories. He played 120 games for the Cardinals, second only to Mike Olliver's 122, and he started 119, still tops in school history. He was a teammate of Tom Sewell, who was one of three No. 1 draft picks of the Philadelphia 76ers in 1984, the others being Charles Barkley and Leon Wood.

"I heard a lot of stories about him, how he used to have a nice little jump shot, how he was a lot more athletic than I am," Kendrick Perkins said of his father. "But I've never seen any film of him or anything like that."

While Kenneth Perkins may have given his son innate and undeniable basketball skills, he was not around to personally pass them on to his son, who was born in November 1984. Kenneth Perkins was never a factor in Kendrick's upbringing and left mother and son when Kendrick was 18 months old to pursue a basketball career overseas, eventually settling in New Zealand.

Kendrick's mother Ercell Minix was murdered when Kendrick was only five, shot in the neck by a neighbor, who was convicted and sentenced to 30 years in prison.

Perkins was raised by his maternal grandparents, Mary and Raymond Lewis. His high school coach, Andre Boutte, stepped in to fill the father void and did an excellent job creating some balance in Perkins' life. Aware that he had a potential first-round draft pick on his hands, Boutte nonetheless made sure that Perkins worked in the gym, in the weight room, ran on the track, and stayed out of trouble. He purposely cut back on the basketball schedule and travel to lessen the attention on Perkins.

But you can't completely hide a large, talented, nearly seven-footer who was called "Baby Shaq" and would become a McDonald's All-American. In Perkins' final three years at Clifford J. Ozen High School in Beaumont, the team won 96 of 99 games and took the state title his sophomore year. He averaged 25.7 points, 16.4 rebounds, and 7.8 blocks per game as a senior, which may explain why the stands at Ozen soon started to fill with both pro and college scouts. Early in his senior year, Perkins committed to the University of Memphis for two main reasons. One, if he ever was going to go to college, he would go there, in part because one of his teammates and close friends, Keena Young, was also committing to Memphis. Two, he did it so he could enjoy his senior year and keep the recruiting wolves away from his door.

"I signed just to stop all the letters and phone calls," Perkins said. "I wanted to stop all the contact. I wanted to make sure I had a pretty good senior year, but I think even back then I knew I was going to put my name in for the draft."

The Celtics thought so as well. GM Chris Wallace saw Perkins play in Beaumont and recalled a big, strong, but raw and unrefined kid with no real offensive game. Memphis coach John Calipari, who was hoping to get Perkins for a year, called him "an absolute monster in high school. He had the long arms, and he had this real mean streak in him. I'm thinking if I can get that kid, we're going to be real good. I was ecstatic when he committed. And then when he called me to tell me he was going pro, well, let's just say I was less than ecstatic."

Perkins said Calipari told him if he went to Memphis for just a year or two, he would be a lottery pick, maybe even the No. 1 pick overall. Said Calipari, "If he'd come for just a year, he would have been top ten, no question. I mean, how many good big guys are there in college basketball?"

As many top high school players did at the time, Perkins turned to adidas' Sonny Vaccaro for advice. It had been Vaccaro who had urged Kevin Garnett to turn pro eight years earlier, and he had the same advice for Perkins, especially since he knew the kid would get picked in the first round, where three years of guaranteed money awaited him. Said Vaccaro, "Kendrick Perkins was never going to college."

By the time the 2003 draft came, the Celtics had quietly worked out a deal with Perkins: they would take him with the second of their two picks in the first round. Perkins ended up being the twenty-seventh player taken, drafted instead by Memphis, but it was one of those deals that the Celtics Leo Papile, the Celtics assistant executive director for basketball operations and the Grizzlies Jerry West had arranged beforehand.

"That's the most amazing part of the story," Calipari said. "He's one of the few to go from high school to the pros having been drafted so low and actually made it. Most of them taken at that point don't make it. Not only that, but he made it going that low and not even playing in his first season. That just shows that it's hard to gauge a kid's drive, desire, and persistence. But he worked his way to fit in on a team whose needs perfectly fit what he can do."

Keena Young, meanwhile, never went to Memphis. After Perkins declared for the NBA draft, Young ended up doing a year of junior college in Texas and then played at Brigham Young for three years. He played professionally in Belgium and Korea.

Perkins' first year in Boston was your classic case of culture shock. To ease with the transition, Boutte and other coaches from high school stayed with him for awhile. The Celtics meanwhile took one look at Perkins' body and decided it was time for an extreme makeover. His first season in Boston was devoted to body work at the hands of strength and conditioning coaches Bryan Doo and Walter Norton. Perkins logged a total of 35 minutes that first year. He also dropped more than 50 pounds, most of it fat.

"It was an adjustment, I'll say that," Perkins said. "I was coming from a situation where I was the man about town and I had the ball in my hands all the time and then you finally get to the NBA and you never play. It was an adjustment I had to make and it was very hard at first. But once I got into basketball shape it was better. But it was tough at first."

There also was the obvious geographical adjustment. Boston and Beaumont could not have been more different, from the size of the cities to the weather to the attitudes of the residents. Back in Texas, Perkins was used to strolling through the Pear Orchard neighborhood where he lived and stopping by a neighbor's home for dessert or just some general chit-chat. His whole life had pretty much been confined to one square mile of Beaumont, in which his house, his church, and his high school all were located. People watched out for him. Now he was pretty much on his own.

"Down south, there's just a whole lot of hospitality," he said. "You can just be somebody who lives down the street and you get invited to a cookout, or stop in to borrow some butter or sugar. Whatever you need. You're always welcome. That's just the kind of place Beaumont is. In Boston, every one seems to be going their own separate way. When you go out to eat, you can tell the people are only focused on what they have to do. You don't see a lot of mingling and getting to know people and stuff like that."

To make things even crazier in Perkins' first year, then head coach Jim O'Brien abruptly resigned midway through the season. It woke him up to one of the trite truisms about professional sports.

"A lot of things surprised me that first year on the court, but off the court, you can never forget that this is a business," he said. "Despite how much fun you might be having or how much you love the team or the organization, it's still a business. That's the way you have to approach it."

Assistant coach John Carroll finished off the year, and the Celtics somehow backed into the playoffs as the No. 8 seed with a grand total of 36 wins. Perkins wasn't even put on the team's playoff roster for what would be a ritualistic four-game massacre of the overmatched Celtics by the top-seeded Indiana Pacers. Instead the team elected to go with veteran Dana Barros, who had signed with the team on the final day of the regular season. Barros never played in the playoff series against Indiana.

With the arrival of Doc Rivers, Perkins gradually started to see more playing time, at least compared to his rookie season. He appeared in 60 games that second season—50 more than in his rookie year—but still logged less than ten minutes a game. Raef LaFrentz, Mark Blount, and a promising rookie named Al Jefferson took up most of the big-man minutes. Perkins did manage to make his first playoff appearance that year, appearing in six of the seven games (but only for a total of 28 minutes) against Indiana, which defeated the Celtics for the second straight season.

Perkins did play a small part in Game 6 of that series, which was highlighted (or lowlighted) by the ejection of Paul Pierce with 12 seconds left. At the time of the ejection, Pierce had been fouled by Jamaal Tinsley, so he was due to take two free throws. Under NBA rules, the opposing coach gets to choose the free-throw shooter in such circumstances. Indiana coach Rick Carlisle, no dummy, chose Perkins, who is not exactly Steve Nash at the free-throw line but, more to the point, had not yet played in the game. Predictably, the nervous Perkins missed both free throws with the score tied at 84–84, although the Celtics did go on to win the game in overtime. The record will show Perkins played one minute, even though the clock never moved while he was in the game.

The next season, Danny Ainge started to clear some room for Perkins as the Celtics wanted to see exactly what they had in the third-year center. Ainge shipped Mark Blount to Minnesota in January 2006. Perkins ended up starting 40 games that third year and had one monster game of 19 rebounds against the 76ers. Doc Rivers said he wanted more games like that. So Perkins delivered a 17-point, 6-block game against the Knicks. Those two games, however, were five months apart, which drove home Rivers' point. He wanted consistency from Perkins, not a big game here and there. To complicate matters for Perkins, he had to battle shoulder problems, which resulted in him missing 13 games.

Just before the start of his fourth season, and recognizing that security was important for him, Perkins decided to forgo free agency and signed a four-year $16 million contract extension. The deal kicked in beginning with the championship season. Perkins will only be 26 when the deal expires in June 2011, although he will have had eight NBA seasons under his belt.

In his fourth year, with Jefferson as his sidekick on and off the floor, Perkins started 53 of 72 games. The improvement was noticeable, and he was looking forward to a prolonged partnership with Jefferson, until he saw the news on television on July 31 that Kevin Garnett was now a Boston Celtic. And Al Jefferson was not.

He was upset to see Jefferson go. The two were born less than two months apart, though were in different high school classes. Both southerners, they bonded during their time in Boston.

"It was really hard for me when Al was traded," Perkins said. "He was here for all the tough times when we were struggling, and he heard all the boos, just like I did. And we caught all of the bad media and stuff like that. It's too bad he didn't get a chance to experience the good times after going through all the bad times. I wish some of them guys who were here could see how it feels to be on the other side. I miss them. But there's nothing you can do about it. And there's definitely nothing to complain about because the team got a lot better. When I saw it was Kevin Garnett, I said, 'Wow!'"

The arrival of Garnett wasn't the only good news for Perkins in the summer of 2007. Long estranged from his father—"I don't have anything to say to him," Perkins said during his rookie year, 2003–2004, the two men had a rapprochement. That made the 2007–2008 season even more special for Perkins. He finally had a relationship with his father.

"He actually attended a few games, and we got a chance to talk and we are on good terms," Perkins said. "He just called me one day, and we ended up talking. He said he'd come to Boston to see me play and he did. We ended up bonding after getting a chance to hang out for a few days. He still lives in New Zealand, where he's a basketball coach. But it's good that we're back on good terms, and now he gets time to spend with his grandchild [Kendrick Perkins Jr., born in September 2007], and he likes my girl, so it's all been growing on him."

In 2007–2008, Perkins stayed healthy and started all 78 games in which he appeared. He established career highs in just about every meaningful statistical category and would have led the NBA in field goal percentage (63.1 percent) except he did not take enough shots to qualify. He was the nineteenth best shot-blocker in the game.

He thrived playing next to Garnett on defense and offensively would often be the recipient of passes for dunks and layups as Garnett, Ray Allen, or Paul Pierce drew double teams on their way to the basket. Early in the season, Toronto coach Sam Mitchell was talking about the huge difference Garnett had already made on the Celtics, and he zeroed right in on Perkins. "You can tell just by looking at him how much he enjoys playing with KG," Mitchell said. "And he's playing a whole lot better because he's playing with KG. Those are the kinds of things KG does for you." Perkins didn't dispute that. He loved everything about his new teammate.

"I never understood how valuable KG was until I had a chance to play with him," Perkins said. "I don't know if a lot of people realize how much he brings to the court. I think people underestimate that at times. He makes life so much easier for everyone on defense because he's so long and he's all over the court, always talking, always patrolling, everything. You never can appreciate how valuable he is until you are on the court with him."

———————

The night of January 5, 2008, has a special meaning for Wyc Grousbeck. It's the night that the Celtics beat the Pistons at the Palace of Auburn Hills, and Grousbeck still carries the ticket stub from that game in his wallet.

It was the first meeting between the two Eastern Conference powers since the Pistons had nipped the Celtics in Boston back on December 19. Neither team had lost since then; the Celtics carried an eight-game winning streak into the game, while the Pistons had an 11-gamer intact. According to the Elias Sports Bureau, it was the first time in 27 years that two teams with 54 combined wins had met as early as January 5.

Both teams had played the night before, but the Celtics encountered some travel difficulties leaving Boston after the victory over the Memphis Grizzlies in Boston. They sat on the plane but eventually were told to go back home and return to the airport in the morning. Ray Allen didn't think it was such a big deal: "An extra night to sleep in your own bed. What's bad about that?"

Doc Rivers also downplayed the delay.

"That's how we used to do it when I played," he said. "I don't think it's any big deal at all."

The game was a nerve-wracking affair, with the Pistons taking an early 12-point lead and the Celtics coming back in the fourth quarter. But it wasn't one of the usual suspects who made the difference for Boston that night. It was a rookie—Glen "Big

Baby" Davis. He played the entire fourth quarter. He scored 16 of his 20 points in the fourth quarter (Detroit as a team had only 19). He had one huge offensive rebound in the fourth quarter. He had three, three-point plays in the fourth quarter.

No one had seen this coming, least of all Davis. He was a rookie, and by no means could he then be considered a regular rotation player, 32 games into the season. In the previous seven games, he had played 28 minutes and never got into two of them. He had played 23 minutes against the Pistons.

He had shown snippets of why he was where he was. There was the power coupled with the finesse. There were the great hands, the great sense of anticipation, the great footwork, and most of all the understanding of how to play the game. He knew it. He got it. Some of that is coachable. Some of it isn't.

But he had done his job for the night. As he was leaving the floor, Kevin Garnett cupped him on the head and said, "You came to play."

As the clock was winding down, James Posey rose and started chanting "Dee-troit Basket-bums" to the fans around the basket who were giving the Celtics some grief. It was a take-off on the annoying Pistons public address announcer, John Mason who blasts out "Detroit Basketball" when the Pistons have forced a turnover or are taking the ball out of bounds.

The Celtics won, 92–85. (You didn't think Grousbeck would carry the ticket stub from a losing game?) Said Davis, "I'm glad Wyc does keep that in his wallet. The game was great. I'm glad we won. But I don't think about the good stuff. I think about the bad stuff, that's what sticks out. The things that molded me, the things that changed me. That's what I take away."

———————

THERE WAS PLENTY of "bad stuff" in Davis' life. His mother battled drug addiction. His father deserted him at an early age. He had to live in shelters and foster homes before eventually settling in with the parents of a fellow AAU player. The player was Garrett Temple, whose father Collis had starred at LSU. Thanks to the efforts of Temple and a local basketball coach Ari Fisher, Davis was able to enroll at the small, exclusive University Lab School on the LSU campus.

"The Temples changed my life in different ways, to the point that it made me the man that I am right now today," Davis said. "I give credit to Mr. Temple and his family because I don't know where I would have been without those guys. Just being around those guys led me in the right direction, because I was going down the wrong path. So I love the Temples, and what can I say, they kind of saved my life."

Davis played both football and basketball for University. He had acquired the moniker "Big Baby" during his PeeWee football days when he had to play against older players because of his girth. One of his coaches told him to stop whining and being a big baby; the nickname stuck. He accepted it then, as he accepts it today. It's a part of who he is.

While he did play some football in high school, his best sport was basketball. He led University to the state championship in 2004. He and Garrett Temple both decided to keep their partnership together and stay in Baton Rouge and play for the LSU Tigers.

"I didn't want to go anywhere else," he said. "It would be a great foundation for Louisiana State, and I wouldn't have to start over, meeting new people. It's just easier being around family and friends. I've always loved basketball. I played football because I could. But my passion was basketball."

When he got to Louisiana State University, he wore No. 0. "It's a symbol of my whole life," he said. "I came from nothing." By then, however, both of his parents had become part of his life again. And by that time, the folks who follow LSU basketball had started to warm to this large (well over 300 pounds), engaging fellow who seemed to be enjoying himself while certainly not taking himself seriously.

Davis played on the same team and roomed with Rajon Rondo when the two played for USA Basketball in the FIBA U–21 Championships in Argentina. Davis was the youngest player on the team and pretty soon was homesick.

"I hadn't been away from home like that, and this was in another country for a long time," Davis said. "And we had these itty-bitty little beds. Sure, I was a little bit homesick. But at the same time, it was a great experience."

His coach in Argentina, Phil Martelli of Saint Joseph's, said "It was a challenge for him to be away from home for so long. But overall, I think he just wanted to please everyone. He wanted his teammates to like him. He probably tried too hard at times, but he added a flair to that team. The trip would have been boring without him."

Davis' coach at Louisiana State, John Brady, said Davis' outgoing personality was "the key to our team." While LSU was making its big run to the Final Four in 2006, Brady told a story about Davis hoisting up an ill-advised three-pointer in a game against Vanderbilt in the SEC Tournament. Davis had been, as they say, "feeling it." But he also knew that the three-pointer was a dumb play, and as he was headed to the bench for a time-out, Davis asked Brady to reprimand him in front of the rest of the team.

"I can't really tell the team what I really want them to do because I keep thinking about the comment that he just shared with me," Brady said. "So I said, 'Glen, by the way, that was a terrible shot you just shot. Get right behind the goal where you need to be to take a better shot.' He smiled and winked. He said, 'You're right, coach.' He went back on the floor.

"He wants to be treated like everyone else," Brady said. "It's good that a player knows that he took a bad shot. Coming off the floor when he shared that with me [asked me to] yell at him in front of the team, it shows the kind of personality that he has. That's the way he is. He kept the locker room light."

Davis toyed with turning pro after that season; LSU had been defeated in the semifinals by UCLA, and one of his closest friends on the team, fellow Baton Rouge native Tyrus Thomas, was going pro after only one season. Thomas didn't have Davis' set of skills, but he could jump out of the gym and was oozing with potential, which made him very Flavor of the Month-ish in the NBA. He ended up being the fourth overall pick in 2006.

"I just didn't feel I was ready after my sophomore year," Davis said. "I wanted to come back and develop myself more, which I did. I felt after my junior year, I was ready."

Davis led the SEC in rebounding as a junior and was third in scoring. He entered the draft, and up to draft night, there were pervasive rumors that some team had promised to take him in the first round. It didn't happen. He slid all the way to No. 35, the fifth pick in the second round, where the Sonics took him as part of the deal with the Celtics that had sent Ray Allen to Boston earlier that night.

"No disappointment whatsoever," Davis said of his draft situation. "Coming from where I came and where I ended up, how could I be disappointed?" That attitude served him well from the first day of training camp to the end of the season.

And in possibly the most anticipated regular-season game of the 2007–2008 season—at least since the last Boston-Detroit meeting—he had come up huge. He would never score 20 points again for the Celtics that season, but what he did that night gave him a lot of currency over the rest of the season.

"I think the second time we played Detroit was the biggest win of the year for us," Paul Pierce said. "They had beaten us at home, and we went in there and beat them pretty easily. Baby was unbelievable. He got to the right spots, and we got the ball to him. We had always felt that Detroit was the best team in the league next to us, and after that game, I was thinking to myself, if we can stay healthy, with all this depth, it's going to be hard for any team to beat us four times in a playoff series."

———————

THE VICTORY OVER THE PISTONS gave the Celtics a 29–3 record. They were off to one of the best starts in NBA history, better even than the 1995–1996 Chicago Bulls, who set an NBA record with 72 wins. No one expected such a start, but even when reality set in during the month of January, it still was somewhat of a shock, given what the Celtics had done over the first two months.

A loss at home to Charlotte followed the Detroit win. The Bobcats gave the Celtics fits in their first two meetings, revealing one of Boston's potential weaknesses—difficulty with athletic, high-octane teams. The Wizards then beat the Celtics back-to-back, resulting in the first losing streak of the season. Next, Toronto beat the Celtics at home, and suddenly Boston looked very, very ordinary. After the loss to the Raptors, the Celtics were only 4–4 in the eight games following the victory in Auburn Hills.

Garnett's old team, the Timberwolves, made their only Boston appearance on January 25, the halfway point of the season. It wasn't a major reunion for Garnett; only three players on the active roster that night had been teammates of his in Minnesota, and none had been with Garnett for more than two years. It was much more of a reunion for the ex-Celtics. Ryan Gomes, Sebastian Telfair, and Al Jefferson all started. And Gerald Green and Antoine Walker, who had come in a trade from Miami, both came off the bench.

Like many of the Celtics games in January, this one was tightly contested. Gone were the routine home blowouts; even a recent 25-point win over Philadelphia was highly deceptive because it had been a close game midway through the fourth quarter.

The Wolves came into the game with only seven victories in 41 games. But they gave the Celtics everything they could handle.

But more troublesome to the Celtics was the situation with Garnett, who had left the game with 6:18 to play after appearing to hurt himself while losing the ball to rookie Corey Brewer. The Celtics trailed by six at the time. In the locker room, Garnett was told he had suffered an abdominal strain, a very dicey injury for a basketball player. It was an abdominal strain that ended the careers of Jerry West and Michael Dickerson. It was an abdominal strain that bothered Shaquille O'Neal in his early career with the Lakers, in part contributing to his missing 51 games in his first two seasons with the Lakers.

"I felt like I got sniped from the rafters or something," Garnett said. "I just felt this sharp pain in my stomach and wanted the doctors to look at it." The Celtics medical team was divided as to whether Garnett should return to the game, which he desperately wanted to do. Garnett was allowed to go back, and with 1:51 to play and the Celtics down 86–81, he made his triumphant return. The Timberwolves did not score again, the Celtics reeled off six straight points, and Garnett preserved the win by poking the ball away from Telfair at half court as time expired.

"I wasn't going to do anything to jeopardize my future," Garnett said. "But my philosophy has always been that if I can run, if I can blink, if I can wake up in the morning, I'm going to play."

Garnett had never before had a serious injury in his career. He had sat out games at the end of the previous two seasons, but those were meaningless affairs for the going-nowhere Timberwolves that, skeptics assumed, were merely trying to get the best lottery odds by continuing to lose. This was different.

"I didn't know what to think at first," Garnett said. "But I put my trust in the doctors and the trainer and did what they told me to do. Just like with everything else, I took my time, considered everything. I knew I'd get back."

The question now for the Celtics was, when? Their terrific start had been a blessing in many ways for Rivers and his veteran-laden team, for now he could afford to take his time bringing back his star. Already Garnett was playing at a pace that would see him log the fewest minutes over an 82-game season since his rookie year. Rivers also was watching the numbers for Ray Allen and Paul Pierce, correctly figuring that it made no sense to burn them out in the regular season.

The Celtics were going to be ultra-careful with Garnett. They had no choice. While he might have been insistent on playing, he also was properly deferential to what he was being told about his injury. He was going to rest. The Celtics put no timetable on a possible return, but it was apparent that Garnett was not coming back anytime soon.

He would miss big home games against Dallas and San Antonio. The Celtics won them both, with Glen Davis doing an admirable job on Tim Duncan. He would miss big road games against the Magic and the Cavaliers. The Celtics lost them both, beaten by a Hail Mary heave by Hedo Turkoglu in Orlando and then by one point in Cleveland in a game in which neither team played any semblance of defense.

Rivers refused to allow the injury to Garnett to be used as an excuse, even though it was clear that in some games, the loss in Cleveland for instance, his absence was huge. One could easily have imagined him throwing a shoe through the television set as the Cavs rang up 114 points, shot 57 percent, and LeBron James nearly had a triple double.

The games still had to be played, with or without Garnett. That's what a team is all about. That's what *ubuntu* was all about. And while Garnett was on the mend, Leon Powe stepped into the breach.

———————

THE WORD SURVIVOR COMES TO MIND when discussing the life of Leon Powe. He overcame two anterior collateral ligament tears, one in high school and the other in college. As a child growing up in the San Francisco Bay area, he was often homeless. He often lived in a car with his mother, who sold geegaws at a flea market by the Oakland Coliseum. He never knew his father.

Powe's best friend from childhood sits in a California jail, convicted of a robbery that he tried to get Powe to help commit. He spent much of his life, like Glen Davis, in foster homes. Soon Powe discovered basketball, helped by a probation counselor and former Oakland playground legend named Bernard Ward. It was Ward who steered Powe to the straight and narrow, convincing him to attend school and study. Powe had missed significant chunks of school growing up to care for his siblings.

"I had to learn just about everything on the streets," Powe said. "But there was a lot of good basketball out there. One of the greatest (players) was a guy named Hook Mitchell. He was a legend. I used to talk to Hook every day, and I still talk to him from time to time. My brother, he talks to him a lot more than me. But as far as I know, he used to be able to jump over cars, do all type of crazy stuff in the air."

Powe's mother died when Powe was a junior in high school. But staying on course, he did well enough at Oakland Tech on the court and in the classroom to earn a scholarship to the University of California. He also played for the Oakland Soldiers, an AAU team whose motto is "Just Get It Done." He toyed with the notion of going to the NBA directly out of high school, but then he felt a pop in his left knee while playing in a high school All-Star tournament that featured LeBron James, Kendrick Perkins, and Dwight Howard. It was a torn ACL, and it forced him to scrap his NBA plans for the time being.

"He overcame so much. He never really had a childhood," said Leo Papile, the chapter chairman of the Leon Powe Fan Club. "Oakland is as rough as it gets in America. When you play an AAU team from Oakland, it's full body contact basketball. It's not dirty. But it's hard. And Leon personifies that style. He has that toughness. That edge. He's a guy that you don't want to fool around with, and to me that's the ultimate compliment."

Powe spent three years at Berkeley. He was Pac 10 Freshman of the Year, becoming the first freshman in history to lead the conference in rebounding. But another ACL tear forced him to redshirt his second season. He then returned for the 2005–2006 season and put up some nifty numbers (20.5 points, 10.1 rebounds a game). He became only the third player in Cal history to earn All-American honors. The others were Darrell Imhoff and Jason Kidd.

"I scouted him a lot during that second season," said Papile. "And I came away thinking that this guy should be a lottery pick. He looked like he did back before he got hurt in high school, when he was one of the elite players in the country along with LeBron and Perk [Kendrick Perkins]. I knew he was undersized. I knew he didn't have much of a stroke. But he had the energy, the perseverance, and he created so much space for himself around the basket that I thought he could be a double-double guy in the league for years to come."

Powe was 22 when he declared for the draft, even though he had two years of college eligibility remaining. Concerns about his knees, not his game, affected his draft status, and he slid into the second round in 2006. The Celtics had just announced the deal for Rajon Rondo and Danny Ainge was answering questions from the media, when back in the draft room, Papile was calling team after team, trying to see if he could procure a second-round pick to get Powe. He finally reached an accommodating colleague in Denver personnel boss Mark Warkentein. The Nuggets had the forty-ninth pick, but would take Powe for Boston if Powe was still there. In return, the Nuggets wanted a second-round pick from the Celtics in 2007.

"Done," said Papile.

Ainge returned to the draft room and found out that the Celtics had taken Powe and said, "You always liked that guy. That's great."

The Celtics did a similar maneuver in 2008 in selecting Billy Walker in the second round. As Papile said, "You have to be on your toes in that second round. There's only two minutes between picks and it moves at the speed of sound."

Second-round picks have played roles on the Celtics in the Danny Ainge era. Ryan Gomes went in the second round. Glen Davis went in the second round. Gabe Pruitt went in the second round. All thought they'd be first-rounders. For Powe, getting picked so low was simply one more hurdle to overcome in a lifetime of them.

The Celtics soon discovered that Powe had tenacity as well as an affinity for rebounding. He just went out and got the ball. They saw that Powe loves to take it to the basket and is not afraid of anyone who might get in his way. But mostly they saw a guy who worked his tail off every day, stayed patient, and was ready when the call came.

A perfect example was the night of January 29, 2008, when the Celtics made their final visit to Miami. Garnett was out. Ray Allen was sick with the flu. Paul Pierce had one forgettable game (7 points on 2-of-9 shooting). Yet Boston won easily, in part because the first man off the bench had 25 points and 11 rebounds in 36 minutes. That man was Leon Powe.

"I'm just happy to get in a game and just happy to be a part of this whole experience, because it's been a long journey for me," he said. "To be able to contribute, whether it's on the defensive end or the offensive end, it don't matter to me. I just go out there and try to play hard, 110 percent every time. I never give up."

Until Garnett got hurt, Powe had played only 110 minutes over 18 games. Doc Rivers had not used Powe at all in 23 games. But once Powe got an opportunity, he made the most of it. While Garnett was out, he averaged 12 points and 7 rebounds in a shade more than 20 minutes a game.

That was enough to convince Rivers that Powe needed to be on the floor. Powe missed only one game the rest of the year due to a coaching decision and two more due to a sore foot. And very soon Garnett would be back, as the Celtics geared up for a difficult second half of the season and, they hoped, a long playoff run in the spring. But it was still winter and a lot of things could, and did, happen.

9

All Stars, Add-ons, and a Fantastic Finish

KEVIN GARNETT HAD ALREADY penciled in New Orleans for All-Star Weekend because, well, he's Kevin Garnett. He's an automatic at All-Star Games. But in 2007–2008, it was a bittersweet weekend for him.

Everywhere in New Orleans, or so it seemed, there were adidas posters with Garnett's face staring down at you. He had been the leading vote getter in the fan balloting and was seen as a legitimate candidate to win his second Most Valuable Player award. He was the moving force behind the team with the best record in the NBA.

And he wasn't going to play.

The abdominal strain was healing, and Garnett was planning on returning to the lineup after the All-Star Break, when the Celtics kicked off a five-game western swing in Denver. Doc Rivers, who was coaching the Eastern Conference team, ran Garnett through a couple of practice sessions over the All-Star weekend and liked what he saw. But he too was going to wait until the season resumed before deciding how much Garnett would play.

The Celtics contingent in New Orleans was significant. Rivers and his coaching staff would lead the East. Paul Pierce had been named as a reserve by the conference coaches in what amounted to a no-brainer. But Ray Allen had not been. Joe Johnson of the Atlanta Hawks, which didn't have a winning record, had gotten the nod.

"Ray should have gotten it instead," Pierce said. "No knock against Joe, but they [Atlanta] are not a .500 team, and I thought it was important what you did as a team. The Pistons had four guys a couple years ago and their record was similar to ours."

Allen took the snub in stride and made plans to go to the Bahamas. But he had to scratch them when, for the second straight year, he was named as a Commissioner's choice to replace an injured player. The year before it had been Steve Nash. This time around it was Caron Butler.

"It's an honor to be chosen," Allen said. Then, on All-Star Sunday, he went out and scored a game-high 28 points in only 18 minutes, making 5-of-6 three-pointers, as the Eastern Conference avenged an embarrassing loss from the year before. Allen finished second to LeBron James in the voting for Game MVP.

"I didn't think about that," Allen said. "I didn't even know how many points I had. I told my family before I left the hotel that this was my eighth All-Star Game. They're so proud of me, they're happy for me to be here. I told them, 'I know you guys want to see me in the game, and you want to be excited about me.'

"But I also told Doc, 'Don't worry about me being on the bench. I'm not going to be mad at you if you don't play me. We're on the same team.' But then I got rolling, and I was happier for them [his family] than I was for myself because I know they were excited that I was playing well."

Rivers almost substituted for Allen just before the hot streak, concerned about his team getting outrebounded. But he didn't and then watched along with everyone else as Allen put on a show.

"It was great for Ray," Rivers said. "He was not an original pick, and he should have been. He's the guy that had sacrificed more for our basketball team offensively so we could win. I thought he should have gotten more credit for that when the original votes were out. He didn't. And he didn't get down about it. He came in, was finally put on the team, and played the way he played."

ALL-STAR WEEKEND IS ABOUT MANY THINGS, some even basketball. The 2008 weekend was also about trying to help New Orleans recover from Hurricane Katrina, which had demolished parts of the city three years earlier. While much of downtown New Orleans was slowly coming back, many of the hardest hit areas of the city remained desolate and deserted.

The NBA devoted an entire day to public service on the Friday of All-Star Weekend, with players, coaches, executives, and league employees donning work gloves and work shoes. Doc Rivers' son rode on one of the buses to a work site and yakked it up with Kobe Bryant.

All-Star Weekend is also about parties—lots of them. One in particular, a charity fund-raiser, was being held Friday night at one of the many hotels on Canal Street. The event was chaired by the wife of former NBA player P.J. Brown, who was enjoying retirement living in the New Orleans suburb of Slidell.

Around 1 a.m., dodging raindrops as he exited the hotel, Brown saw a big black SUV limousine come to a halt as he was ready to cross the street. One of the tinted windows in the rear came down and out popped the face of Paul Pierce. "P.J.? What's up," Pierce said. "Look man, we could really use you in Boston. We need you, man." Then the window went up and the limousine disappeared into the night.

"I didn't know what to think," Brown said. "I mean it was late and it was All-Star Weekend and he might have been feeling good."

Brown had been on the Celtics wish list since the beginning of the season, but had declined all offers to return for a sixteenth season. The Lakers, Spurs, Suns, and Mavericks had called, along with the Celtics. "He was 99.99 percent retired," said his agent Mark Bartelstein.

Brown's heart wasn't in it. But the Celtics, even with the league's best record, were still trying to add veterans for the antici- pated playoff run, and Brown was as good as they came. He *was* *ubuntu*—selfless, classy, professional, articulate, the recipient of league awards for both citizenship and sportsmanship. The Celtics thought he might still have something left in the tank.

"The worst case scenario if we ever got him," Doc Rivers said, "is that we'd be adding a great guy to the locker room."

Brown was flattered by what he heard from Pierce, and the next night he got a similar recruiting pitch from Ray Allen when the two met at a party sponsored by the NBA Players Association. "I know Paul gave you a holler last night," Allen told Brown. "But he's for real. We want you. We think you'd fit right in. You'll like playing for Doc, you'll like the way he handles the veterans."

Brown told Allen he still wasn't sure if he really wanted to do it. He hadn't played since last May. He wasn't sure if his 38-year-old body would respond. He wasn't sure if he even wanted to play again.

"I felt I had put my time in and people knew what I did and that I really didn't have anything else to prove," Brown said. "I knew I had given it my all over the last 15 years and that it was time for me to move on to something else. In my mind, it was pretty much over."

Celtics assistant coach Clifford Ray, who had developed a relationship with Brown when the two were in New Jersey, also went on the recruiting trail. But when All-Star Sunday rolled around, Brown was still up in the air.

The Hornets were interested as well, and geographically it made all the sense in the world. But New Orleans was also going to get a chance to re-sign Chris "Birdman" Andersen, who had missed the last two years due to a suspension for violating the league's drug policy. Eventually, the Hornets decided they'd go in that direction. That left Brown with the option of staying retired or joining the Celtics, who were rolling along at a 41–9 clip. He at least had narrowed it down by then.

"I wasn't even sure that if I did come back, I could even make a difference," Brown said. "I still had doubts. And I was concerned about the team's chemistry. A team bonds a certain way throughout the season, and this team was doing very, very well. I was scared that I would mess that up. That was a big concern."

Once the weekend was over, Brown returned home. He watched the Celtics lose at Denver, then at Golden State, then again at Phoenix. Garnett had returned, but he was nowhere near the player he had been in the first two months of the season. He had been out almost a month. The first of those losses, to the Nuggets in Denver, was the first Celtic loss to a Western Conference team all season. They had won their first 13 games against teams from the deeper, tougher West.

Slowly but surely, Brown came to envision himself in Celtic green and white. He gathered his wife Dee, who like Brown had played at Louisiana Tech, and the four children and asked them what they all thought about a possible return to the NBA for dear old dad. In Boston. They green-lighted the whole thing.

"I did a lot of praying," Brown said. "I tossed and turned at night. But, to me, if I was going to try it, Boston was the best situation. Then it was on me to make the final decision."

He called Bartelstein and told him to contact the Celtics. He would be coming back for one last hurrah. On February 27, some 12 days after he had seen Pierce in the limousine on Canal Street, Brown agreed to terms with the Celtics for the rest of the season.

———————

THE CELTICS WOULD BE Brown's fifth team, but seventh NBA location, as he had lived in three different places (Charlotte, New

Orleans, and Oklahoma City) while playing for the Hornets. He had thought the Celtics might actually draft him in 1992, when he had finished his career at Louisiana Tech as the school's second most prolific shot-blocker and fifth most prolific rebounder.

He had been a classic "late bloomer," taking up basketball as a junior in high school only after he went from six-foot-three to six-foot-six, and only after some friends had worked on him ceaselessly to try out for the varsity at Winnfield Senior High School in Winnfield, Louisiana. "Sort of like the same way Paul and Ray recruited me," he said.

He played well enough to generate some enthusiasm from a few schools, but signed early with Louisiana Tech because it was close to home. There he played in 121 of a possible 122 games, establishing a reputation for dependability and durability that would continue throughout his 15 years in the NBA. He never missed more than eight games in any one season.

Brown was drafted twenty-ninth overall, the second pick of the second round in 1992, by the New Jersey Nets. He saw the player drafted before him, Marlon Maxey, get a guaranteed deal. He saw the player drafted after him, Sean Rooks, get a guaranteed deal. The NBA minimum at the time was $140,000. The Nets would not guarantee that much to Brown, even though he was the team's top pick; there had been no first-rounder.

"I felt I had done everything possible to prove to all the teams that I was NBA material," Brown said. "I wasn't a Street & Smith's All-American. I wasn't on Dick Vitale's first, second, or third teams. I was just one of those guys in the gray area. People said I was too skinny. People said I was too frail. I had put so much hard work in and now they were telling me they couldn't even guarantee me the minimum? I thought that was unfair. I went overseas. It was a big gamble at the time, but I told myself that it was what I had to do and to look at it like a great opportunity."

But there was even more adventure ahead. Brown first signed on with a team in Israel, which quickly got a case of buyer's remorse. The team lodged a steroid charge against Brown and got out of the contract. Bartelstein went to court. Brown went to Greece to play for Panionios in Athens. "I liked the city, but it was tough being alone, far from home, halfway around the world," he said.

When he went back to the Nets in 1993, coach Chuck Daly was much more receptive this time around. He told Brown if he practiced hard, did the little things, and hustled, then Daly would find a spot for him.

"And that's what I did for the next 15 years," Brown said.

Over that span, he played for Hall of Famers in Daly and Pat Riley. He had his most success with Riley in Miami, where he played for four years. He remembers Riley dunking his head in a bucket of water to demonstrate what trust was all about. Brown still doesn't know what was more amazing, that Riley did it—or that he did it during a regular season game against the Pistons. He usually saves his best stuff for the playoffs. Brown remembered the heartache of seeing Allan Houston's last-second shot fall through as the Knicks upset the Heat in the first round of the 1999 playoffs. Twice, the Heat fell to New York in the first round, losing the clinching Game 5 at home.

"It was especially painful for him that we never could get over that hump," Riley said. "I feel bad about that because he's the best of the best, maybe the classiest guy I ever coached. He really is what the Celtics are all about."

BROWN WASN'T THE ONLY VETERAN the Celtics sought. While Danny Ainge had been careful not to bring in a veteran point guard to back up Rajon Rondo, and had been proven correct in that decision, the playoffs were an entirely different matter in his eyes. Rondo had never been in a playoff game. Ainge felt it was imperative that someone with playoff experience be added.

The Celtics arrived in Los Angeles on Monday, February 25. They had ended their three-game losing streak the night before with a victory in Portland and now were closing out the trip against the Clippers, who were back to their usual losing ways. The trading deadline had come and gone the previous Thursday.

Earlier in the winter, the Celtics had decided not to sign Damon Stoudamire, who had been released by Memphis and eventually caught on with the Spurs. There were two players out there who Ainge felt might be available and who he liked—Brent Barry and Sam Cassell.

Barry had been traded to Seattle by the Spurs and then was quickly waived. Ainge has been a Barry fan for years and talked to him after Seattle waived him. "I would have loved to have had him for his shooting, his passing, his length," Ainge said of Barry. "But he told us he was probably going to go back to San Antonio. That's where his family was. He knew their team. He was going to be healthy in time for the playoffs, which is what we were looking for."

Barry did go back to the Spurs. That left Cassell, who, when the Celtics arrived in Los Angeles, was still a member of the Clippers. He wasn't playing (he was said to have a sprained right wrist), and it was common knowledge that his agent David Falk was talking to the Clippers about buying out the remainder of Cassell's contract, which was up at the end of the season.

"I didn't want a run-of-the-mill veteran," Ainge said. "I wanted it to be a significant veteran. And I felt that if we played well, one might become available. We talked to Damon [Stoudamire], and we took a chance because we lost Damon and there was no guarantee we'd get Sam. But I'd rather have Sam. I was thinking playoff insurance and health insurance. I thought Sam was the best option."

The trick was convincing Clippers owner Donald Sterling that it was the best move for everyone. Cassell was not going to be brought back. He had given the Clippers two-and-a-half seasons, playing well in 2006, when they came within a game of the Western Conference Finals.

Sterling claimed not to understand the nature of a buyout, wondering why Cassell had to be paid at all if he was leaving the team. Eventually, there was a meeting of the minds and Cassell and the Clippers agreed to a figure. He was put on waivers and then promptly signed with Boston.

THE CELTICS HAD HAD A SHOT at Cassell when he came out of Florida State in 1993. A lot of teams did. Most took a pass. The Houston Rockets chose Cassell with the twenty-fourth pick. Cassell had played two years in junior college (San Jacinto in Texas) and then moved on to Florida State. The Rockets quickly discovered what they had: a confident, brash young guard who was unafraid of just about anything. He played in 66 games for the Rockets as a rookie and all 22 of their playoff games, winning a ring in his first season.

"That team was a lot like the Celtics because we had unbelievable chemistry," Cassell said of his initial Houston team. "We never argued on the court. If someone turned it over, he turned it over. Hakeem [Olajuwon] was the one who picked us all up, saying, 'It's OK, don't worry about it.' He was the star and he led the team. When the playoffs started that first year, he came up to me and said, 'You're not a rookie any more. You're a veteran if you know your role, play your role, just keep doing what you've been doing all along. Don't start doing new things. Don't try anything new.'"

Cassell then won another ring in his second year in the league, before the Rockets team started to disband. One of the great what if's of the 1990s is what would have happened had Michael Jordan's Bulls met Hakeem Olajuwon's Rockets in the Finals. Those two teams were the only NBA titlists for eight straight years, yet never met in the NBA Finals. Houston's titles came in the two years following Jordan's first retirement in 1993; Jordan did return late in the 1994–1995 season, but his Bulls lost in the second round.

"That would have been one awesome series," Cassell said. "If we had kept that team together, added a power forward, someone like Kevin Willis, that's all we needed. We had Chucky Brown, but we needed a big, strong guy."

The Rockets did indeed get Willis, but not until 1996. By that time Cassell was gone, having been traded to Phoenix in a mega-deal that relocated Charles Barkley from the Suns to the Rockets, where he linked up with Hakeem Olajuwon and Clyde Drexler. That was another "Big Three," but the Rockets never got back to the Finals.

"That trade for Barkley would have been a good trade if they had made the Finals. But they didn't. So it was a bad trade," Cassell said.

Cassell then bounced around over the next several years. He came close to getting back to the Finals with the Bucks (and Ray Allen) in 2001 and then in 2004 with the Timberwolves (and Kevin Garnett). The Celtics would be his eighth NBA team after two-plus seasons with the Clippers, where he had been part of the best team in Clipper history in 2006, reaching Game 7 of the second round of the Western Conference playoffs before losing to the Suns.

But things had gone back to normal for the Clippers since then, and 2007–2008 was an utter disaster. Elton Brand, the team's best player, tore an Achilles tendon over the summer and missed virtually the entire season. Promising point guard Shaun Living-ston missed the entire season recovering from a knee injury. Cassell was almost traded to Memphis for Mike Miller at the trading dead-line, but the deal fell through. Thus, once the deadline expired, the only way he could get out of LA was for the Clippers to buy him out. He was not in their plans. And, in talking to Garnett, he had an inkling he might be in Boston's plans if he could wiggle out of his deal.

"Kevin and I were talking at least once a week," Cassell said. "And I told him about my situation and that I thought I might be able to get out of my contract because I knew I wasn't a part of the

Clippers' future. So he was like, 'Really? We could sure use you.' So we kept talking."

When he showed up for his first Boston practice, it wasn't as if Cassell needed to wear a name tag. There were some familiar faces among his new teammates—and bosses.

"I played with Kevin. I played with Ray. Paul is a neighbor in California," Cassell said. "I knew a lot of these guys. It wasn't hard at all. I competed against Doc Rivers. I competed against Danny Ainge. I won championships playing against both of them [against Ainge in 1994 and Rivers in 1995]. And I had one of my best games against Doc [when Rivers was with the Spurs in 1995]. I remind him of that a lot."

Cassell also saw his move to Boston as getting one step closer to what he eventually wanted to do, once he couldn't play anymore: coaching. Rivers in fact had told him he'd find a place for him on the Boston bench once Cassell did retire. Even as he said it, Rivers wondered what coaches' meetings were going to be like with the motor-mouth Cassell in the room. And, Rivers conceded, he'd probably have to let his assistants start talking to reporters.

THE CONCLUDING TWO VICTORIES on the western swing over Portland and the Clippers started the Celtics on what would be a season-best, 10-game winning streak, the longest since the 1985–1986 team had rattled off 14 straight victories. There was a rousing home victory over a tired Pistons team on March 5, a game highlighted by an end-to-end running dunk by Rajon Rondo. (Detroit had played the night before and had travel problems getting to Boston.) That started a string of four straight games in which the Celtics never trailed. Boston reestablished its dominance at home, going 6–0 during the streak, and won the last four games of the streak by margins of 23, 30, 14, and 29 points.

But on the eve of the Celtics' departure for a road trip that would test their mettle against some of the best teams in the West, the Utah Jazz arrived in Boston and spanked the Celtics, 110–92. It was their biggest margin of defeat all season, as Deron Williams went for 32 points and 8 assists. In that game, Ray Allen played only 12 minutes after jamming his left ankle.

———————

THE TEXAS TRIP WAS THE CHANCE for the Celtics to finally play some of the iron of the league, away from the comfy confines of home. It was a bruiser—five games in eight days starting with what would be a glorified tune-up against the hapless Bucks and then heading straight into the belly of the beast with games against the Spurs, Rockets, Mavericks, and Hornets, all among the elite in the Western Conference.

The Celtics won handily in Milwaukee and then arrived in San Antonio for a St. Patrick's Day showdown with the Spurs. The two had met on the same date the year before in San Antonio, and the Celtics, then one of the NBA's worst, beat the eventual champion Spurs, defeating Tim Duncan for the first time.

San Antonio had not lost at home in six weeks, and the Celtics had not swept a season series from the Spurs since 1988–1989. Neither of those stats appeared to be in jeopardy when San Antonio jumped to a 28–11 lead after one quarter, gradually expanding the lead to 35–13 in the second. Tony Parker was having his way. Manu Ginóbili was making big shots. And the Spurs were cruising.

The Celtics chipped away however and trailed by 10 at half-time. A strong start in the third gave Boston its first lead on a Paul Pierce dunk, but San Antonio recovered and built a 9-point lead in the fourth. The resilience of the Celtics had already been tested once. But could the team rally again without Ray Allen, who was in street clothes for the second straight game? They could and they would.

The Spurs held a one-point lead in the final minute until some excellent ball movement by the Celtics found Cassell wide open outside the three-point arc. Cassell and Doc Rivers were thinking the same thing when Cassell unhesitatingly let it go and knocked it down—"That's why he's here." The Celtics held a two-point lead at the end, when Garnett, forgetting to call time-out, tried to inbound the ball from under the Boston basket. The pass was stolen by Bruce Bowen, who also did not call a time-out. He instead passed it to a wide-open Robert Horry, who let go a three-pointer as time expired.

This was almost identical to the ending of the Celtics–Bobcats game the previous November, when the Celtics had stolen an inbound pass and Allen had made a game-winner as time expired. Horry has a reputation for making big shots at the end of games, two of the biggest being game winners for the Lakers (in Game 4 of the 2001 Western Conference Finals against the Kings) and the Spurs (in Game 5 of the 2004 NBA Finals against the Pistons.) That's why they call him "Big Shot Bob." But Horry didn't connect this time, and the Celtics escaped with a two-point victory.

The rampaging Houston Rockets were next in what promised to be a mid-March classic. Houston had won 22 straight games, the second longest winning streak in NBA history, topped only by the 33-gamer of the 1971–1972 Los Angeles Lakers. No team had failed to win an NBA title if it had managed to win 19 straight in one season; Houston was well past that.

The Rockets had not lost since January 27 and had won the last 11 games without center Yao Ming, who had suffered a season-ending foot injury. A franchise record crowd of 18,525 filed into the Toyota Center, hoping to see Houston continue its winning ways against the team with the best record in the league—and a 22–4 record against teams from the Western Conference. Houston icon Hakeem Olajuwon was sitting at courtside. The Celtics meanwhile would once again be without Allen, who missed his third straight game nursing his sore left ankle.

Before the game, Garnett had to deal with some rather unflattering words from Timberwolves owner Glen Taylor, who accused his former franchise forward of tanking games by sitting out at the end of the season. It was common knowledge in Minnesota the previous two years that the Wolves did tank games at the end of the season to protect their draft position. What better way to ensure losing than by resting your best player?

Garnett rightfully took umbrage at the remarks. While he wasn't deemed to be seriously hurt in either of the last two seasons, the idea that he could be personally tanking games was inconceivable. As he put it when he was injured in January, "If I can blink, I can play." And he wasted no time in answering Taylor's ridiculous charge.

"That's nonsense," Garnett said. "I don't even know why he would bring that up, but you know, it shows the taste of some people . . . Glen Taylor was good to me while I was a Timberwolf. I'm a Boston Celtic now. I'm not going to be going back and forth and saying tasteless things. That's not in my character. I'll let him speak if he wants to. I have nothing to do with the Minnesota Timberwolves. That's my past and I'm in a new chapter in my life. I thank him for the opportunity . . . when I was younger the chance to not only explore my dream, but to make it to where I am today. And that's all I'm going to say about that."

Garnett doesn't like it when he has to deviate from his scripted pregame routine, but it didn't show in his play that night. He had 22 points, 11 rebounds, 3 steals, and 2 blocked shots as the Celtics crushed the Rockets, 97–74, ending Houston's celebrated streak. The game had been tied, 40–40 at the half, but the Celtics defense clamped down on Tracy McGrady, who was limited to eight points and left the game for good with 8:45 remaining.

"I've never seen a defense like that," McGrady said after the Celtics had held Houston to a season-low 34 points in the second quarter on 33 percent shooting. "I mean, if they play defense like that, night in and night out, the NBA is in trouble because that was defense at its finest."

They had been playing defense like that all season. That was why they were where they were.

After an off-day, the Celtics met Dallas at American Airlines Center, a building where they had never won. Ray Allen was back in the lineup, and he made the game's biggest shot near the end of what was a truly ugly game. The Celtics shot 34.5 percent, the Mavericks, 39.3 percent. Rajon Rondo missed all seven of his shots, and Sam Cassell missed eight of nine. Jason Kidd, who had been with the Mavericks for a month, missed seven of eight shots.

But it was Allen, with 21 points, who mirrored what Cassell had done in San Antonio a few nights earlier, connecting on a three-pointer in the final minute to turn a one-point deficit into a two-point lead. The Celtics then settled things at the free-throw line and won 94–90, completing a sweep of the Texas teams at home and on the road. No team had done that since Ray Allen's Bucks in 2000. And it had been seven years since any team had beaten all three Texas teams on the road in successive games.

"It's something for the rest of the NBA to watch," Allen said.

The trip concluded two nights later in New Orleans, a homecoming of sorts for P.J. Brown, who had played so many seasons for a Hornets team in three different locales. The biggest crowd of the season, 18,250, showed up, which in itself was newsworthy, given the Hornets' tough attendance situation. Even though New Orleans then was battling for the top spot in the Western Conference and had a dynamic young team led by All-Stars Chris Paul and David West, it was not translating into putting bodies in the seats. Only Indiana, Memphis, and Seattle drew fewer fans in the 2007–2008 season, and the Hornets' long-term future in New Orleans is tied to improved attendance.

But there was Mardi Gras–like gaiety and enthusiasm when the Celtics came to town for what would be the first meeting between the teams. The Celtics led by 15 late in the first half and by 13 in the second half, but couldn't close the deal. Perhaps a little fatigued by playing five games in eight days, they wilted down the stretch. Paul hit two big shots. West was a monster all game with 37 points; only one player, LeBron James, would score more against the Celtics in a regular season game. He had 38.

———————

Boston returned home and then was blindsided by Philadelphia, whose athleticism was simply too much on this particular night. It's almost an article of faith in the NBA that the first home game after a long road trip is still a road game. The Celtics just didn't have it all night, losing 96–90. As much as Doc Rivers instructed the team to live in the moment, it might have been hard to ignore the next two games, visits by the Suns and the Hornets, both of whom had wins over the Celtics in their first meetings.

The Phoenix game was close in the first half, but the Celtics put it away in the fourth quarter behind a tour de force from Paul Pierce. In one stretch of less than four minutes, Pierce simply took over, scoring 12 points and assisting on the only two baskets he didn't score for the Celtics in that stretch. The run began with the Celtics nursing an 11-point lead with 10:11 to play and concluded with 6:35 to play and the Celtics ahead by 19 points.

Watching from the bench, Cassell was dazzled by what he saw. He had played with both Allen and Garnett before, but this was his introduction to Paul Pierce.

"That game was something. It was score, score, assist, score again. Me and P.J. [Brown] looked at each other and I said, 'Wow, can it be any easier than that?' I saw how easily the game comes to him, but sometimes I get upset at him because he can be too lackadaisical," Cassell said. "He has that killer instinct, but sometimes he lets guys live too long, instead of going right at 'em. Bam. Bam. Then he'll coast for a while. But in that game against Phoenix, he was a killer. He's bigger than people think he is. He's stronger than people think he is. He's faster than people think he is. And he can jump higher than people think he can."

The Celtics won by 20. Garnett had 30 points, but afterward Shaquille O'Neal dismissed the Big Ticket as a worthy MVP candidate because his numbers weren't up to those of Kobe Bryant (Shaq's choice) or teammate Amare Stoudemire. When it was suggested to O'Neal that Garnett's numbers were down because his minutes were down, and that his real importance was as a defensive force, Shaq sniffed, "He doesn't play defense." Which made one wonder: what had he been watching all season?

Two nights later, the Celtics got revenge on the Hornets, winning again by 20. That gave the Celtics the distinction of having beaten every team in the league.

At this point, the Celtics really had their eyes on the post-season, for there was little to play for in the remaining ten games. They had clinched a playoff spot. They had clinched the division. The softness of their April schedule—nine games, one against a team with a winning record—ensured they would soon clinch the best record in the league. It translated to a few weeks of exhibition games.

Boston would finish winning nine of its last ten, the only loss coming to the Wizards in Washington on April 9. One of the few mysteries of the 2007–2008 was the Celtics' inability to beat Washington, which finished the season with a 3–1 record against the Celtics. No one else had a season's advantage over them, and only two teams, Orlando and Cleveland, managed two wins.

Coach Doc Rivers was well into player preservation mode. He rested his Big Three against Charlotte on April 5, and the

Celtics had a much easier time with the Bobcats in Charlotte than they did when all three of them played the previous November, winning 101–78. All three rested again for the penultimate game of the regular season on April 14 in Madison Square Garden against the Knicks.

Much had changed in New York since Boston's last visit in January. Respected executive Donnie Walsh was now in control of the basketball operations, a much-needed change from the chaos of the Isiah Thomas years. Thomas was still coaching, but clearly was walking the plank, Walsh simply letting him finish the horrible season.

Masters golf champion Trevor Immelman had a courtside seat for the game; he was in New York to appear on *The David Letterman Show* a day after winning at Augusta. Rivers invited Immelman to the Celtics locker room in yet another of his motivational ploys. "I wanted them to shake the hand of a champion. I wanted them to see a champion," Rivers said. "But Ray got the poor guy cornered, and now I'm worried that might have ruined his game." Rivers was joking, but Immelman had only one other top ten finish through the end of July after winning at Augusta in April.

After the 99–93 victory over the Knicks, Isiah Thomas spotted Garnett in a corridor outside the Celtics locker room and went up to chat. Thomas has long had a healthy respect for the Celtics organization, even as it thwarted him year after year until the Pistons finally broke through in 1988.

"I just said to him that there are certain players who fit what the Celtics model is all about," Thomas said. "Garnett, he's in that same lineage along with Russell, the Joneses, Havlicek, and Cowens. [It was noticed he didn't mention Larry Bird, who had fired him from his head coaching job in Indiana.] When you look at [Garnett], you see Celtics. That's what I told him. He's a Celtic. He looks and acts as if he should have been drafted by them, because he is one."

The Celtics then flew home and coasted to a season-ending finale over the Nets. No starter played more than 20 minutes; Garnett would end up playing the fewest minutes since his rookie year. Rondo and James Posey were given the night off.

All thoughts were now on the post-season, something the Celtics had not seen in three years. They had every intention of sticking around for a while.

10

Bandwagon Fans and
Menacing Gestures

T HE ATLANTA HAWKS were the Celtics' opponent in the
first round of the playoffs, and it appeared on the surface
to be a colossal mismatch. The Hawks may have been
the eighth best team in the East, but going by their
37–45 record, there were 16 better teams in the NBA. The Celtics
had won all three regular-season games between the teams by an
average of more than 14 points a game.

The Hawks looked to one and all to be the classic case of
a team "just happy to be here," making their first post-season
appearance since 1999, the year of the lockout. They had not won
a playoff series since 1997 and had not won a best-of-seven series
since 1970.

The Hawks were young, athletic, but vastly inexperienced in
the ways of the post-season, which is a different season unto itself.
That's a lesson one can learn only by playing in the playoffs, and
only two members of the Hawks, Mike Bibby and Joe Johnson, had

any measurable playoff experience—Bibby's with the Sacramento Kings and Johnson's with the Phoenix Suns.

The mid-season acquisition of Bibby solidified the Hawks' backcourt; this was after all the team that passed on both Chris Paul and Deron Williams for Marvin Williams in the 2005 draft. Atlanta played nearly .500 basketball (16–17) after Bibby came aboard.

But it was Johnson, still only 26 when the playoffs began, who had quietly emerged as the face of the franchise. He had been named the team's captain. He was its only representative at the All-Star Game, and he had been among a group of players invited to try out for the national team. He played on the USA Team that qualified for the Beijing Olympics, but was not chosen to play on the Olympic team.

Going up against Boston in his first playoff series for the Hawks represented something of a full circle for Johnson. It had been the Celtics who drafted him in 2001, selecting him with the tenth overall pick. He had played two years at Arkansas, posting modest numbers, but developing a reputation as a terrific all-around player whose only flaw might be that he was a little too unselfish at times.

The Celtics thought they had themselves a certifiable star. In the middle of November, Johnson had 22 points, 8 rebounds, and 6 assists in a game against the Indiana Pacers. Leo Papile, then the team's assistant general manager, walked by a group of reporters saying, "R-O-Y. R-O-Y." As in "Rookie of the Year."

"I remember that game," Johnson said. "But I don't remember much else about my time here. It was so short, it's like it didn't happen."

He's right. He was in the starting lineup in December, on the bench in January, and on the move in February. Coach Jim O'Brien leaned heavily on veterans, having had to sit next to Rick Pitino for the previous three-and-a-half years, watching young players make countless mistakes and watching the Celtics lose a lot more than they won. He stressed defense and toughness, and as a rookie,

Johnson was lacking in each area. The Celtics then were also a team of strong personalities, not an easy fit for a quiet southerner.

By February 2002, midway through Johnson's rookie season, the Celtics were en route to their first playoff berth in six years and had an opportunity to add depth and experience to their roster. The Eastern Conference looked to be wide open; the Nets—the Nets!—had emerged as the top team with the arrival of Jason Kidd.

The Celtics nearly pulled off a trade with Denver for Nick Van Exel, but instead struck a deal with the Phoenix Suns, acquiring Rodney Rogers and Tony Delk. The Celtics sent Johnson, their No. 1 pick in the 2002 draft, Milt Palacio, and Randy Brown to Phoenix. Johnson's Celtics career was over after only 48 games, 33 of which he had started.

The Celtics recent history is littered with what ifs. What if Len Bias had lived? What if Reggie Lewis had lived? What if Larry Nance had not stepped on Kevin McHale's foot in 1987, when McHale was as automatic and deadly inside as anyone has ever been?

The Johnson trade became another one because the Suns were not actively seeking him. Phoenix would just as soon have taken Kedrick Brown, a rookie who had been the No. 11 pick in 2001 and thus had a salary very close to what Johnson earned. The Suns didn't care; they wanted to get rid of Delk's contract and did not want to deal with Rogers, who was entering free agency at the end of the season. Had the deal been made in November or even December, Kedrick Brown would have been in the package. But by February, Johnson had fallen out of favor, and the Celtics saw some things in Brown (athleticism, defense, three-point capability) that at the time worked to his advantage. So Brown stayed.

Johnson developed into a star in Phoenix, thriving in their offense (especially after the arrival of Steve Nash in 2004). Brown was soon out of the league and, while the Celtics and Hawks were preparing to play in the 2008 playoffs, was completing his first season in the NBA's development league.

With the Suns, Johnson's numbers rose dramatically, and once Nash arrived, he found himself on the receiving end of no-look passes and on one of the best teams in the league. The 2004–2005 Suns won 62 games, tops in the league. Nash was an MVP. Johnson averaged 17 points a game, and his three-point shooting percentage rose from 31 percent in the year before Nash to 48 percent in Nash's first year. Only three players in the league logged more minutes.

But in the second round of the playoffs, Johnson was fouled by Dallas' Jerry Stackhouse on a drive to the basket and fell face first to the floor. He got up, made one of two free throws, and then left the game. The next day, he underwent surgery to repair a displaced fracture in the bone around his left eye.

He returned to play in the final three games of the Western Conference Finals against the Spurs, wearing a protective mask. But by then, the Suns were already down 2–0 in the series and would lose in five games. There's still a belief in Phoenix that had Johnson not been hurt, the Suns might have won it all that year. He had become that critical to them.

He also was establishing a reputation around the league and that summer became a restricted free agent. The Suns held the cards in this situation; they could match any offer from another team. That ability usually scared away most teams. Atlanta however had plenty of cash to offer and showered it on Johnson, signing him to a five-year deal worth more than $67 million. To discourage the Suns from matching, the Hawks gave Johnson a signing bonus of more than $13 million, along with a first-year salary of $12 million. Thus, the financial commitment for Year 1 of the deal was more than $25 million.

Phoenix wasn't going to pay that kind of money, so a sign-and-trade deal was arranged where the Suns re-signed Johnson and then promptly traded him to the Hawks for Boris Diaw and two No. 1 picks. Johnson was going from one of the best teams in the league to one of the worst. He was going from a situation where he was an ideal wingman in an ideal system to a situation where he'd have to be Mr. Everything with the big contract. He read and heard that he'd made a huge mistake. He instead looked at it as a challenge: "If you don't believe in yourself," he said, "no one else will."

The 2007–2008 season was Johnson's third in Atlanta and he had helped lead the Hawks into the playoffs. But no one expected them to go very far or last very long. This series was seen by most as simply a tune-up for the Celtics on their way to bigger and better things. And in a roundabout way, that is exactly what it was.

"People forget that this was our first time together, in the playoffs, as a unit," Paul Pierce said of the Celtics. "It's a totally different game in the post-season. And people also forget that it had been a long time since we'd played a game that really meant anything. We just had to find ourselves again on the floor and that took some time. You have to change your game plan, and we had to try and figure out who we were again."

The Hawks were easily one of the most athletic teams in the playoffs. They could run and jump with players like Johnson, the acrobatic Josh Smith, Josh Childress, and the impressive rookie, Al Horford. Bibby supplied a steady hand. Athletic teams potentially could give the veteran Celtics some trouble, as Philadelphia and Charlotte had done in the regular season.

And Atlanta did just that, although from early appearances, it sure looked like the series was going to be a Boston blowout.

The Celtics cruised to a 23-point victory in Game 1, as the Hawks looked to be every bit the ingénue that many had predicted. Rajon Rondo had thoroughly outplayed Mike Bibby, prompting chants from the crowd of "Rondo's better, Rondo's better" every time Bibby had the ball. Rondo had prepped for his first playoff game by watching the New Orleans–Dallas series over at Ray Allen's house, with Allen's mom Flo doing the cooking.

Bibby and Rondo actually had some history together, for Mike Bibby's cousin Doug was Rondo's high school coach in Louisville. And Doug Bibby had sent Rondo out to Sacramento for a few summers to play with Mike Bibby. It was a memorable mentoring experience for Rondo. "I played with Mike a couple summers," Rondo said. "He was great to me, telling me to keep working."

Bibby had another Celtic tie-in: Eddie House was married to his sister. And considering that Rondo and Josh Smith were roommates at Oak Hill Academy, there were all kinds of story lines.

After Game 1, Bibby referred to the Boston fans as "bandwagon jumpers," which made things even more dicey for his future appearances in the TD Banknorth Garden. "I played here last year too, and I didn't see three-fourths of them. I remember them coming to games with bags on their heads," he said.

Before Game 2, another Boston rout, Kevin Garnett was named as the NBA's Defensive Player of the Year. It was no surprise. He had been the anchor on the league's top defensive team and received 90 of a possible 124 first-place votes. But it was an honor that no Celtics player had ever won, mainly because the team usually paid lip service to defense. One figured Adam Sandler would win an Oscar before a Celtic won a Defensive Player of the Year award.

Garnett changed all that. And when he was presented with the trophy before the start of Game 2, he called out his teammates to join him on the floor, bringing back memories of Olympic hockey captain Mike Eruzione at Lake Placid in 1980. Garnett had 19 points and 10 rebounds in the 96–77 Boston victory, but had missed his first seven shots. But he doesn't like attention drawn to himself, especially on the day of a game when routine is everything.

"Obviously [the presentation ceremony] is for the fans and the people to show their appreciation," Garnett said. "It is gratifying. We all have a routine and we like to stick to it, but it's cool. It wasn't that big of a distraction."

He did admit however that the pregame presentation of the 2004 MVP Trophy had been a distraction, because he had to arrive earlier than usual, chit-chat with Commissioner David Stern, and pose for a lot of pictures. "And then go out and try to prepare for a game? That wasn't easy."

Leading 2–0, the series shifted to Atlanta where, for the first time in the twenty-first century, Hawks fans got to watch playoff basketball. They showed up in droves, energized their team and made Philips Arena a charnel house for the Celtics. It was a shocking turnaround. The Celtics had been a terrific road team all season. Josh Smith, invisible in Boston in the first two games, scored 27 points in Game 3, going right at the newly minted Defensive Player of the Year in a 102–93 Atlanta victory. Al Horford nailed a big jumper with 22 seconds left, then barked at Pierce on his way back to the huddle after a Celtics timeout.

Pierce, too, started to go to the Atlanta huddle. He got about halfway there, then gave a sign with his hand, his index finger and thumb enclosed in a circle and the other three fingers pointing down. Few noticed it at the time. But the eagle-eyed guys in the NBA offices saw it, and the next day, it was announced that Pierce would be fined $25,000 for making what the league called "a menacing gesture."

Commissioner David Stern, in Atlanta for Game 4, couldn't really define what a menacing gesture really was except that he knew when he saw one. He said the league "was sending a message to one of the best players in the world to play the game." In the blogosphere, it was written that Pierce had made a gang sign of some sort, though it wasn't clear. Stu Jackson, the league's vice president of operations and de facto disciplinarian, said Pierce was fined because the NBA doesn't want players doing anything that "might incite an altercation."

Pierce denied his gesture was gang-related, going so far as to issue a statement. But the incident soon became old news when the Hawks rallied from a 10-point deficit in the fourth quarter to win Game 4, 97–92, behind 35 points from Joe Johnson. It was now a series that would go at least six games.

The Celtics came back and stomped Atlanta again in Game 5 in what was becoming a recurring theme in the series: blowout wins for the Celtics at home and close losses for the Celtics on the road. The three wins at home for Boston had been by margins of 23, 19, and 25 points. The two losses were by 9 and 5 points. By the time the Celtics went back to Atlanta, the city was mobilized and energized as never before.

"The noise in that arena was by far the loudest of any of the buildings we played in during the playoffs," said Wyc Grousbeck.

The Hawks announced on the eve of Game 6 that they had sold more than $100,000 worth of season tickets for 2008–2009. Television ratings were up 85 percent over the regular season. One sign in the arena said it all: "ATL–We Know Drama."

Then the Hawks went out and beat the Celtics again, taking a 103–100 victory. Johnson again came up big as the Celtics looked confused and discombobulated away from the friendly confines of home. Pierce fouled out and then didn't help matters by getting whistled for a technical foul for throwing his headband. Garnett was being viewed as a roundball Alex Rodriguez, a player who does wonderful things in the regular season but fails to come through in the postseason. The unthinkable was going to happen: a Game 7 between the best team in the playoffs and the worst team in the playoffs.

The Celtics had played the 2007–2008 regular season better than anyone else, but now they were being called frauds and pretenders. They were now deemed to be vulnerable, beatable, and fragile, a team that couldn't win close games on the road.

A loss to Atlanta in Game 7 would go down as one of the greatest choke jobs in the history of any sport, let alone the NBA. The Celtics had lost as many games in ten days as they did in two-and-a-half months, when they started the season 29–3. The Lakers, Pistons, Spurs, and even the Cavaliers had all won their first-round series in six games or less.

"The night before Game 7 against Atlanta was the most stressful night for me in the whole playoffs," Danny Ainge said. "We had had leads in the fourth quarters of Games 4 and 6, and we stopped playing our game. But we had played so well at home that

I felt we would have to play really, really bad to lose. Could it happen? Sure. And it would have been devastating. Absolutely devastating."

Ainge wasn't the only one who had a fitful night. Garnett and Kendrick Perkins didn't sleep. Ray Allen spent half the night sending text messages to teammates. Doc Rivers did sleep, thanks to a pill.

The Celtics' long history is littered with Game 7s, and they were 14–3 at home in such winner-take-all-affairs. But this group had not been in one together. All the pressure seemed to be on the Celtics.

Then the Celtics went out and overwhelmed the Hawks, who had that deer-in-the-headlights look throughout the game. The final score was 99–65, a true indicator of how badly Atlanta had played. The Hawks scored only 26 points in the first half. Bibby scored only 2 points. Josh Smith looked so nervous that he might as well have stayed home; he missed 8 of 11 shots and had only 7 points. Marvin Williams was ejected in the third quarter for a hard takedown of Rajon Rondo; after the series, the league announced Williams would be suspended for the 2008–2009 opener because of the foul. No Celtic played more than 33 minutes. In a series of routs at home, Game 7 was the most lopsided of them all.

Rivers had calmed his nervous team before the game, essentially reminding them of what Ainge had said: they were the better team, they were at home, they had each other's backs, and that if they just played their game, they'd win. "I just wanted to let them know that we were all right," Rivers said.

For Rivers, the Game 7 win meant he could coach another round. It was a first for him; before the victory, he had had the distinction of coaching the most playoff games without ever winning a series. That night, when he returned home, he got a call from Flip Saunders, the coach of the Pistons.

Saunders congratulated his friend, saying he could empathize. He had lost his first seven playoff series before winning one.

Rivers would go on. But the bloom was off the Celtic rose. A team with 66 victories had needed seven games to beat a team with 37 victories. A team that had played well on the road in the regular season (remember the Texas sweep?) had gone winless on the road. The thinking was if the Celtics had this much trouble against a mediocre (at best) Atlanta team, what was going to happen when they actually had to play a team that was any good?

The answer was about to come. LeBron James was coming to town.

11

LeBron and
Another Grinder

THE SEVEN-GAME SERIES AGAINST THE HAWKS had given the Celtics virtually no time to prepare for the Cleveland Cavaliers. The clinching win against Atlanta had come on a Sunday afternoon. The first game of the conference semifinal would be on Tuesday night.

Rivers cast the continuous playing in a favorable light, noting that the team plays a similar schedule during the regular season, so players are accustomed to it. But with a veteran-heavy team, there's no doubt that the coach and many of his players would have preferred to have some downtime before the next series. The Cavs had not played since eliminating Washington on the road the previous Friday, the same night the Celtics could not eliminate the Hawks on the road.

Playing Cleveland was going to be a stark contrast in style to the Hawks. The Cavs had a solid defensive mind-set and were one of the best rebounding teams in the league. They preferred a slow place, even if they had in LeBron James one of the game's most electrifying open-court performers. James had noted the previous summer how much fun it had been to play with Jason Kidd at the Olympics qualifier. "You run, he'll find you," James said of Kidd. "That's the best part of my game, running the floor. I don't have that luxury in Cleveland, so this is a treat for me. It's going to be tough to go back to the way we play in Cleveland."

But that was how Cavaliers coach Mike Brown did it, and it was hard to argue with his record. In his first three years, Brown already had recorded the best winning percentage of any coach in Cleveland history, which unfortunately said as much about the sorry affairs of the Cavs than it did about Brown's coaching ability. Still, in the spring of 2008, the Cavs were one of only three teams in the Eastern Conference to have made the playoffs from 2006–2008, the others being the Pistons and the Wizards. And in Brown's tenure, only five teams in the league had better records from 2005–2008, and only one of those, the Pistons, was in the Eastern Conference.

But the 2007–2008 season had proven to be the toughest for Brown, whose first two Cavaliers teams had each won 50 games in the regular season. The team tied a franchise record with 23 players appearing in at least one game, a record held by the immortal 1981–1982 Cavaliers, who had gone 15–67. That team was owned by Ted Stepien, among the most universally ridiculed and inept NBA owners in league history. Due to the Cavs' trading ways under Stepien—at one point, Cleveland traded its No. 1 draft pick in five straight seasons, 1982–1986—the NBA instituted what's now known as the Ted Stepien Rule, which prevents a team from trading No. 1 picks in successive seasons. It was a rule intended to save Stepien from himself. Eventually, Stepien sold the team to the Gund brothers, Gordon and George, who in turn sold it to present owner Dan Gilbert in 2006.

The Cavs had overcome early-season holdouts from valuable rotation players Anderson Varejão and Sasha Pavlovic and then, shortly before the trading deadline expired, pulled off a huge three-way deal with Chicago and Seattle that netted them Wally Szczerbiak, Delonte West, Joe Smith, and Ben Wallace. That deal, while not of the magnitude of the Celtics' deals for Allen and Garnett, or even the Lakers' earlier theft of Pau Gasol from the Memphis Grizzlies, seemed to put Cleveland in much better position to make a run at a second straight Eastern Conference championship. James, who, like Paul Pierce, had been pleading for better teammates for some time, even appeared mollified.

The Cavs didn't fear the Celtics either, having beaten them twice in Cleveland (once without Garnett), while losing twice in Boston (once without James and once when the Celtics were on their ten-game tear in February and March). New additions Wallace and Smith could help with the interior defense. Szczerbiak supplied some outside shooting. West, while not your classic point guard, was an upgrade at the position, something that would soon be apparent when he was put in the starting lineup.

While the trade appeared to improve the Cavaliers on paper, they actually had a lower winning percentage after the deal (15–13) than before the deal (30–24). And before the deal, 6 of those 24 losses had come in games James had missed due to a finger injury. (He was hurt in a blowout loss at Detroit on November 28 and then missed the next five games.) But Wallace and Smith did improve the team's already strong defense and rebounding numbers and all four newcomers had gradually worked their way into a new system.

Constantly throughout the year, Doc Rivers had talked wistfully about what the Cavaliers (and Pistons) had done in years past, while his Celtics had in fact done nothing. The Cavaliers had defied the odds and somehow gotten to the 2007 NBA Finals, where they were promptly broomed by the San Antonio Spurs. They had gotten that far thanks to a favorable draw (playing the injury-ravaged Wizards and the Nets) and then improbably rallying from a 2–0 deficit against Detroit to take four straight.

The victory over the Pistons featured what still may be James' single greatest game and undeniably one of the greatest individual performances in NBA playoff history. In Game 5, he scored 48 points in a 109–107 double-overtime victory. But he also scored 29 of Cleveland's last 30 and the last 25 overall, something no other player has ever done in NBA playoff history. The Cavs then went home and got a surprising 31 points from rookie Daniel Gibson in Game 6, 19 in the fourth quarter, to send the bewildered Pistons home. But the Cavaliers were no match for the efficient, experienced Spurs, whose success and philosophy Brown had attempted to replicate in Cleveland. He had worked under San Antonio coach Gregg Popovich for three seasons.

The Cavs had then defeated the Wizards in six games in the first round in 2008—the third straight year they had eliminated Washington—and then turned their attention to Boston. And Boston turned its attention, unavoidably, to LeBron.

———————

PROBABLY NO TEAM IN THE LEAGUE depended on one player more than the Cavaliers depended on LeBron James. Kobe Bryant and the Lakers might be the closest comparison, but it would be hard to imagine the Cavs leading a quality team by more than 20 points in the first half of a big playoff game without a basket from James. (The Lakers did that in Game 4 of the 2008 Finals.)

James was coming off a truly historic season, even by his own lofty standards. In his fifth year in the NBA, James led the league in scoring, averaging 30 points a game, becoming the first Cavalier player to do so. He also averaged 7.9 rebounds and 7.2 assists, meaning he accounted for no fewer than 44 points a game. Only Oscar Robertson and Michael Jordan had ever averaged as many points, rebounds, and assists in a season.

He became the franchise's all-time leading scorer in March— in less than five full seasons—surpassing Brad Daugherty, who had

played in 134 more games than James. He became the first player
in four years to have triple-doubles in consecutive games and the
first player in 20 years to do it twice in the same season. He was
the MVP of the All-Star Game for the second time in three years.
And he still was only 23 years old, even though he had the body and
look of someone much older. Paul Pierce called him a beast, as
high a compliment as an opposing player could make.

James had been a household name in basketball circles well
before he set foot in the NBA, directly out of St. Vincent–St. Mary
High School in Akron, Ohio. In his freshman year, word about a
15-year-old phenom from Ohio filtered out of summer camps as
James played as good or better than players three years older.

He started as a freshman in high school at six-foot-two.
The team went undefeated and won the state title. He grew to
six-foot-six by the time he was a sophomore and again led
St. Vincent–St. Mary to the state title. He was voted Ohio's
Mr. Basketball as a sophomore. By this time, even his high
school coach was telling smitten college coaches to forget about
it; James was not even going to consider college.

Then James truly became a national celebrity when *Sports
Illustrated* put him on its cover during his junior season. The cover
had the words "The Chosen One" with a big picture of James. In
the article, Danny Ainge, then working for TNT, was quoted as
saying, "There are only four or five players in the NBA I wouldn't
trade to get LeBron James right now."

It was widely assumed at the time that had James been eligible
for the NBA draft, he would have gone No. 1 overall, even ahead
of the No. 1 pick in 2002, Yao Ming. But he had to wait another
year due to NBA age rules.

Back for one final year at St. Vincent–St. Mary, James and the
basketball team became a truly national phenomenon, a traveling
road show not unlike Oak Hill Academy—with one big difference.
ESPN picked up a couple of James' games, including one against
Oak Hill, then undefeated. St. Vincent–St. Mary won the game.

Their home games were moved to the University of Akron to accommodate the overflow crowds of up to 5,500. (At the same time, the Cavaliers had fewer than 2,000 season ticket holders.) Some of their games were even put on regional cable, pay-per-view. And it wasn't to see Willie McGree, Sian Cotton, or Dru Joyce III. It was to see LeBron, who even back then had become such a force that he had now entered the company of other celebrities for whom one name sufficed.

Senior year had James holding formal press conferences due to an unusually high number of media outlets covering his games. His team again won the state title, and it wasn't because James had a lot of help. There were no national recruits, like at Oak Hill, on this team. It was an Akron-based team, and only two players went on to play any meaningful time at a Division I school—the University of Akron.

There were however some controversies for James that year. His team forfeited a couple of games when it was revealed he accepted throwback uniform jerseys in exchange for autographed pictures. He also was seen driving around in a Hummer, purchased for him by his mother, who was 16 at the time LeBron was born. (James' father has never been publicly identified.) It was rumored that Gloria James leveraged her son's future fortune, which no doubt was going to be substantial, to pay for the vehicle. Nothing came of L'Affaire Hummer in part because LeBron James' future provided surefire collateral.

Then, shortly before the May draft lottery, James really struck gold, signing a $100 million deal with Nike. The Oregon-based shoe/apparel giant had beat out Reebok and adidas, even though adidas had longtime James' friend Sonny Vaccaro pushing its product. But adidas wouldn't go where Nike went. James had always idolized Michael Jordan, and this was his chance, and the company's, to pick up where Jordan had left off.

James then fell into the hands of the Cavs when Cleveland won the 2003 draft lottery. Only a month earlier he had held a news conference to announce he was entering his name in the NBA draft. Then when the Ping-Pong balls delivered James to Cleveland, things started to change almost overnight, for what then was one of the NBA's most sorry franchises. Cleveland had been dead last in the league in attendance in 2002–2003 and had gone 17–65.

By the time the Cavaliers were preparing to play the Celtics in the spring of 2008, they ranked third in league attendance, averaging 20,465 a game with 30-plus sellouts in each of the last three seasons. Only four teams drew better on the road than the Cavs.

James had already made the case that he was among the most physically talented individuals to ever play the game. But like Paul Pierce, Ray Allen, and Kevin Garnett, he was missing that one career-defining piece of jewelry—a championship ring. He had come closer than the other three, which in 2008 made him all the hungrier.

THE FIRST SIX GAMES of the Boston–Cleveland series played out the same way as the first six games of the Boston–Atlanta series, with a few minor tweaks. The teams all won their home games, although the Cavaliers were much more competitive than Atlanta had been in Boston, and the Celtics were a lot less competitive in Cleveland than they had been in Atlanta.

James had two lamentable games to start the series, going 2-of-18 in the opener, which the Celtics won, 76–72, and then following up with a marginally better performance, going 6-of-24 in a 16-point defeat, 89–73.

The two poor performances somewhat overshadowed a puzzling shooting slump on the part of Ray Allen, who had taken only four shots in 37 minutes of Game 1 and missed them all and then was 4-of-10 in Game 2. Cleveland had made a decision before the series started: they were going to focus on Allen, who had averaged a team-high 23.8 points a game in the four regular-season games, while shooting 52 percent from the field. Someone else was going to have to beat them.

"They took away most of the opportunities I had," Allen said. "I wasn't getting my normal number of shots a game. If I missed six or seven shots in a game before, it was no big deal because I was taking 15, 16, 17 shots. But I was only shooting seven or eight times a game against Cleveland. It was a matter of me trying to do the other things to help the team win. That's how it was in my eyes. I never really saw it as a slump. I saw it as me not getting enough looks, not getting enough shots. My routine never changed. I didn't change anything. But it was frustrating."

Most everyone else saw it as a slump, mainly because every time Allen elevates for a shot, you think it's going in. But his numbers in the Cleveland series were indeed dreadful. He never made more than four baskets in any of the seven games. He never took more than 12 shots in any of the seven games. He never scored more than 16 points in any of the seven games. He averaged 9.3 points a game while shooting 32.8 percent from the field and a very unAllen-like 16.7 percent from three-point range. When you're talking about Ray Allen, those numbers constitute a slump.

The Cavs rallied to tie the series, blowing the Celtics out in Game 3 and then winning Game 4 by 11 in a game in which James, who scored 21, delivered a thunderous tomahawk dunk on Kevin Garnett in the closing minutes. There also was a humorous incident late in the game when Paul Pierce, grabbing James to prevent a layup, carried him into the courtside seats, where James' mother Gloria was sitting. As she barked at Pierce, James snapped at her and told her to zip it, using words, he later admitted, that a son should never use when speaking to his mother.

With the series knotted 2–2, Cleveland proceeded to take a 14-point lead in the second quarter of Game 5, making the TD Banknorth Garden a very nervous place. James already had

23 points and finally appeared to be having the big game that many felt was long overdue. But Boston got offense from an unexpected source, with Rajon Rondo hitting two big three-pointers before the half, making it just a three-point Cleveland lead at the break. The Celtics then overran the Cavaliers in the second half and won, 96–89.

Before leaving TD Banknorth Garden, James said, "A LeBron James team is never desperate." Then in Game 6, he scored 32 points in a 74–69 Cleveland win. (Ray Allen wasn't the only one slumping. The Celtics averaged 100.5 points a game in the regular season, but only 84 a game against the Cavaliers. The slower pace was definitely affecting them.)

The stage was set for another Game 7 in Boston, and this would prove to be an epic, recalling memories of another Game 7, 20 years earlier, in which Larry Bird and Dominique Wilkins had gone mano a mano, with the Celtics barely surviving, 118–116. This time around, the two protagonists would be James and Paul Pierce.

While James had had his early troubles in the series, he had righted things with some 30-point games. Pierce, on the other hand, had not presented himself to be anything close to a worthy offensive match, maybe in part because he spent so much time trying to stop James from scoring. He had averaged only 14 points a game in three losses in Cleveland and had scored only 4 points in Game 1. But Allen's shooting woes had been more pronounced and thus had gained more attention.

But when Game 7 rolled around, Pierce was ready. He had 9 of the Celtics first 14 points, getting the Celtics off to an early lead they would never relinquish. He had 26 points at the half and 35 after three quarters. All the while, James was humming the classic Irving Berlin tune, "Anything You Can Do, I Can Do Better." While Pierce would finish with 41 points, James would end up with 45. And after he stole the ball from Pierce with 2:20 left and went in for a rim-rattling dunk, the Cavaliers trailed by only a point, 89–88.

While James and Pierce were the unquestioned alpha players on this day, combining for 45 percent of the points in the game, another hero emerged for the Celtics in the final two minutes. Without two big plays by P.J. Brown, Boston might never have advanced. The first came with 2:45 left, when Brown rebounded a short Rajon Rondo air ball and laid it in. "Right place at the right time," Brown said. "Just like my whole career."

But the second basket was even bigger. After James missed a three-pointer that would have given Cleveland the lead, Brown was at his favorite spot, the elbow, about 15 feet away as the shot-clock was winding down.

"My job was to get Eddie [House] open, and I thought I set a great screen to do just that," Brown said. "You knew the Cavs were going to swarm Paul, Ray, and Kevin. I thought I got Eddie pretty open and when Eddie is open, he usually shoots it. I don't know why I didn't go to the basket then, because he always shoots it. But I stayed where I was and then I saw that he was sending it back to me.

"I've taken that shot a million times, and I didn't even think about it," Brown continued. "You could feel the tension in the building after LeBron had stolen the ball, and I have to believe a lot of people were holding their breath even more when they saw P.J. Brown take this shot with 1:20 left in the game. But you don't think like that. You just shoot it."

Needless to say, he made it, restoring Boston's tenuous three-point lead. James missed again and the Celtics sealed it with Ray Allen, House, and Pierce all making two free throws the rest of the way. The Celtics had done it again, though not as easily as before, winning Game 7, 97–92.

Pierce's day belonged in the vault of clutch Celtics playoff performances, certainly his best under the circumstances. In addition to the 41 points, he had 5 assists and 2 steals. He made 11 of 12 free throws. "It probably outshines anything else because of the stage it was on and the fact that it was a Game 7," he said.

Pierce would later say that he was looking forward to a massage and a hot tub after Game 7. As was the case in the previous series, the Celtics having to go seven games cut down their preparation time against their next foe, the Pistons, who had been off for more than a week after eliminating the Orlando Magic.

Detroit would be rested. Detroit was battle-tested. Detroit had already won once in Boston in the regular season, something neither Atlanta nor Cleveland had been able to do. Detroit had no fear whatsoever of the Celtics and had been looking forward to playing them in exactly this situation—the Eastern Conference Finals.

12

The Real NBA Finals

A S FAR BACK AS AUGUST, or after Kevin Garnett had been traded to the Celtics, the players on the Pistons and the Celtics had been gearing up for a much-anticipated showdown in the Eastern Conference Finals. It seemed almost preordained.

The Celtics had the best record in the NBA. The Pistons had the second best record. The Pistons led the league in points allowed per game. The Celtics were second in points allowed per game.

You could easily make the case, despite the obvious depth and strength of the marquee teams in the Western Conference, that the league's two best teams resided in the Eastern Conference and that a playoff series between the two would be the equivalent of the NBA Finals.

The current Pistons represented a standard of excellence that the current Celtics were only hoping to emulate. Detroit was appearing in its sixth consecutive conference final, matching the

Lakers for the most such appearances since the 16-team playoff format was introduced in 1984. They had done so under three different coaches, the latest being Flip Saunders, who had coached Garnett for most of Garnett's career in Minnesota.

The Pistons had won 50 or more games in seven straight seasons and had 59 victories in 2007–2008, only seven fewer than the Celtics. They were 22–8 against the Western Conference (the Celtics were 25–5) and for the third straight year ranked No. 1 in the NBA in fewest turnovers committed per game.

Beyond the recent superb play of the two teams, there were more than a few story lines that would be examined (and reexamined) in a series between the teams. Chauncey Billups, arguably the Pistons' best player, had been one of the most vocal advocates for pushing Garnett to accept a trade to Boston. The two were very good friends.

Billups had started his career in Boston and even spent some time in Orlando when Rivers was the head coach. Saunders and Doc Rivers had coached a United States national team in the 2001 Goodwill Games in Australia. Saunders was the head coach, Rivers the top assistant.

When Richard Hamilton was considering colleges, one of the people who showed him the alluring sights of Storrs, Connecticut, was Ray Allen. Now, both UConn legends, they'd be guarding each other in the series.

There also was the history element, although it was pretty much ancient history to the players involved in 2008. The last time the teams had met in the playoffs was in 2002, when the Celtics won in five games. Paul Pierce was the only player on either team who played in that particular series.

The two franchises waged some epic battles in the 1980s and 1990s, with the Celtics prevailing in 1985 and 1987, and the Pistons coming out on top in 1988, 1990, and 1991. The 1987 Eastern Conference Finals resulted in a grueling, bruising seven-game series between two teams that did not like each other. It was a series that featured Robert Parish punching out Bill Laimbeer, Larry Bird stealing the ball from Isiah Thomas to save Game 5, and Pistons players Vinnie Johnson and Adrian Dantley bumping heads in a collision in Game 7, with Dantley getting taken to the hospital. After the Celtics had finally prevailed in Game 7, Dennis Rodman declared that Bird would be just another player, had he not been a Caucasian. Isiah Thomas seconded Rodman.

That series however marked a turning point of sorts. The two teams met again in the conference finals in 1988, and it was the Pistons who ended Boston's reign of the 1980s by winning in six games, taking the clincher in a raucous Pontiac Silverdome. The Celtics needed 15 years to reach their next conference finals and then another six to do so again. This time, however, the Celtics had the home-court advantage.

Boston had won two of the three games played between the teams during the regular season, including the huge January 5 victory at the Palace of Auburn Hills. The Pistons, however, had been the first team to beat the newly constituted Celtics in Boston.

But those results meant nothing when the series opened in Boston on May 20. The Celtics again had only a day to prepare, having been stretched to seven games by the Cavaliers. The Pistons had been off for a week, after dispatching Orlando in five games.

What did mean something however was the status of Billups, who had strained his hamstring in Game 3 of the series against Orlando and missed the rest of that game and the final two games. That game had been played on May 7, so Billups had almost two weeks of inactivity before the series with the Celtics began. But hamstrings can be very balky and if Billups was still bothered by the injury, he was not about to tell anyone. One would have to wait until the games began.

———————

Chauncey billups' nba story was one of missteps, wrong decisions, and bad situations but ultimately one of perseverance and triumph. There was a time in his career when he was available to just about anyone for a very reasonable price. He was one step removed from being Eddie House, trying to latch on to whatever team wanted him, unable to find employment in any one location for more than two years. He came in with high expectations, the third pick in the 1997 NBA draft, which happened to be Rick Pitino's first draft as the head coach and president of the Celtics.

Pitino soon soured on Billups for one main reason—he wasn't a classic point guard. (That Pitino didn't know that when he drafted him is a bit surprising.) Celtics legend Bob Cousy told Pitino he thought Billups would never become a classic point guard, although he thought Billups had NBA skills. Pitino decided to jettison Billups in February after only 51 games, dealing him to Toronto for Kenny Anderson, a point guard, but a vastly overrated and vastly overpaid one.

From there, Billups was dealt to Denver, which was home for him, having played at George Washington High where he led the team to a pair of state titles, and then attending college for two years down the road at the University of Colorado at Boulder. His stint with the Nuggets didn't work out too well either, and in February 2000, he was traded to Orlando. He was one of the many "just passing through" players who would soon be gone to make way for the Magic's run at Tim Duncan in the summer of 2000. But he made an impression on Orlando's first-year head coach, Doc Rivers.

"I had him for three months," Rivers recalled. "He never played in a game because he was injured, but that's when I became very fond of him. He knew when he was traded to us that he was injured, that he wasn't going to play, that he would probably go somewhere else at the end of the season. Yet he didn't miss a practice. He didn't miss a meeting. He actually spoke up at times. And from that day forward, I had the utmost respect for him because I don't think a lot of guys would have done that. He came and worked out every day, did his rehab every day along with everybody else. I thought that not only meant a lot to me personally, but it was really important to our team. And I've told him that many times."

Orlando, as expected, let him go and he signed as a free agent in Minnesota. After two seasons with the Timberwolves, however, his coach at the time, Flip Saunders, convinced General Manager Kevin McHale to let Billups go because Billups wasn't a classic point guard. To his everlasting dismay, McHale acceded to his coach's wishes and allowed Billups to become a free agent in 2003.

The Pistons then swooped in, with a two-pronged attack led by coach Rick Carlisle and general manager Joe Dumars. They didn't care that Billups wasn't a classic point guard. Dumars saw a lot of Billups in himself, an old-fashioned guard-guard who could play either backcourt position, but didn't fall neatly into one category or the other. Billups had good size and lived for the big moments.

"A lot of coaches didn't know if he was a point guard or a [shooting guard]," Rivers said. "I never even got a chance to look at him. But I think what everyone found out was that he was a heckuva basketball player."

The Pistons gave Billups something no other team did— security. They signed him to a five-year deal. Two years into the deal, the Pistons stunned everyone and won the NBA championship, upsetting the heavily favored Lakers in five games. Billups was named the Most Valuable Player in the NBA Finals. They almost pulled it off the next year, losing to San Antonio in seven games.

Billups has been viewed as a borderline elite player ever since, participating in three All-Star Games, becoming just the third player in NBA history to make an All-Star debut after having played for five different teams. The other two are Anthony Mason and Sam Cassell. Billups played for the United States national team in the 2007 Olympic qualifier and was a likely member of the 2008

Olympic team, had he not decided to withdraw for personal reasons. He made a couple of All-NBA and All-Defensive teams.

In the summer of 2007, he re-signed with the Pistons for five more years, returning the loyalty they showed him in 2002. In his first six seasons with the Pistons, he played in 461 games, starting every one of them.

"When I signed, I signed with the expectation it was pretty much established I was going to finish my career a Piston," Billups said. "Now you never know what can happen. This is the NBA, this is basketball, this is business; you never know what can happen. But it was understood that's why I was signing—to end my career as a Detroit Piston. That's what it was all about and that's why I did it."

In 2007–2008, Billups was second to backcourt mate Richard Hamilton in team scoring, while leading the team in assists and steals. He and Hamilton, who came to the Pistons in separate deals nearly two months apart in 2002, formed one of the best backcourts in the league. Healthy, they were as good as it got in the NBA. But as the 2008 Eastern Conference Finals approached, no one was sure just how healthy Billups really was.

———————

ASIDE FROM BILLUPS' HAMSTRING, the overriding question going into Game 1 was whether the well-rested Pistons would be able to take advantage of the supposedly fatigued Celtics and steal Game 1 in Boston. They couldn't. Kevin Garnett made big plays down the stretch, and Billups looked substantially less than 100 percent as the Celtics won, 88–79. The only concern for Boston was Ray Allen's continuing shooting woes; he was 3-of-10. Two nights later, Detroit evened the series dealing the Celtics their first home loss of the playoffs. Hamilton scored 25. Billups, with 19, looked more like the Billups of old, although he aggravated the hamstring late in the game. Ray Allen appeared to come out of his slump, scoring 25, including his first three-pointer since Game 5 of the Cleveland series. But the Pistons made the big plays down the stretch.

The Detroit victory in Game 2 now put the Celtics into a must-win situation on the road, something they had not faced against either Atlanta or Cleveland. In hindsight, Doc Rivers considered it almost a blessing to have lost in Game 2, because it forced the team to focus on getting a road win or else their season would be over.

"There was a different sense of urgency after that game, where we knew we had to win on the road," he said. "Our security blanket had been taken away. I always felt that we would win on the road. I just didn't know that we'd *have* to win on the road."

Faced with a new predicament, the Celtics came up big in Game 3, led by Garnett, and won easily, building a 24-point lead and taking a 94–80 victory. The Pistons looked stale, weary, inexcusably flat, and Billups again looked like he was bothered by his leg, managing only 6 points. Now it was the Pistons' turn to rally and, with an appreciative home crowd behind them, they came back to tie the series with a rousing 94–75 victory. Antonio McDyess had 21 points and 16 rebounds for the Pistons, while the Celtics shot horribly (31.6 percent) and stayed competitive only because of a major imbalance in free throw attempts (39 to 26).

That set the stage for what would be another epic game in the TD Banknorth Garden. When the Celtics took the floor, the cold-shooting Allen, who had been 2-of-8 from the field in Game 4, was seen sporting a long white sleeve on his left arm. Was it a response to his shooting woes, even though it was on his nonshooting arm? Absolutely not.

"It was because Rip was living up to his nickname," Allen said of the Pistons Richard Hamilton. "He doesn't cut his fingernails. You ask anyone around the league and they'll tell you that he has the longest fingernails of anyone. I had these scratches and bumps and welts all over my body, and after every game, I'd find these new scratches on my arm. He'd dig those nails into my arm trying to get around a screen or bump me off a play, and then I just figured I had to do something about it. After I put the sleeve on, he couldn't dig into it anymore."

But while Allen wore the sleeve out of self-preservation, fans and others noted a remarkable coincidence: his shooting eye had returned at the same time. He had 29 points, including a huge basket in the final 62 seconds.

The Celtics had come out with a purpose and got some Chamberlain-esque play from Kendrick Perkins, who out-rebounded the entire Pistons team in the first half. He finished with 18 points and 16 rebounds. The Celtics used an overwhelming rebounding edge to build a 17-point lead in the third, with Allen scoring 16 points in the quarter, then watched in horror as the Pistons chipped away, gradually pulling to within a point with 83 seconds remaining on a three-pointer by precocious Detroit rookie Rodney Stuckey.

Then it was Allen time. With the Celtics nursing a one-point lead and the shot-clock winding down, Allen found himself in the left corner, with Theo Ratliff flying out at him to contest his shot. He let it go. In the previous two weeks, Celtics fans might have winced at that scenario, although his teammates had never lost faith. Garnett had approached Allen during the shooting slump and in his own inimitable fashion said, "Hey, bleep, bleep. Shoot the bleep bleep." Asked to sanitize the remarks, Garnett said, "I don't have a clean version."

But Allen had made 8 of 14 shots to that point and 5 of 6 three-pointers, and circumstances dictated that he shoot this one. It went down, giving Boston a three-point lead with 1:02 to play. He and Garnett then made free throws, and the Celtics escaped with a 106–102 victory.

All that remained now for yet another seven-game extravaganza was for the Pistons to hold service at home. Before the game, the NBA announced that Rasheed Wallace, who had been alternately good and invisible over five games, had been fined $25,000 for criticizing the officiating in Game 4, the game where the Celtics had a seemingly endless parade to the free-throw line. "The cats are flopping all over the floor, and they're calling that," Wallace said of the Game 4 officials. "That ain't basketball out there. It's all entertainment. You all should know that."

Many of Wallace's hefty paychecks have had an "NBA Fine" line in the deductions section; he is always among the league leaders in technical fouls and was one technical away of getting suspended for a game in the Celtics series. Maybe that's why he came up so flaccid in Game 6, with just 4 points and 3 turnovers. He might as well have called in sick.

Still, despite Wallace's no-show, the other Pistons did play, and early in the fourth quarter, Detroit led by 10. It appeared to one and all that there would be another Game 7 in the Celtics' future. But Pierce got on a roll, and the Celtics went on a 19–4 run to lead by five. It was a four-point Boston lead with 1:40 left when James Posey surprised Tayshaun Prince, coming in from behind to steal the ball, giving the Celtics another 24 seconds. It may have been the play that sealed the game—and the series.

Clutch steals have been a big part of Celtics playoff lore, from John Havlicek's celebrated theft in Game 7 of the 1965 Eastern Conference Finals, to Gerald Henderson's steal of a James Worthy pass in Game 2 of the 1984 NBA Finals, to Larry Bird's steal of Isiah Thomas' inbound pass in Game 5 of the 1987 Eastern Conference Finals.

Posey was soon getting tons of text messages about the play, and of course the steal was prominently and repeatedly shown on television over the next 24 hours, along with the other three. This one soon had its own place in Celtics history. "I mean, you look at the season he had, and it seemed like every single game, he made three or four James Posey plays that helped win the game," Celtics principal owner Wyc Grousbeck said.

The steal helped the Celtics hold on, and they won, 89–81. It was Boston's first conference championship since 1987. In a jubilant

Boston locker room, John Havlicek and Grousbeck accepted the conference trophy. Garnett, Pierce, and Allen all reflected on going somewhere they'd never been before and how rewarding it was to have done it together for the very first time.

But as the tee shirts and hats were being passed out, and the celebratory talk continued, it was Posey who rose and demanded to be heard. He had been here before, two years earlier, and was doing a lot of the same things that his teammates were doing. Then, Shaquille O'Neal had risen in the Miami locker room and reminded his Heat teammates that they really hadn't won anything yet. Now it was Posey's turn to say the same thing.

"I remember Shaq telling me that it was just getting started," Posey said. "He told me it was OK to be excited, but let's not forget what the ultimate goal is—to win it all. I just tried to put it out there in the [Celtics] locker room because everyone was so excited. I told them the same thing Shaq told me: 'Yeah, this is cool, but we didn't play for this. We play to win a championship. We still have work to do. Sure, it's all right to be excited and happy as far as making it to the Finals. But it's just a beginning.'"

There was indeed more work to do. A lot more. The NBA Finals awaited, with Kobe Bryant, the league's Most Valuable Player, determined to prove he could win a title for the Lakers without Shaquille O'Neal. He had never had the chance before.

But in the week leading up to the NBA's showcase series, more than a few people believed he and the Lakers would do it in 2008.

13

Finishing the Race

FROM THE END OF THE EASTERN CONFERENCE FINALS until the start of the NBA Finals, sports aficionados and so-called experts from around the country weighed in on the likely outcome of the Boston–Los Angeles series.

The overwhelming sentiment: it would be a cruise for the Lakers.

Las Vegas installed the Lakers as 2 to 1 favorites. A panel of eight "experts" from ESPN.com picked the Lakers by a margin of 7 to 1. The Lakers had the best player, Kobe Bryant. The Lakers had the best coach, Phil Jackson. The Lakers had blown through the best conference, the Western. To many, Los Angeles was an obvious favorite.

But those who boarded the Lakers' bandwagon had not been paying real close attention to the Celtics. Yes, they had struggled mightily, some might even say unnecessarily, to eliminate Atlanta and Cleveland. But how could anyone not come away impressed with the way they dispatched Detroit, who had the league's second best record?

Once the Celtics had eliminated Detroit, Danny Ainge felt the hardest part of the post-season had just been completed. He didn't see any way the Celtics would lose to the Lakers.

"I was concerned about Cleveland because they played good defense and they had played us tough all year," Ainge said. "And because LeBron is so scary. But I felt Detroit was going to be our biggest challenge. And I told Wyc, 'If we can get by Detroit, we're going to win it.'"

Sitting in his office two days before the start of the NBA Finals, Doc Rivers too had heard about all the Laker love out there. "I like where we are," he said. "I'm confident." He did however concede that his players might take offense at all the pro-Laker predictions.

"They do care," Rivers said "You can use it (as a motivational tool), but at the end of the day you've still got to play basketball. Whether they pick you or don't, you still have to play basketball. But guys take it personal, they do. They understand that eight out of ten, nine out of ten people have picked the Lakers. Whatever. Like I told them at the start of the year, the questions will never stop. They'll never stop about Rondo, they'll never stop about me, they'll never stop about Kevin, they'll never stop about Paul, they'll never stop about our team, and you can't take any of it personally. It's part of it. Just go out and just keep playing, and that's all you can do. You can control it with your play."

The most glaring concern for the Celtics—or any Lakers' opponent—was the multidimensional, multitalented Bryant, whose play in 2007–2008 earned him his first Most Valuable Player award. Bryant had come a long way since the Celtics worked him out prior to the 1996 draft, an occasion that then coach/general manager M.L. Carr still remembers quite well.

"His workout was off the charts," Carr said. "But his interview was even better. We were really, really impressed with the kid."

But Bryant ended up going to Los Angeles and now, in his twelfth season with the Lakers, appeared to be one of the few superstars who would play for one team throughout his entire career.

Doc Rivers worried that Bryant had the talent and drive to single-handedly take over a series, as Hakeem Olajuwon had done to Rivers' San Antonio Spurs in 1995. But Rivers also knew his team. He knew how it had handled Bryant during the regular season. He just couldn't see Bryant asserting his will on the Celtics.

The Celtics had easily beaten the Lakers in their two regular-season meetings, though Pau Gasol, who had been acquired on February 1 from Memphis, had yet to join the team. So, the thinking went, the Celtics had not seen the *real* Lakers, the Lakers who, with Gasol roaming the middle, had finished the season going 29–9 over the final 38 games, while emerging as the No. 1 seed in the Western Conference.

But, the Celtics countered, they had been missing Rajon Rondo for the second meeting and had won convincingly in the Staples Center, even though they had played Utah the night before while the Lakers were off. And didn't the Lakers have Andrew Bynum for both of those games? The whiz-kid center who was smothered by Kendrick Perkins? And hadn't Bryant shot 15-of-46 against the vaunted Boston defense?

"I think after the Cleveland and Detroit series, that's when I thought we found ourselves," Pierce said. "We had won big games. We had won on the road. It just took us a little longer because we were so new to all this and new to each other."

REGARDLESS OF WHO WAS FAVORED, the NBA was getting a dream NBA Finals. The Lakers and the Celtics together accounted for more than half of the NBA titles and were the two Goliaths of the league. The franchises had cachet, star appeal, and a history that dated back half a century, when the Lakers were in Minneapolis. It was without question the matchup that just about every basketball fan wanted to see.

"Even though the names have changed as players and coaches, when you think about it, most fans around the world who watch basketball, if you ask them what team would they want to see in the finals, they would pick these two teams," said Lakers Hall of Famer Earvin "Magic" Johnson.

To many current sports fans, the Lakers–Celtics rivalry meant two names: Magic and Larry. Magic Johnson and Larry Bird had played against each other three times in the 1980s, with the Celtics winning in 1984 and the Lakers triumphing in 1985 and 1987. Those two individuals were credited with saving the NBA, for in the early 1980s, the league was so discredited that it had to put the Finals on tape delay because no one bothered to watch. Casual fans thought the NBA a drug-infested league whose players did not (or could not) relate to the ticket-paying fan.

Bird and Johnson changed all that, starting with the electrifying seven-game series in 1984. From then on, Boston–LA was must-see viewing, whether it was the two regular-season games or the playoffs. In 1985, the teams actually played each other four times in the exhibition season, which led to an altercation in one of the games.

"It was always the Celtics and the Lakers," Bird said. "That's really how we were taught."

Johnson wholeheartedly concurred. "Our team was into it big-time," he said of the rivalry with the Celtics. "We didn't sleep for two weeks [before] playing them. We talked about it every day. That's all we watched. Where are the Celtics? We didn't even bother celebrating when we won the Western Conference Finals because that was nothing to us. It was about beating Boston, winning the championship, looking forward to playing them. That's how our team was. We always wanted to play the best. And so did the Celtics."

But the Lakers–Celtics rivalry had sprouted long before Bird or Johnson ever thought about the game. The teams met seven times in the NBA Finals between 1959 and 1969. The Celtics, with the great Bill Russell leading the way, won all seven of those series.

The 1959 Finals, when the Lakers were still in Minneapolis, resulted in a four-game sweep, the first in NBA Finals history. The Celtics needed only five games to win the 1965 NBA Finals, taking the clincher by a 33-point margin. But the Lakers came agonizingly close in 1962, losing Game 7 in Boston in overtime, and in 1969, when Los Angeles had leads of 2–0 and 3–2 and still couldn't finish off the Celtics. On the night of Game 7 in 1969, Lakers owner Jack Kent Cooke had balloons ready to be released from the rafters of the LA Sports Arena once the Lakers won. A 108–106 Celtics triumph ensured the balloons never left the rafters.

Russell retired after that game, and the Celtics–Lakers rivalry went dormant. Los Angeles finally got its first NBA title in 1972 and then, with the arrival of Johnson and Kareem Abdul-Jabbar, would win five more in the 1980s, while Bird's Celtics claimed three. Rosters back then were stocked with future Hall of Famers or should-be Hall of Famers, and the games were rough and tumble. Neither side won again until Bryant and Shaquille O'Neal combined for three more for the Lakers from 2000 to 2002. By that time, the league had added six new teams, diluting the talent base.

Hoop historians will look back on the 1980s as the golden era of the NBA, an era where the caliber of play stood by itself, when there was no need for mascots, eardrum-splitting music, boisterous public address announcers, or clueless fans hoping to see their mugs on overhead scoreboards. It was all about basketball back then. By the time 2008 rolled around, basketball had long been supplanted by entertainment. In that sense, Rasheed Wallace was correct. It was all about the entertainment.

The celtics and lakers represented an entertaining pairing, to be sure. Among the Celtics, only James Posey and Sam Cassell had ever been to an NBA Finals. The Lakers had Kobe Bryant and Derek Fisher from the championship teams earlier in the decade, but their team was similarly devoid of grizzled playoff veterans. But, the Lakers did have the really grizzled Phil Jackson, who was coaching in his eleventh NBA Finals and was determined to add a tenth championship to his Hall of Fame résumé, one more than Celtics legend Red Auerbach.

Jackson's pursuit of a record tenth NBA championship was one more story line, a story line the Celtics were determined would not get written on their watch. Jackson had irritated Auerbach, who felt it had come too easy for the coach nicknamed Big Chief Triangle. Jackson had played for the Knicks, and Auerbach hated everything about the franchise (even though he came close to join-ing the Knicks in the late 1970s). But there would be no tweaking of Auerbach by Jackson in 2008, for it would be a decidedly one-sided affair.

———————

Before the series opened, the media reexamined the once frosty relationship between Ray Allen and Kobe Bryant, who had gone against each other many times while both players were in the Western Conference. In October 2004, the two had exchanged words and elbows during an exhibition game, and after the game, the usually circumspect Allen delivered a broadside.

"He feels like he needs to show the league and the country that he is better off without Shaq, that he can win a championship without Shaq," Allen said of Bryant. This had come a few months after Shaquille O'Neal had been traded to Miami. "So, offensively, he's going to jump out and say, 'I can average 30 points a game. I can still carry the load on this team,'" Allen said. If [the Lakers don't get] two-and-a-half good players to be a legitimate playoff contender or win a championship, in about a year or two he'll be calling out to [Lakers owner] Jerry Buss that, 'We need some help in here.' Or, 'Trade me.' And we'll all be saying, 'I told you so,' when he says that."

Bryant was not pleased when apprised of the remarks, saying, "Don't even put me and that dude in the same place." But Allen proved prophetic when Bryant did in fact demand a trade in the spring of 2007. The Lakers resisted, traded for Pau Gasol, and now had developed to the point where Bryant was placated. And by the 2008 Finals, the feud had pretty much been forgotten by the two protagonists.

The Lakers' future also looked extremely bright with Andrew Bynum, out with a knee injury but due back for 2008–2009, and several other talented young players. But Bryant is all about the here and now, and he felt that that didn't look too bad either. He liked the Lakers' chances after seeing what they had done in getting to this point.

"You can want it worse than anybody on this planet, but if you don't have a group of guys or a team that collectively executes well enough to win, you're not going to win," Bryant said.

He thought he had that group of guys.

The eleventh meeting between the Lakers and Celtics in the NBA Finals began on June 5. The Lakers looked the calmer, more composed of the teams, and it showed, as they led 51–46 at half-time. Then a collective gasp came over the 18,624 in attendance midway through the third quarter when Paul Pierce collapsed under the Boston basket, his teammate Kendrick Perkins having fallen on him.

"I heard this scream," said Danny Ainge, who was sitting maybe 15 feet away. "Paul told me he heard something pop." Down at the other end of the court, Celtics principal owner

Wyc Grousbeck said to himself, "This is not good news." Doc Rivers pulled his team aside and reminded them again of *ubuntu* and fighting through adversity and tough times. But he sensed the worst as well. "You see it's a knee and that's never good," Rivers said.

Two Celtics subs, Brian Scalabrine and Tony Allen, lifted Pierce up off the floor. Team physician Dr. Brian McKeon, not wanting to take any chances, ordered a wheelchair for Pierce. As he was being wheeled from the floor to the Celtics locker room, Pierce kept yelling, "It can't end this way! It can't end this way!"

Once inside the locker room, McKeon started feeling the knee area and turned to Pierce, saying, "Your knee is stable." That was all Pierce needed to hear. He later admitted that it was fear more than pain that was driving his thinking and once he got the good news, the fear disappeared.

"Let me get back out there then," Pierce said.

But McKeon made Pierce do some exercises, such as standing on one leg and shuffling from side to side. Eventually, the doctor too was convinced. Pierce flew out of the locker room and came back out of the tunnel. Three minutes of real time had passed.

When Pierce returned the Garden erupted and Kevin Garnett raised a fist to the skies.

"We saw him being carried off and we didn't know what the situation was," Garnett said. "We kept asking, 'Is he all right?' Doc was trying to get us back to the huddle. One thing we know about (Pierce) is he's very tough and we'd seen him play through numerous injuries throughout the season. There were times when we thought he wasn't going to play, (but) he played.

"When he came out, you just heard the roar of the crowd. He was walking, he was up on his own strength, and he rejuvenated us, I think to the point where he gave everybody life. The defense picked up a little bit. I could tell that everybody was rejuvenated. It was good to see that he was okay."

Once back in the game, Pierce had the crowd roaring even more, as he drained two big three-pointers. The Celtics blew out the Lakers in the second half and won Game 1, 98–88.

Immediately, the Los Angeles media called out Pierce for being a drama queen. Years earlier, M.L. Carr had nicknamed the LA team "the Fakers," but this time, Pierce was being accused of overacting, to the point where some felt he had done it deliberately to stir up the masses as well as his teammates. The Lakers led 62–58 when Pierce went out of the game with 6:49 left. He returned with 5:04 left, the Celtics having regained the lead, thanks to Ray Allen.

Pierce was most definitely not faking it. "I thought I tore it. I couldn't move," Pierce said. It was listed as a sprain, but Phil Jackson, never one to let slide a chance for a quip, said, "Was Oral Roberts back there?"

Pierce recovered quite nicely and, as the Lakers would soon discover, quite effectively as well. Beating the Lakers in the opener gave the Celtics a historical boost, although they probably were unaware of it. Jackson had a 40–0 record in playoff series when his teams won Game 1. But he was only 5–8 when his teams lost Game 1.

The Celtics dominated Game 2—until falling apart in the fourth quarter and nearly blowing a 24-point lead. Bryant, who was 9-of-26 in Game 1, continued to struggle against the Celtics swarming defense. Gasol and Lamar Odom found the inside to be particularly hard to navigate. And Leon Powe was in the process of cementing his Celtics legacy with a boffo performance off the bench, helping the Celtics to a 22-point lead after three.

Not only was Powe getting his way, he was getting to the line with increasing frequency, something that clearly irritated Jackson. Weren't the stars supposed to be accorded this kind of treatment? Powe attempted 13 free throws in only 15 minutes of play. The Lakers *team* attempted 10 the entire game. Powe finished with 21 points. Rajon Rondo had 16 assists. Pierce's knee held up fine

(28 points in 41 minutes), and the Celtics seemingly were on their way to another easy win.

Then the Lakers started making three-pointers, the Celtics started making turnovers, and pretty soon the lead was down to single figures. Two free throws by Bryant with 38 seconds left made it a 104–102 game, as the Lakers had made up 22 of the 24 points in a shade more than seven minutes.

But Pierce then bulled his way to the basket, got fouled, and made both free throws. (The Celtics attempted 28 free throws as a team.) Pierce then grazed a Sasha Vujacic three-pointer enough to get a block. James Posey rebounded, was fouled, made them both, and the Celtics had a 106–102 win and 2–0 series lead. Afterward, Jackson questioned the free-throw differential and deliberately (he does nothing uncalculated) mispronounced Powe's name. He quickly corrected himself, but the message was clear. The Lakers can't be beaten by some guy few had even heard of.

The Lakers clearly were hoping for the home court to be the difference when the series shifted to Los Angeles. They had not lost at home in the playoffs.

The change in venue meant a return to his roots for Pierce, who still was getting roasted on the airwaves for his remarkable recovery from what looked to be a serious knee injury. He had always played well in Los Angeles and had scored 33 points when the Celtics had beaten the Lakers in the Staples Center back in late December, and his career average was almost 28 points a game in Los Angeles. He would have plenty of time to hang with his friends and visit one of his favorite eateries, Roscoe's Chicken and Waffles. But he also had a warning for anyone who hoped for game tickets.

"There'll be tickets for friends," he said. "After that, it's high-def."

But he clearly was excited to be playing for an NBA title in his hometown. As a youngster growing up in Inglewood, he had often snuck into Lakers games at the nearby Forum and, like most of his friends, worshipped Magic Johnson and detested the Celtics. Now, he was playing for the team he once loathed against the team he once loved.

"It means everything to Boston fans," Pierce said. "To me, I think that's what pretty much got me started in basketball, growing up in Los Angeles, watching the Lakers and the Celtics. It's ironic, now we're playing against the Lakers in the Finals. As a kid, I hated the Celtics. I'm going home to play against my team that I grew up watching. I think that rivalry really revolutionized the game of basketball and now I'm a part of it. Just thinking about it, it's a dream come true. It's your hometown. I couldn't have scripted it any better."

With all the talk about the Celtics' free-throw advantage in Game 2, it was widely presumed merely exhaling on any Laker would be deemed to be a foul on the Celtics when play resumed in the Staples Center. That's just the way things go in the NBA.

The Lakers clawed back into the series with an 87–81 win in Game 3. It was not a thing of beauty, as both teams appeared fatigued from having to crisscross the country and then play the next day. Pierce struggled most of all, getting booed every time he touched the ball and finishing with only 6 points, missing 12 of 14 shots. He also battled foul trouble in the game and admitted to being a little nervous in his first NBA Finals appearance in his hometown.

"I was probably a little more anxious than normal, being that I'm at home in front of more family and more friends," Pierce said. "But I've got to block that out and go out there and leave it on the court. I've done it in the past. I've been here and played well despite having family and friends. It's time for me to do it again."

LA got a huge three-pointer from Sasha Vujacic with 1:53 left to turn a two-point game into a five-point game, and Bryant added 36, including 11-of-18 from the line. The Lakers took 34 free throws, the Celtics only 22. The Celtics also lost Rajon Rondo to an ankle injury. He played only 22 minutes and the injury would continue to bother him over the next two games.

On the positive side for Boston, it appeared that Allen, still wearing his sleeve, had resoundingly emerged from whatever had bothered him against Cleveland. He always contended it had been the number of attempts that resulted in his poor shooting. He averaged 12.3 shots a game in the first three games against the Lakers after averaging less than 9 per game against Cleveland.

Game 4 of the 2008 NBA Finals will be remembered in Boston as The Comeback and in Los Angeles as The Collapse. It was a game in which Allen, playing wire-to-wire, made two gigantic baskets down the stretch. It was a game in which the Lakers led by 21 after one and 24 in the second period. Bryant was content to play the facilitator, registering six assists, but no baskets, as the Lakers built what looked to be a very comfortable and certainly commanding lead. But the Celtics rallied, and one of the big stories of the game was Eddie House, up to then known as the Forgotten Man. With Rondo bothered by the ankle injury and Sam Cassell having difficulty staying with the quicker, younger Lakers guards, House was resurrected for the Finals. Some thought it should have happened much sooner.

House had been a key part of the Celtics regular-season success, but his time in the post-season had been limited. He had played only 17 minutes in the Detroit series as Doc Rivers went with Cassell, who had been brought in just for such situations. House occasionally would go into the game for one play only, never touch the ball, and then return to the bench. He remained publicly upbeat, cheering on the sideline, but inside he was confused and upset.

"The hardest thing about it was getting the rug snatched from under my feet when I didn't feel I did anything to warrant me losing my job," he said. "And I didn't feel he [Cassell] had done anything to come in and take my job. I could have lived with it if we had competed every day and he outplayed me. I can live with someone being better than me. But that wasn't the case.

"Regardless of what you did all season, and how you played, that rubbed me the wrong way at first. But then I realized, I couldn't have all these negative thoughts, all day, come to practice thinking about it, going home, thinking about it, and not thinking about doing my job and being prepared. You can't be in that mode. So I set it aside; I can't control that. What I can control is coming to work every day early, getting my shots up, running on the treadmill, staying in shape, lifting weights, and just working on my game, and taking care of my body so when I did get called, I was ready. In my mind, I was always in the game."

With the Celtics trailing by 20 points midway through the third quarter, Doc Rivers made a decision that changed the outcome of the game and the series. He already had substituted James Posey for P.J. Brown, who was in the game because Kendrick Perkins had injured his left shoulder while fouling Lamar Odom with 2:25 gone in the third quarter. With Rondo still hobbled, Rivers inserted House into the lineup. The thinking was that this particular lineup would prevent the Lakers from continuing to trap and swarm the Big Three while leaving Rondo, Perkins, or Brown alone. House and Posey demanded attention because they could shoot.

Additionally, Pierce had come up to Rivers at halftime and asked that he be allowed to guard Bryant in the second half. While Bryant's scoring wasn't an issue in the Lakers' taking their huge lead, his overall game had been. Pierce figured he could put a little more pressure on Bryant and that might disrupt things.

Still, trailing by 20 with 19 minutes left represented a formidable margin for the Celtics to overcome. But the lineup change worked wonders. Boston closed the third quarter with a 23–5 run, holding the Lakers to a single basket (a Pau Gasol dunk) in the final seven minutes. Bryant missed his last five shots, one of which was blocked by Pierce. House made two big three-pointers, Posey added another hoop, and, after an authoritative slam by Brown in the closing seconds, the Celtics trailed only 73–71 heading into the fourth quarter.

"Their defense was up to the task in the second half. It changed the momentum of the game," Phil Jackson would say later.

The Celtics finally broke through with 4:07 left when Eddie House hit a jump shot, giving them their first lead of the game, 84–83. They would not give it back.

Allen followed with a Jordan-esque baseline drive in which he went under the basket and somehow put the proper amount of spin on the ball to get the layup off the glass while avoiding an Odom block. Posey, who finished with 18 points, had two huge three-pointers, the second of which, with 73 seconds left, gave the Celtics a 92–87 lead. But it was a play in the final 20 seconds by Allen that sealed the improbable win. Isolated on Vujacic because the Lakers had to respect House and Posey on the perimeter, Allen blew by the overmatched Lakers guard for a stunningly easy basket. The hoop gave the Celtics a 96–91 lead with 15 seconds remaining and the Lakers were done. The final score, 97–91, represented the greatest comeback in an NBA Finals game since Elias Sports Bureau started tracking these kinds of things back in 1971. Boston now had a 3–1 series lead and could practically taste the champagne, although there was concern about the status of Perkins, who had not returned, and Rondo, who played only 17 minutes.

After the incredible victory, the Celtics owners returned to the team's headquarters at the Beverly Wilshire Hotel. Wyc Grousbeck tossed his credit card on the bar and announced to one and all that the drinks were on the Celtics. It had been that kind of night. Then, once the Celtics' entourage noticed there was a huge picture of Jack Nicholson over the bar, they couldn't resist. Out came the digital cameras and cellphones and, one-by-one, photos were taken of celebrating Celtics, raising their glasses in front of a picture of the most famous Lakers fan of all.

———————

RAY ALLEN'S REMARKABLE PERFORMANCE in Game 4 (19 points, 9 rebounds in 48 minutes) soon became yesterday's news when he became so concerned for the health of his son Walker that he took the child to the hospital on the morning of Game 5. Allen's family had made the trip for Games 3–5 and Walker Allen had been lethargic and vomiting for much of the time in Los Angeles. But his father chalked it up to exhaustion and, perhaps, even the excitement from the Celtics' big comeback win in Game 4. He figured it was a virus.

But eventually, the vomiting didn't stop, so Allen deposited his son at the hospital and then tried to get his mind straight for Game 5. His son, he discovered after a day of tests, had been diagnosed with juvenile diabetes. "It was extremely hard for me to concentrate that night," he said of Game 5, when he shot 4-of-13 from the field. "I just didn't feel like I was a part of it. My mind was elsewhere."

His teammates put up a valiant fight, with Pierce going wire-to-wire and scoring 38 points. Kendrick Perkins, still bothered by his left shoulder, did not play; Leon Powe started in his place. Rajon Rondo did start, but played only 15 minutes. Somehow, with Allen's mind wandering and two starters ailing, the Celtics nearly won the game. They once again overcame a big, early deficit (17 points after one quarter, 19 in the first half) and briefly led the game in the second half. They trailed by two points with 40 seconds left when Bryant stole the ball from Pierce and went in for a dunk. LA prevailed, 97–91, sending the series back to Boston.

Allen, however, returned to the hospital immediately after the game, spending the night there while trying to arrange medical care for his son when the family returned to Boston. He eventually took a red-eye flight home from Los Angeles on Monday, landing in Boston around 10 a.m. on the day of Game 6. By this time, word had filtered out that his son was sick, and Allen felt an obligation to discuss the ailment, if for no other reason than to alert other parents whose children may be showing similar symptoms.

"If we had waited any longer, it's likely he would have gone into a coma, and there's a chance he wouldn't be here with us today," Allen said. "The Lord dropped this in our laps right after the biggest game of my career. I felt there must have been a reason for that. It was a life and death situation, and it needed to be talked about."

The relief of identifying Walker's illness and having the resources to deal with it was palpable for Allen in Game 6. He was everywhere, scoring 26 points, making 8-of-12 shots. Kendrick Perkins returned and played 13 minutes. Rondo was a whirling dervish and the Celtics clinched the championship with their 132–91 rout of the visitors.

———————

"ONE OF MY IMMEDIATE THOUGHTS after it was over was, 'This is tough. This is really, really tough,'" Doc Rivers said. "It's really tough to win a title. You have to be a man. Your team has to be a team of men. They have to sacrifice, commit, give up their bodies, give up their time, leave their families. There were so many things just in that series. There was Paul's knee. There was Ray's child. There was Perk's shoulder. There was Rajon's ankle. So many things. You look at all the games we could have lost in the playoffs and it was certain plays that were the difference. Some were simple picks. Some were guys being in the right spot, making the effort. It had to do with knowing your role and playing your role. But I'll tell you this: I have a new appreciation for guys who do it over and over again. I don't know how they do it."

Rivers later posed with a cigar in front of a picture of Red Auerbach, one winning coach saluting the other. He had, indeed, finished the race, as Grady Rivers always told his son he needed to do.

Epilogue

ESS THAN 48 HOURS after their annihilation of the Lakers in Game 6, the Celtics reconvened at the site of the massacre—TD Banknorth Garden—for their victory parade through the streets of Boston.

The route wasn't quite the same one that Doc Rivers had plotted the previous fall, when he took Ray Allen, Paul Pierce, and Kevin Garnett on a Duck Boat ride through the city's downtown. This parade would start at the Garden and wind its way to Copley Square.

Sixteen Duck Boats were on hand for the "rolling rally." Players, wives, family members, and Celtics employees piled on the boats, as tens of thousands of fans lined the streets to cheer them. Glen Davis provided the comic relief, removing his shirt and gyrating for the fans. The whole thing, which cost more than $300,000, was over in 90 minutes.

Then it was time for the public appearances. Garnett and Allen flew to New York to join David Letterman. Pierce went home to Los Angeles and made an appearance on *The Jimmy Kimmel Show*, coming out from behind the curtains in a wheelchair when he was introduced. "That was my idea," Pierce said. "You know, they all think I'm a faker in LA."

Pierce also took part in a pool tournament in Los Angeles. He fashions himself as a pretty adroit hustler, and he quickly advanced to the championship match, where $20,000 was at stake.

"This guy comes into play against me, and he's got his own personal cue in a bag," Pierce said. "He takes it out and starts putting it together, and I'm like, which one should I use that's hanging on the wall here? He made his first shot, missed the next one, and he never got another chance. Then, I find out I get $20,000 for my foundation, a nice watch, and a gold-plated iPod. And I'm thinking, I gotta go play the lottery now because I am on a roll."

In the last weekend of June, a group of the Celtics met in Las Vegas to watch Filipino boxer Manny Pacquiao, who was fighting David Diaz at the Mandalay Bay Special Events Center. Pacquiao, whose trainer is from Massachusetts, is a big Celtics fan and offered to get tickets for the players. The casino put many of them, including Garnett and Pierce, in ringside seats for the bout.

Pacquiao then proceeded to knock out Diaz in the ninth round to win the WBC Lightweight Championship. Several Celtics gathered with Pacquiao in his dressing room after the bout, chanting, "Manny, Manny." Garnett said, "I'm a huge Pacman fan. That's why I'm here."

Among the notable absentees at the championship fight was Glen Davis, who was back in Massachusetts, working out at the team's training facility. "I can't party with the vets yet," he said. "I'm still a rookie." He did, however, manage a quick trip to the Bahamas after the Finals, where, he said, "Everyone knew who I was. It's amazing."

Most of the team then went out to Los Angeles in mid July for the taping of the annual ESPY Awards, which are the Oscars/Emmys/Tonys of the sports world. Fans vote and then celebrities announce the winners. The Celtics were one of six nominees for Team of the Year, the others being the Boston Red Sox, the Detroit Red Wings, the New York Giants, the Lady Vols NCAA champion basketball team from the University of Tennessee, and the NCAA men's basketball champs from Pierce's alma mater, the University of Kansas.

Justin Timberlake, who hosted the event, parodied the Celtics' Big Three, rapping about his injured knee while dressing up as Pierce. He was flanked by life-sized puppets of Allen and Garnett. At the end of his routine, he held the Garnett puppet in front of his face and screamed, "Anything is possible."

The presenters for the Team of the Year award were Kiefer Sutherland, star of the Fox hit, *24*, and the music star Fergie. It was Fergie who announced that the fans had named the Celtics the winners.

Ray Allen accepted the award and spoke for everyone, opening with, "It's great to get another win in LA." That drew a lot of laughs from the crowd. However, the cameras also zeroed in on the Lakers Derek Fisher, who didn't think it was funny at all.

There was a bit of discouraging news that day as well, because James Posey, who was with his teammates in Los Angeles for the ceremony, had decided to accept an offer from the New Orleans Hornets. He was the first defection from the roster.

One of the really critical guys on the 2007–2008 team was leaving. When Danny Ainge had said, "Without James Posey, we don't win a title," he wasn't kidding. Posey had more than delivered the goods on and off the court.

He was able to cash in on his terrific season, getting a guaranteed four-year deal from New Orleans worth $25 million. The Celtics offered him a three-year, guaranteed deal, but declined to go any further. Posey will be 35 when the deal expires in 2012.

"At the end of the day, there is a business side," Posey said. "That's part of it. It helps. Most importantly, basketball-wise, it was a great opportunity . . . I was able to watch some of the [Hornets] games during the course of the regular season, and also saw the games in the playoffs against San Antonio. You could just see it. It's right there. Hopefully I can be that missing piece, a little bit to further that journey."

Only a few days before, Posey had joined a number of teammates for the premiere of the championship season DVD in Boston. Season ticket holders were also there and chanted "Re-sign Posey," when he entered the room. But Posey did what just about any other NBA player would do: he took the better offer. And it's not like he's joining a bad team. The Hornets are an up-and-coming team with an exciting future.

Soon after, the Celtics announced that they had re-signed Tony Allen and Eddie House. Tony Allen was long presumed to be a goner, as he had rarely played in the post-season, and the Celtics had not even bothered to make him a qualifying offer to retain matching rights. He was an unrestricted free agent, able to sign with anyone. Then, the Celtics went out and drafted a Tony Allen–like player in J.R. Giddens from the University of New Mexico, which seemed to make him even more expendable.

But with Posey gone, Tony Allen came back into play. The team also signed free-agent center Patrick O'Bryant, a lottery pick (No. 9 overall in 2006) of the Golden State Warriors. He never fit into Don Nelson's run-and-gun system and appeared in only 40 games in his two seasons there.

House meanwhile will return to the same team for the second straight season for the first time since 2003. "Everybody knows how big Eddie was for us in the Finals," Danny Ainge said. "I'm excited to have him back."

One thing seemed abundantly clear: Ainge was not going to have the hectic summer he had in 2007. After the House and Tony Allen signings, he announced that he was taking time off and that he was through chasing players for the time being. The Celtics roster of 2008–2009 would look a lot like the one from the year before—and that was fine with him. P.J. Brown was expected to really retire this time around. Cassell's status was up in the air.

Before taking some downtime, however, Ainge and Doc Rivers welcomed a group of undrafted rookies and veterans for a small minicamp at the team's practice facility. Ainge and Rivers had decided earlier in the year that they would not send a team to the NBA's Summer League in Las Vegas, mainly because they felt they didn't have enough players. Giddens, however, did not participate in the camp because his contract had not been settled.

On the first day of the camp, Davis and Gabe Pruitt joined the newcomers for drills on the very same floor where, only a few weeks earlier, the eventual NBA champions had practiced. There was, however, one notable difference in the décor. The last time Davis and Pruitt had been there, the spotlight had shone on the empty space on the wall where, it was hoped, a seventeenth championship banner would hang. Now, there was no longer a spotlight—or an empty space. The 2008 championship banner was already on the wall.

Boston Celtics Championships

1957: Celtics defeat St. Louis Hawks, 4–3. Bill Russell and Tommy Heinsohn are rookies and Bob Cousy is the league's Most Valuable Player.

1959: Celtics defeat Minneapolis Lakers, 4–0. The first ever 4–0 sweep in the NBA Finals.

1960: Celtics defeat St. Louis Hawks, 4–3. Bill Russell has 22 points and 35 rebounds in Game 7.

1961: Celtics defeat St. Louis Hawks, 4–1. Bill Sharman's last year with the team.

1962: Celtics defeat Los Angeles Lakers, 4–3. Celtics rally from 2–1 and 3–2 deficits and win Game 7 in overtime.

1963: Celtics defeat Los Angeles Lakers, 4–2. Bob Cousy's last year with the team.

1964: Celtics defeat San Francisco Warriors, 4–1. The first meeting in the NBA Finals between Bill Russell and Wilt Chamberlain.

1965: Celtics defeat Los Angeles Lakers, 4–1. Biggest test comes in conference finals against Philadelphia, with John Havlicek stealing the ball in Game 7.

1966: Celtics defeat Los Angeles Lakers, 4–3. Eighth straight title and ninth overall for Red Auerbach, who retires as head coach at the end of the season.

1968: Celtics defeat Los Angeles Lakers, 4–2. Celtics recover from a 3–1 hole in conference finals against the Philadelphia 76ers.

1969: Celtics defeat Los Angeles Lakers, 4–3. Celtics trail 2–0 and 3–2 in the NBA Finals but win Game 7 on the road in Bill Russell's final season.

1974: Celtics defeat Milwaukee Bucks, 4–3. The first championship of the Dave Cowens–John Havlicek era.

1976: Celtics defeat Phoenix Suns, 4–2. A series most remembered for the triple overtime Boston victory in Game 5, arguably the greatest playoff game ever.

1981: Celtics defeat Houston Rockets, 4–2. The first of three titles won by the Big Three of Larry Bird, Kevin McHale (a rookie that year), and Robert Parish.

1984: Celtics defeat Los Angeles Lakers, 4–3. Epic series featuring first Finals matchup between Larry Bird and Magic Johnson.

1986: Celtics defeat Houston Rockets, 4–2. A fitting conclusion for the best team in Celtics history and, quite possibly, of all time.

2008: Celtics defeat Los Angeles Lakers, 4–2. Ten-year veteran Paul Pierce is Finals Most Valuable Player and joins 13-year-veteran Kevin Garnett and 12-year veteran Ray Allen in winning first championship. Also the first championship for coach Doc Rivers.

Acknowledgments

IN TRYING TO RE-CREATE an amazing and special season in a short period of time, many, many people stepped up to make this project possible. The Boston Celtics were more than accommodating, offering stories and insights. In particular, owners Wyc Grousbeck and Steve Pagliuca were generous with their time as was general manager Danny Ainge and coach Doc Rivers. Heather Walker in the team's public relations department was instrumental in helping secure interviews with the players, especially after the season ended. That is no small feat. Jeff Twiss and Brian Olive in the Celtics' public relations department also provided helpful insights. Keith Sliney of the Celtics and Joe Amati of the NBA were helpful with the pictorial display.

Kevin Hanover of Da Capo Press first proposed this idea and championed it through to the end, sweating out two Game 7's (along with the author). And Kate Burke of Da Capo Press also deserves thanks for her assistance. Thanks also to my agent, Colleen Mohyde, of the Doe Coover Agency, and to my former colleagues at the *Boston Globe*, Bob Ryan, Shira Springer, and Marc Spears. Finally, many, many thanks to the diligent Jeffrey Pickette of Brandeis University, without whose work this project could not have been completed in the allotted time.

Index